COUNTER CULTURE

COUNTER CULTURE

FOLLOWING CHRIST
IN AN ANTI-CHRISTIAN AGE

DAVID PLATT

TYNDALE
MOMENTUM™

The nonfiction imprint of
Tyndale House Publishers, Inc.

Visit Tyndale online at www.tyndale.com.

Visit Tyndale Momentum online at www.tyndalemomentum.com.

TYNDALE, Tyndale Momentum, and Tyndale's quill logo are registered trademarks of Tyndale House Publishers, Inc. The Tyndale Momentum logo is a trademark of Tyndale House Publishers, Inc. Tyndale Momentum is the nonfiction imprint of Tyndale House Publishers, Inc., Carol Stream, Illinois.

Counter Culture: Following Christ in an Anti-Christian Age

Designed by Julie Chen

Published in association with Yates & Yates (www.yates2.com).

Unless otherwise indicated, all Scripture quotations are taken from *The Holy Bible,* English Standard Version® (ESV®), copyright © 2001 by Crossway, a publishing ministry of Good News Publishers. Used by permission. All rights reserved.

Scripture quotations marked NIV are taken from the Holy Bible, *New International Version,*® *NIV.*® Copyright © 1973, 1978, 1984 by Biblica, Inc.® Used by permission. All rights reserved worldwide.

Scripture quotations marked HCSB are taken from the Holman Christian Standard Bible,® copyright © 1999, 2000, 2002, 2003, 2009 by Holman Bible Publishers. Used by permission. Holman Christian Standard Bible,® Holman CSB,® and HCSB® are federally registered trademarks of Holman Bible Publishers.

Scripture quotations marked NASB are taken from the New American Standard Bible,® copyright © 1960, 1962, 1963, 1968, 1971, 1972, 1973, 1975, 1977, 1995 by The Lockman Foundation. Used by permission.

Scripture quotations marked NKJV are taken from the New King James Version,® copyright © 1982 by Thomas Nelson, Inc. Used by permission. All rights reserved.

For information about special discounts for bulk purchases, please contact Tyndale House Publishers at csresponse@tyndale.com or call 800-323-9400.

Library of Congress Cataloging-in-Publication Data
Platt, David, date.
    Counter culture : a compassionate call to counter culture in a world of poverty, same-sex marriage, racism, sex slavery, immigration, abortion, persecution, orphans, and pornography / David Platt.
        pages cm
    Includes bibliographical references.
    ISBN 978-1-4143-7329-4 (hc)
1. Christian life—United States.   2. Christianity and culture—United States.   3. Culture conflict—Religious aspects—Christianity.   I. Title.
    BV4501.3.P628 2015
    261.0973—dc23   2014038804

ISBN 978-1-4143-9038-3 (Softcover)

ISBN 978-1-4964-0104-5 (International Trade Paper Edition)

Printed in the United States of America

24	23	22	21	20	19	18	17
8	7	6	5	4	3	2	

All of the author's royalties from this book will go toward promoting the glory of Christ in all nations.

To all who long and work for justice and mercy in the world

while loving and proclaiming the Judge and Savior of the world

CONTENTS

THE GOOD NEWS THAT THE JUST AND

GRACIOUS CREATOR OF THE UNIVERSE

HAS LOOKED UPON HOPELESSLY

SINFUL MEN AND WOMEN AND HAS

SENT HIS SON, JESUS CHRIST, GOD

IN THE FLESH, TO BEAR HIS WRATH

AGAINST SIN ON THE CROSS AND

TO SHOW HIS POWER OVER SIN

IN THE RESURRECTION, SO THAT

EVERYONE WHO TURNS FROM THEIR

SIN AND THEMSELVES AND TRUSTS

IN JESUS AS SAVIOR AND LORD WILL

BE RECONCILED TO GOD FOREVER.

RETREAT OR RISK?

Consciously countercultural. This is the only possible posture for individuals, families, and churches who have any hope of following Christ in contemporary America.

I make the statement above without hesitation or reservation. In 2014, I wrote the first edition of this book to encourage Christians in America to live out their faith amid the significant social issues that surround us. At that time, the Supreme Court was about to consider arguments concerning so-called same-sex marriage, and transgender sexuality was rarely even discussed. Two short years later, so-called same-sex marriage has become law across the country, and the federal government now threatens to withhold children's education money from states who do not allow men who wish they were women to use public bathrooms alongside young girls. The rate of social and moral change in contemporary America is both staggeringly swift and historically unprecedented. Indeed, only God knows where we will be by the time you're reading this book.

So how should Christians respond to such a rapidly changing American culture? Do we resign ourselves to pessimism, convinced that many of the moral foundations upon which our society once stood have collapsed and are now irrecoverable? Or do we reassure ourselves with optimism, confident that we can still win the culture war if we'll just unite together spiritually, personally, politically, and philosophically? I propose that neither pessimism nor optimism is the answer. Instead, realism is.

Followers of Christ need to face the reality that contemporary American culture is increasingly anti-Christian. As we will see in the pages ahead, the Supreme Court of the United States has called Christians who believe what the Bible teaches about marriage "bigots" and "enemies of the human race."[1] Similarly, in a recent ruling on religious liberty, a state supreme court declared that Christians should be "compelled by law to compromise the very religious beliefs that inspire their lives."[2] These legal statements merely reflect the anti-Christian sentiments that the media, business, and entertainment industries are aggressively promoting in the minds and hearts of American individuals, families, and institutions every single day.

Such anti-Christian sentiments are obviously not limited to America. Across the world, followers of Christ live in settings that are hostile to Christianity (many of them far more hostile than the United States). After all, Christianity was born into a culture of opposition two thousand years ago. Across the centuries, Christians in countless cultures have lived out their faith in settings where belief in the Bible has been viewed as offensive and commitment to Christ has proved to be costly.

So how should followers of Christ today live in an American or any other culture that is intentionally and increasingly anti-Christian? I am convinced that every professing Christian in any such culture has two clear options: retreat or risk.

On the one hand, we can retreat. We can retreat from Christ altogether, although I'm guessing that for most professing Christians, we won't reject Christ outright and all at once. Instead, our retreat can be far more slow and subtle. In the name of "progressive" faith, "inclusive" belief, and "open" minds, we can begin trading in the timeless truths of God's Word for the changing opinions of the world. The ruins of such retreat are already evident across contemporary Christianity, as many professing "Christians" deny that God is the Author of Scripture or that Christ is necessary for salvation. In efforts to accommodate the culture, scores of individuals and churches have already abandoned Christ. Most dangerous of all is that they've done so under the semblance of supposed Christianity.

Even if we don't retreat from Christ, we might retreat from culture. In the face of anti-Christian sentiments and social challenges, many Christians who hold to a belief in the Bible may choose to hide in the comfortable confines of privatized faith. We might stand up and speak with Christian conviction in the privacy of our homes and churches yet sit back and stay silent about Christian conviction in more public settings. When the conversation at the café switches to the topic of homosexuality, for example, we might sheepishly, almost apologetically, stumble through a vague notion of what the Bible teaches, or probably more likely, we might say nothing at all. Or when our boss at work asks us what we believe and we realize that our job may be in jeopardy based on how we answer, we might find ourselves masking, or at least minimizing, the parts of our faith that could be most offensive to him or her. Or maybe our retreat will simply involve scrolling through headlines on social media each day where we see news of rampant poverty, refugee crises, racist violence, and regulated abortions (if abortion ever even shows up in the news we receive), and instead of deciding to do something in response to these realities, we might sympathetically shake our heads and move on as if there's nothing we can (or should) do.

One of the reasons I've written this book is because I see temptation to retreat in the above ways all around me. I see it in Christian students who don't want to be labeled narrow-minded or intolerant and who are slowly (or sometimes swiftly) concluding that Christianity is outdated and irrelevant. I see it in Christian singles who think the Bible's teaching on sex is overly restrictive and Christian couples who believe the Bible's teaching on marriage is offensively chauvinistic. I see it in Christian parents who either isolate their children from cultural challenges or send their children into the culture ill-equipped to face those challenges. I see it in Christian leaders who are proud to stand up and speak out on social issues like poverty and slavery when they will be commended by the culture but prone to sit back and stay silent on social issues like abortion and sexuality when they will be criticized by the culture. I see it in churches who have practically given up the battle with materialism and others who have fundamentally contributed to the problem of racism. Ultimately, I see temptation in my own life to retreat from following Christ in the culture around me. I see a tendency in me, my family, and my church to prioritize my comforts over Christ's commands and to elevate my thoughts over his truth, and I know that retreat on any of the above levels isn't right.

But if we don't retreat, only one option remains: risk. Neutrality is not a possibility. Either we retreat from Christ or from the culture, or we risk following Christ by countering the culture. And *risk* is the right word. As followers of Christ, we are fooling ourselves if we don't face the reality that belief in and obedience to the Bible in an anti-Christian age will inevitably lead to risk in one's family, future, relationships, reputation, career, and comfort in this world.

That risk is what this book is all about. This book is about encouraging and equipping followers of Christ to counter the culture around us, even when that inevitably and inescapably means cost in the culture around us. The first chapter of this book is about helping you and me begin by loving the gospel in the church even when it's hated in the culture. Then subsequent chapters are about helping us think through how to live out that gospel in our lives, families, and churches in an age of sexual confusion, legal abortion, rampant materialism, violent racism, escalating refugee crises, diminishing religious liberties, and a number of other significant social issues. This book is about refusing to retreat from these realities, instead choosing to face them with a fearless faith that is full of hope in Christ and free to love even those who would belittle Christian belief.

To be sure, I don't claim to be the expert on how to live Christlike in an anti-Christian age. Nor do I claim to know all the ways my culture (or other cultures, for that matter) will continue to change in the days, months, and years ahead. Yet I do know timeless truth that is guaranteed to stand the test of cultural trends. And I am on a journey to discover how to humbly, lovingly, faithfully, and fearlessly put that truth into practice in a way that exalts Christ in the age and place in which God has put me. I invite you to join the journey with me in the pages ahead.

THE GREATEST OFFENSE: THE GOSPEL AND CULTURE

The gospel is the lifeblood of Christianity, and it provides the foundation for countering culture. For when we truly believe the gospel, we begin to realize that the gospel not only *compels* Christians to confront social issues in the culture around us. The gospel actually *creates* confrontation with the culture around—and within—us.

It is increasingly common for biblical views on social issues to be labeled insulting. We know that it's offensive to an ever-expanding number of people to say that a woman who has feelings for another woman should not express love for her in marriage. It doesn't take long for a Christian to be backed into a corner on this issue, not wanting to be offensive yet wondering how to respond.

But this is where we must recognize that a biblical view of homosexuality is not the greatest offense in Christianity. In fact, it's nowhere close to the greatest offense in Christianity. The gospel itself is a much, much greater offense. We need to start, then, with exploring what the gospel is, and we need to ask ourselves, Do we actually believe it? Our answer to this question fundamentally determines how we live in our culture.

IN THE BEGINNING, GOD

The gospel's offense begins with the very first words of the Bible.[1] "In the beginning, God . . ." (Genesis 1:1). The initial affront of the gospel is that there is a God by, through, and for whom all things begin. "The LORD is the everlasting God, the Creator of the ends of the earth" (Isaiah 40:28). Because all things begin with God and ultimately exist for God, nothing in all creation is irrelevant to him.

What is this Creator like? "I am the LORD, your Holy One," God says in Isaiah 43:15. In other words, he is wholly unique—unlike us and incomparable to us. He is of another kind. God is absolutely pure, and there is nothing wrong in him. Nothing. Everything God is and everything God does is right. He is without error and without equal.

This holy God is also good. "The LORD is good to all, and his mercy is over all that he has made" (Psalm 145:9). God's goodness is evident from the start of Scripture, where everything he creates is called "good," culminating in man and woman, who are called "very good" (see Genesis 1:4, 10, 12, 18, 21, 25, 31). The universal grandeur of creation testifies to the undeniable goodness of the Creator.

God's goodness is expressed in his justice. "The LORD judges the peoples" (Psalm 7:8), and he judges them perfectly. God justifies the innocent and condemns the guilty. Consequently, "he who justifies the wicked and he who condemns the righteous are both alike an abomination to the LORD" (Proverbs 17:15). As a good Judge, God is outraged by injustice. He detests those who say to the wicked, "You are good," and those who say to the good, "You are wicked." God is a perfect Judge.

God's goodness is also expressed in his grace. He shows free and unmerited favor to those who could never deserve it. He is compassionate and patient, desiring all people everywhere to know and enjoy his kindness, mercy, and love (see 2 Peter 3:9).

Consider, then, the confrontation created by the reality of God in each of our lives. Because God is our Creator, we belong to him. The one who created us owns us. We are not, as the poem "Invictus" describes, the masters of our own fate or the captains of our own souls. The Author of all creation possesses authority over all creation, including you and me. And we are accountable to him as our Judge. One of the core truths of the gospel is that God will judge every person, and he will be just. This puts us in a position where we desperately need his grace.

Now we see the offense of the gospel coming to the forefront. Tell any modern person that there is a God who sustains, owns, defines, rules, and one day will judge him or her, and that person will balk in offense. Any person would—and every person has. This is our natural reaction to God.

OUR NATURAL REACTION TO GOD

Look at the opening pages of human history, and you will see the ultimate problem of the human heart. When God creates man, God puts him in the Garden of Eden and says, "You are free to eat from any tree in the garden; but you must not eat from the tree of the knowledge of good and evil, for when you eat of it you will surely die" (Genesis 2:16-17, NIV). Here we see God's holiness, goodness, justice, and grace on display. God has authority to define what is right and wrong, good and evil, based upon his pure and holy character. God makes clear to man that he will be judged based upon his obedience to the command God has given. God's grace is evident, for he does not hide his law. In love, God tells man the way to life and exhorts him to walk in it.

So how does the created respond to the Creator? Within a matter of only a few verses, temptation to sin sits on the table. The serpent asks the first woman, "Did God really say, 'You must not eat from any tree in the garden'? . . . You will not surely die. . . . For God knows that when you eat of it your eyes will be opened, and you will be like God, knowing good and evil" (Genesis 3:1, 4-5, NIV).

Do you see the role reversal here? It all begins when the command of God is reduced to questions about God. Is God really holy? Does he really know what is right? Is God really good? Does he really want what is best for me? Amid such questions, man and woman subtly assert themselves not as the ones to be judged by God but as the ones who sit in judgment of him.

The serpent's question revolves around the tree of the knowledge of good and evil. We may read the tree's name and think, *What's so wrong with knowing the difference between good and evil?* But the meaning of Scripture here goes beyond *information* about good and evil to the *determination* of good and evil. In other words, for the man and woman to eat from this tree was to reject God as the one who determines good and evil and to assume this responsibility themselves. The temptation in the Garden was to rebel against God's authority and in the process make humans the arbiters of morality.

When we understand this first sin, we realize that the moral relativism of the twenty-first century is nothing new. When we attempt to usurp (or even eliminate) God, we lose objectivity for determining what is good and evil, right and wrong, moral and immoral. Noted agnostic philosopher of science Michael Ruse echoes this when he says, "The position of the modern evolutionist, therefore, is that . . . morality is a biological adaptation no less than are hands and feet and teeth. . . . Considered as a rationally justifiable set of claims about an objective something, it is illusory."[2] Similarly, noted atheist Richard Dawkins writes:

> In a universe of blind physical forces and genetic replication, some people are going to get hurt, other people are going to get lucky, and you won't find any rhyme or reason in it, nor any justice. The universe we observe has precisely the properties we should expect if there is, at the bottom, no design, no purpose, no evil, and no other good. Nothing but blind, pitiless indifference. DNA neither knows nor cares. DNA just is. And we dance to its music.[3]

Godless worldviews thus leave us with a hopeless subjectivity concerning good and evil that is wholly dependent on social constructs. Whatever a culture deems right is right, and whatever a culture deems wrong is wrong. This is precisely the worldview that prevails in American culture today, where rapid shifts in the moral landscape clearly communicate that we no longer believe certain things are inherently right or wrong. Instead, rightness and wrongness is determined by social developments around us.

But aren't the implications of this approach to morality frightening? Consider sex trafficking around the world. Are we willing to conclude that as long as a society approves of this industry, it is no longer immoral? Are we willing to tell young girls sold into sex slavery that they and the men who take advantage of them are merely dancing to their DNA, that what is happening to them is not inherently evil, and that they are just products of a blind, pitiless indifference that's left them unlucky in the world? Surely this is not what you would say to one of these girls. But this is the fruit of the worldview that many people increasingly profess.

"Doing no harm to others, be true to yourself," a friend and self-identified pagan suggested to me as a philosophy of life one day in the French Quarter of New Orleans. This supposedly simple philosophy was sufficient, so my friend thought, to make value judgments and moral decisions in all of life. The glaring problem behind his worldview, though, is who defines *harm* and to what extent we should be true to ourselves. Wouldn't a pimp in northern Nepal claim that he's creating a better life for a young girl whose chance of living was slim to begin with? Might he also claim that she has a job that he believes she enjoys? And what's to keep the pimp from arguing that he and this girl are helping scores of men be true to the sexual cravings they have within themselves?

Such a godless perspective on morality proves utterly hollow when faced with the harsh realities of evil in this world. Thankfully, the gospel is completely countercultural in this respect. For God's Word tells us that God has beautifully and wonderfully made each precious girl in his personal image, and he loves her. He has uniquely and biologically formed her not for forced sexual violation from countless random men but for joyful sexual union with a husband who cherishes, serves, and loves her. This is the good design of a gracious God, yet it has been grossly debauched by sinful humanity. Sin is real rebellion against the good Creator of all things and the final Judge of all people. Sex trafficking is unjust because God is just, and he will call sinners to account before him.

Such an understanding of sin helps inform why Christians and churches must work to end sex trafficking. Yet a quick perusal through the previous paragraph reveals why these same Christians and churches must also work to oppose abortion and defend marriage. Isn't the God who personally creates every precious girl in his image also the God who personally forms every precious baby in the womb? Isn't the design of God that makes sexual violation wrong in prostitution also the design of God that makes sexual union right in marriage? And isn't sin in all its forms—whether selling a young girl into slavery, ripping a baby's body from the womb, or disregarding God's prescribed pattern for marriage—real rebellion against the good Creator and final Judge of all people?

THE SIN OF SELF

Here again we're confronted with the countercultural offense of the gospel. For even as the gospel grounds the definition of good and evil in the character of God, it also claims that evil is not limited to certain types of sin and select groups of sinners. Evil is unfortunately inherent in all of us and therefore unavoidably a part of any culture we create.[4]

Though we have all been created by God, we have also been corrupted by sin. As much as we would like to deny this, our nature constantly demonstrates it. We possess both dignity and depravity; we are prone to both good and evil. This is the irony of the human condition. John Stott expresses this well in his summary of basic Christianity:

> We are able to think, choose, create, love and worship; but we are also able to hate, covet, fight and kill. Human beings are the inventors of hospitals for the care of the sick, of universities for the acquisition of wisdom, and of churches for the worship of God. But they have also invented torture chambers, concentration camps, and nuclear arsenals.

This is the paradox of our humanness. We are both
noble and ignoble, both rational and irrational, both
moral and immoral, both creative and destructive,
both loving and selfish, both Godlike and bestial.[5]

Why is this so? The gospel answers that although God created
us in his image, we have rebelled against him in our independence. Though it looks different in each of our lives, we all are
just like the man and woman in the Garden. We think, *Even if
God says not to do something, I'm going to do it anyway.* In essence
we're saying, "God's not Lord over me, and God doesn't know
what's best for me. I define what's right and wrong, good and
evil." The foundation of our morality thus shifts from the objective truth God has given us in his Word to the subjective notions
we create in our minds. Even when we don't realize the implications of our ideas, we inescapably come to one conclusion: whatever *seems* right to me or *feels* right to me *is* right for me.

In the end, for each of us, it's ultimately about *me.*

This is why the Bible diagnoses the human condition simply
by saying that we "all have turned aside" to ourselves (Romans
3:12). The essence of what the Bible calls sin is the exaltation
of self. God has designed us to put him first in our lives, others
next, and ourselves last. Yet sin reverses that order: we put ourselves first, others next (many times in an attempt to use them
for ourselves), and God somewhere (if anywhere) in the distant
background. We turn from worshiping God to worshiping self.

Now, we probably wouldn't put it that way. Most people don't
publicly profess, "I worship myself." But, as John Stott points out,
it doesn't take long as we look at our lives and listen to our language
for the truth to become evident. Our dictionary contains hundreds of words that start with self: self-esteem, self-confidence, self-
advertisement, self-gratification, self-glorification, self-motivation,

self-pity, self-applause, self-centeredness, self-indulgence, self-righteousness—on and on. We have created a host of terms to express the extent of our preoccupation with ourselves.[6]

The tragedy in all this is that in our constant quest to satisfy ourselves, we actually become slaves to sin. This is why Jesus teaches, "I say to you, everyone who practices sin is a slave to sin" (John 8:34). We know this to be true. This is easy to see in the alcoholic, for example. He becomes drunk, believing it is the path to personal satisfaction, only to find himself enslaved to an addiction that leads to his ruin.

But sin works similarly in each of our lives—in small ways and in big ways. We tell ourselves, no matter what God says, that a lustful thought, a harsh word, or a selfish action will satisfy us. We persuade ourselves, no matter what God says, that the money we have (regardless of what it takes to get it) and the sex we experience (with whomever we want to enjoy it) will gratify us. We convince ourselves, no matter what God says, that we will be pleased with this person or that possession, this pleasure or that pursuit. We chase all these things, thinking that we're free. But we're blind to our own bondage. For in all our running to serve ourselves, we're actually rebelling against the only One who can satisfy our souls.

In the end, we are all guilty of rebellion against God. Not just the pimp in northern Nepal, but you and me. All of us have turned from God, all of us are guilty before God, and all of us know it. We feel this guilt, and although we inevitably deny it, we instinctively experience it.

Some deny guilt altogether, saying there is no such thing as right or wrong, that all ethics are illusory and arbitrary and only personal preferences remain. However, people who believe this often turn around and argue that it's right for you to agree with them and wrong for you to disagree with them. Ironic, isn't it?

Others try to remove guilt by shifting the standards of right and wrong in the name of cultural progression. One of the easiest ways to assuage guilt is to convince ourselves that our moral standards are impractical or outdated. Greed is not wrong; it's necessary in the good of ambition. Promoting ourselves is the only way to be successful. Lust is natural for contemporary men and women, and sex is expected regardless of marriage or gender. We attempt to remove our guilt by redefining right and wrong according to cultural fads.

Yet guilt remains. No matter how hard we try, we can't successfully erase the sense of "ought" that God has written on the human soul. One need only look in the eyes of a little girl being sold into sex slavery to know that this "ought" not to be, for right and wrong do exist as objective standards for all people in all places at all times. We cannot remove the reality of guilt before God, and this is why we need Jesus. Yet this is where the gospel counters culture in an even more offensive way.

IS JESUS UNIQUE?

Almost all people in the world who know anything about Jesus, including the most secular of scholars, would say that Jesus was a good man. People find Jesus easy to identify with—a man familiar with sorrow, struggle, and suffering. Moreover, people *like* Jesus. He was loving and kind. He championed the cause of the poor and needy. He made friends with the neglected, the weak, and the downtrodden. He hung out with the despised and rejected. He loved his enemies, and he taught others to do the same.[7]

Yet alongside Jesus' remarkably humble character, we also see wildly egocentric claims. You don't have to read very far through the stories of Jesus' life before you start to conclude that he sure does talk a lot about himself. "I am this, I am that," he says over and over again. "Follow me, come to me," he calls to everyone around him. Stott describes this best:

> One of the most extraordinary things Jesus did in his teaching (and did it so unobtrusively that many people read the Gospels without even noticing it) was to set himself apart from everybody else. For example, by claiming to be the good shepherd who went out into the desert to seek his lost sheep, he was implying that the world was lost, that he wasn't, and that he could seek and save it.
>
> In other words, he put himself in a moral category in which he was alone. Everybody else was in darkness; he was the light of the world. Everybody else was hungry; he was the bread of life. Everybody else was thirsty; he could quench their thirst. Everybody else was sinful; he could forgive their sins. Indeed, on two separate occasions he did so, and both times observers were scandalized. They asked, "Why does this fellow talk like that? He's blaspheming! Who can forgive sins but God alone?" (Mark 2:5-7; Luke 7:48-49).
>
> If Jesus claimed authority to forgive the penitent, he also claimed authority to judge the impenitent. Several of his parables implied that he expected to return at the end of history. On that day, he said, he would sit on his glorious throne. All nations would stand before him, and he would separate them from one another as a shepherd separates his sheep from his goats. In other words, he would settle their eternal destiny. Thus he made himself the central figure on the day of judgment.[8]

Even if no one else did, Jesus certainly believed he was unique. He makes maybe his most extravagant claim in John 14:6: "I am the way, and the truth, and the life. No one comes to the Father except through me."

What a statement. As if the gospel were not already offensive enough with the announcement of who God is and who we are, now we hear that Jesus is the only person who is able to reconcile us to God. No other leader is supreme, and no other path is sufficient. If you want to know God, you must come through Jesus.

How can this be? How can a man in his right mind two thousand years ago make this claim? And how can people in their right minds two thousand years later believe it?

It makes sense only if everything we've already seen in the Bible is true.

We have seen that God is completely holy and infinitely good, perfectly just and lovingly gracious. We have also seen that we are each created by God, but we are all corrupted by sin. We have all turned away from God and stand guilty before him. These twin realities set up the ultimate question: How can a holy God reconcile rebellious sinners to himself when they deserve his judgment?

Remember Proverbs 17:15: "He who justifies the wicked and he who condemns the righteous are both alike an abomination to the LORD." In other words, God detests those who call the guilty "innocent" and the innocent "guilty." God detests them because he is a good Judge; he calls the guilty and the innocent what they are.

So when God comes to us as a good Judge, what will he say to us? "Guilty." If he were to say, "Innocent," he would be an abomination to himself. Now we begin to sense the underlying tension of the Bible. Every man and woman is guilty before God. How, then, can God express his perfect justice without condemning every sinner in the world?

Many people answer, "Well, God is loving. He can simply forgive our sins." But as soon as we say this, we must realize that God's forgiveness of sinners is a potential threat to his perfect character. If God simply overlooks sin, then he would be neither holy nor just. If there were a courtroom judge today who knowingly acquitted guilty criminals, we would have that judge off the bench in a heartbeat. Why? Because he is not just. Once we grasp the holy justice of God and the sinful nature of humanity, in the words of Stott, "no longer do we ask *why* God finds it difficult to forgive sins but *how* he finds it possible."[9]

This tension leads us to ask, "How then can God love us when his justice requires condemning us?" This is the fundamental problem in the universe. Now to be sure, it's not the problem most people identify. Most people in our culture are not losing sleep over how it's possible for God to be just and loving toward sinners at the same time. Instead, most people are accusing God, asking, "How can you punish sinners? How can you let good people go to hell?" But the question the Bible asks is exactly the opposite: "God, how can you be just and still let guilty sinners into heaven?"

And the only answer to that question is Jesus Christ.

Jesus' life is truly unique. He is God in the flesh—fully human and fully God. As perfect man, he alone is able to stand in the place of guilty men and women. As perfect God, he alone is able to satisfy divine justice.

That makes Jesus' death unique, which is why his crucifixion is the climax of the gospel. It's strange when you think about it. For all other religious leaders, death was the tragic end of the story. The focus in other religions is always on their leaders' lives. With Jesus, though, it is completely the opposite. He was constantly anticipating his death, and the accounts of his life put a disproportionate emphasis on it. Ever since his death two thousand years ago, the central symbol of Christianity has been the cross, and the church's central celebration revolves around bread and wine, commemorating the body and blood of Jesus.[10] Why is the death of Christ on the cross so significant?

Because the cross is where Jesus, God in the flesh, took the just punishment due sinners upon himself. At the cross of Christ, God fully expressed his holy judgment upon sin. At the same time, God in Christ fully endured his holy judgment against sin. In the process, God through Christ made salvation possible for all sinners—the penalty for sin was paid. We know this to be true because God raised Jesus from the dead. This is the greatest news in all the world, and it's why we call it the gospel (which means "good news"). The holy, just, and gracious Creator of the universe has made a way in Christ for anyone anywhere to be reconciled to him.

But again, we cannot escape the offense of this gospel. "Are you really saying there's *only one way* to God?" people immediately ask. Yet even as we ask the question, we reveal the problem. If there were 1,000 ways to God, we would want 1,001. The issue is not how many ways lead to God; the issue is our autonomy before God. We want to make our *own* way. This is the essence of sin in the first place—trusting our ways more than God's way. But we will not be rescued from our sin by turning to ourselves and trusting our ways even more. Instead, we will only be rescued by turning from ourselves and trusting God's way evermore.

THE ETERNAL OFFENSE

All that we've seen so far in the gospel is not particularly popular. Just the idea that God became a man is outlandish to multitudes around the world. Over a billion Muslims believe that God would never debase himself by becoming a man. Hundreds of millions of others think it preposterous that a man could be divine.

But the gospel's offense goes further. The gospel asserts that not only has God become a man but that this God-man has been crucified. This is foolishness to contemporary men and women. Imagine taking a successful, well-dressed American man with a nice job, big house, and cool car and a free-thinking American woman who thrives on her independence and leading them to a garbage dump, where a naked man hangs by nails on a tree, covered in blood, and telling them, "This is your God." They will laugh at you, may possibly feel sorry for the man, and almost certainly will move on with their lives.

Yet the offense of the gospel reaches its peak when you tell them that their eternal destiny is dependent on whether they believe the man hanging there is their God—the Lord, Judge, Savior, and King of all creation. As soon as you say, "If you follow him, you will experience eternal life; if not, you will experience everlasting hell," you will find yourself across a line of utmost contention in contemporary culture (and in the contemporary church).

The gospel claims that eternity is at stake in how you and I respond to Jesus.

According to the Bible, heaven is a glorious reality for those who trust in Jesus. It is a place of full reconciliation and complete restoration where sin, suffering, pain, and sorrow will finally cease, and men and women who have trusted in Christ will live in perfect harmony with God and each other forever and ever.

The Bible also teaches that hell is a dreadful reality for those who turn from Jesus. It's a reality about which Jesus spoke much. Tim Keller observes, "If Jesus, the Lord of Love and Author of Grace spoke about hell more often, and in a more vivid, blood-curdling manner than anyone else, it must be a crucial truth."[11]

This "crucial truth" flows directly from all we've discovered to this point.

Every man and woman has turned from God to self, and if nothing changes before they die, hell will be the God-given punishment for this sinful, self-exalting choice. Those who rebel against God on earth will receive the just penalty for the path they have chosen. Now of course no one, no matter how evil, would choose hell knowing the horror it entails. Scripture describes hell as a place where people will weep and gnash their teeth in a smoke of torment that rises without rest for all who reside there (see Matthew 8:12; Revelation 14:11). No one knowingly wills to experience this. Yet by ultimately willing against God on earth, sinners' de facto destination is damnation in eternity.

When you put all these truths in the gospel together, you realize that the most offensive and countercultural claim in Christianity is not what Christians believe about homosexuality or abortion, marriage or religious liberty. Instead, the most offensive claim in Christianity is that God is the Creator, Owner, and Judge of every person on the planet. Every one of us stands before him guilty of sin, and the only way to be reconciled to him is through faith in Jesus, the crucified Savior and risen King. All who trust in his love will experience everlasting life while all who turn from his lordship will suffer everlasting death.

DO YOU BELIEVE THE GOSPEL?

So we return to the fundamental question from the beginning of this chapter: Do you believe the gospel?

I envision three categories of readers for this book. The first category includes readers who don't believe the gospel. You don't currently profess to be a Christian, yet for any number of reasons you're reading this book. I'm very thankful you are, and I hope you will get a helpful perspective on the most pressing social issues of our culture and world. As you'll read in the chapter on religious liberty, I deeply respect differing religions, and I believe there are healthy ways not only to coexist but also to cooperate in genuine friendship and valuable partnership in society and culture. At the same time, I'd be less than honest if I didn't say I'm praying that in the process of reading this book, you might come to know God's mysterious, unfathomable, unexplainable, and personal love for you in Jesus. I'm hoping that, maybe even unbeknownst to you, one of the reasons you're reading this book is that God is sovereignly drawing you to faith in him.

The second category of reader is similar to the first in that you don't believe the gospel. The difference, however, is that you currently profess to be a Christian. As I referenced in the introduction, maybe you label yourself a "progressive Christian" or an "open-minded Christian" or a "churchgoing Christian" or any number of other modifiers you might put before your status as a Christian. With all due respect—and I'm not sure how to write this without being blunt—my hope is that you will stop calling yourself a Christian until you believe the gospel.

Some "Christians" don't believe God is the Creator of the universe or the Author of the Bible, other "Christians" don't believe sin is a serious problem before God, many "Christians" believe Jesus is only one of many ways to God, and a host of "Christians" totally reject what Jesus says about hell (while conveniently keeping what Jesus says about heaven). I put "Christians" in quotation marks simply because such "Christians" are not Christians. It is impossible to be a follower of Christ while denying, disregarding, discrediting, and disbelieving the words of Christ.

So if this is you, my aim is similar to what I shared with the first category of reader. I sincerely hope that you will come to know God's mysterious, unfathomable, unexplainable, and personal love for you in Jesus; that you will believe the gospel despite all of its offense; and that you will follow Jesus for who he is, not for who we might prefer him to be. Until this happens, my hope is that you will not blaspheme his name by claiming to be in Christ (Christian) when you do not believe Christ.

The final category of reader includes those who *do* believe the gospel. I assume this comprises many of those reading this book, and this is certainly the main audience for whom I am writing. In the pages that follow, my goal is to bring the gospel to bear on many social issues in our culture, ranging from poverty, slavery, abortion, and sexual immorality to the degradation of marriage and the denial of civil rights. In the process, I want to demonstrate how a full-orbed understanding of the gospel doesn't allow us to sit on the sidelines of our culture.

Moreover, the gospel doesn't allow us as Christians to be selective regarding different social issues. When I look at the church today, I see much emphasis on social justice, but our social stances seem strangely subjective. On popular issues like poverty and slavery, where Christians are likely to be applauded for our social action, we are quick to stand up and speak out. Yet on controversial issues like sexuality and abortion, where Christians are likely to be criticized for our involvement, we are content to sit down and stay quiet. It's as if we've decided to pick and choose which social issues we'll counter and which we'll concede, and our choice normally revolves around what is most comfortable—and least costly—for us in our culture.

But the gospel doesn't give us this option. The same heart of God that moves us to counter sex trafficking moves us to counter sexual immorality, and the same gospel that compels us to combat poverty compels us to defend marriage. We need to see how the gospel moves Christians to consistently counter not some but all of these issues in our culture with conviction, compassion, and courage.

A CALL TO CONVICTION, COMPASSION, AND COURAGE

As you and I consider these issues, I want to call us to conviction. As we've already established, we live in a unique time in Western culture as the moral landscape around us is rapidly changing. As a result, we have many opportunities to stand upon and speak about divine truth, and we can't let this moment pass. Elizabeth Rundle Charles, commenting on Martin Luther's confrontation of key issues in his day, says:

> It is the truth which is assailed in any age which tests our fidelity. . . . If I profess with the loudest voice and clearest exposition every portion of the truth of God except precisely that point which the world and the devil are at that moment attacking, I am not confessing Christ, however boldly I may be professing Christianity. Where the battle rages, there the loyalty of the soldier is proven, and to be steady on all the battle fronts besides is mere flight and disgrace if he flinches at that point.[12]

Indeed, battles are raging over a number of social issues in our culture today. Just decades ago, Francis Schaeffer wrote:

> We as Bible-believing evangelical Christians are locked in a battle. This is not a friendly gentleman's discussion. It is a life and death conflict between the spiritual hosts of wickedness and those who claim the name of Christ. . . . But do we really believe that we are in a life and

death battle? Do we really believe that the part we play in the battle has consequences for whether or not men and women will spend eternity in hell? Or whether or not those who do live will live in a climate of moral perversion and degradation? Sadly, we must say that very few in the evangelical world have acted as if these things are true. . . . Where is the clear voice speaking to the crucial issues of the day with distinctively biblical, Christian answers? With tears we must say it is not there and that a large segment of the evangelical world has become seduced by the world spirit of this present age. And more than this, we can expect the future to be a further disaster if the evangelical world does not take a stand for biblical truth and morality in the full spectrum of life.[13]

May this not be said of you and me today. May we not sin through silence. May we realize that not to speak is to speak. Ultimately, may it be said of us that we not only held firm *to* the gospel, but that we spoke clearly *with* the gospel to the most pressing issues of our day.

In addition to calling us to conviction, I want to call us to compassion. Matthew 9 tells us that "when [Jesus] saw the crowds, he had compassion for them, because they were harassed and helpless, like sheep without a shepherd" (Matthew 9:36). One of my hopes in this book is that God would give us grace to see what he sees. To see the poor, the hungry, and the neglected as he sees them. To perceive those crushed by political, economic, or ethnic oppression from his perspective. To care for the baby in the womb as well as the baby's mother as God cares for them. To love the orphan and the widow, the immigrant and the immoral, the heterosexual, homosexual, bisexual, and transsexual person as God loves them.

Based upon his love, I want to call us to action. "You shall love your neighbor as yourself," Jesus commands (Matthew 22:39). John writes, "Let us not love in word or talk but in deed and in truth" (1 John 3:18). The last thing I want to do is to divorce biblical, theological, and ethical principles from individual, family, and church practice. The goal of this book is not information about the gospel and social issues; it is application of the gospel to social issues. We need to explore all of these issues not with a self-righteous complacency that is content to wring our hands in pious concern, but with a self-sacrificing commitment to do whatever God tells us to do.

Inevitably, God will lead us to act in different ways. Not every one of us will respond in the same way to all of these issues. No one person can fight sex trafficking while fostering and adopting children in the middle of starting a ministry to widows and counseling unwed mothers while traveling around the world to support the persecuted church—and so on. Nor *should* any one of us do all of these things, for God sovereignly puts us in unique positions and places with unique privileges and opportunities to influence the culture around us. But what is necessary for *all* of us is to view each of these cultural issues through the lens of biblical truth and to speak such truth with conviction whenever we have the chance to do so. Then, based on consistent conviction, we seek how individually as Christians and collectively in our churches the Spirit of Christ is leading us to compassionate action in our culture.

In order to help us in this, each chapter in this book concludes by offering some initial suggestions for practical requests you and I can pray in light of these issues, potential ways you or I might engage culture with the gospel, and biblical truths we must proclaim regarding every one of these issues. These suggestions will also direct you to a website (CounterCultureBook.com) where you can explore more specific steps you might take. There you will also find information about the *Counter Culture Scripture and Prayer Guide* that will help you dive deeper into countercultural living as an individual, family, or church. In all of this, I want to exhort you to humbly, boldly, seriously, and prayerfully consider how God is directing you to pray, speak, and live in light of each of these issues. Let's not merely contemplate the Word of God in the world around us; let's do what it says (see James 1:22-25).

Acting with conviction and compassion will require courage, to be sure. As we have seen, the cost of biblical conviction in contemporary culture is growing steeper every day, and we are not far removed from sharing more soberly in the sufferings of Christ. Doubtless this is why more and more "Christians" today are stepping away from the gospel. Fear is a powerful force, leading more and more "churches" today to accommodation and adaptation instead of confrontation with the surrounding culture. Consequently, I believe Schaeffer's words are appropriate:

We need a young generation and others who will be willing to stand in loving confrontation, but real confrontation, in contrast to the mentality of constant accommodation with the current forms of the world spirit as they surround us today, and in contrast to the way in which so much of *evangelicalism* has developed the automatic mentality to accommodate at each successive point.[14]

My hope is that we would heed this challenge. For it is not ultimately a challenge from Schaeffer; it is a challenge from Christ:

Do not fear those who kill the body but cannot kill the soul. Rather fear him who can destroy both soul and body in hell. . . . Everyone who acknowledges me before men, I also will acknowledge before my Father who is in heaven, but whoever denies me before men, I also will deny before my Father who is in heaven. . . . Whoever finds his life will lose it, and whoever loses his life for my sake will find it.   MATTHEW 10:28, 32-33, 39

The gospel of Christ is not a call to cultural compromise in the face of fear. It is a call to countercultural crucifixion—death to self in the face of earthly opposition for the sake of eternal reward.

My hope is that we would believe the gospel of Christ and that our belief would move us to counter our culture. My prayer is that in this journey we are on, God might open our eyes to the needs of people in our culture and around the world, bring us to our knees in tears and prayers on their behalf, and cause us to rise with conviction, compassion, and courage to humbly spread the truth of God while selflessly showing the love of God, all in hopeful anticipation of the day when sin, suffering, immorality, and injustice will finally be no more.

WHERE RICH
AND POOR COLLIDE:
THE GOSPEL
AND POVERTY

Trekking through a snow-covered Asian village, I saw poverty personified.

As soon as we entered the village, a man stepped out of his house. He wore a tattered beige shirt and a torn brown jacket filled with holes that no doubt prevented it from fulfilling its purpose. His jet-black hair, aging gray beard, and rough bronze skin had not been washed for weeks. His name was Sameer.

When I saw Sameer, though, what stood out most was none of those attributes. Instead, when I looked into Sameer's eyes, I could see into Sameer's skull. Not long before, Sameer's right eye had become infected. With no access to basic medicine, the infection worsened. Eventually, his eyeball fell out of its socket. A gaping hole now stood on the right side of Sameer's face, and the infection was spreading farther. Sameer's cheek was beginning to cave. His hearing was beginning to fail. It was evident that whatever sickness was causing this would soon overtake his head and eventually end his life.

We were dreadfully aware of our limited ability to help Sameer physically. The people I was hiking with were working to build a hospital close to his village, but for the time being, there were no options for medical care anywhere nearby.

As we talked with Sameer, we told him the story of Jesus healing a blind man. Sameer had never heard of Jesus, so we shared who Jesus is and how Jesus healed disease as a demonstration of his power to conquer death. We shared with Sameer how Jesus' death had paid the price for people's sin against God. We shared how Jesus' resurrection gives hope that one day all who trust in him will be with him in a land where there is no more sin, suffering, disease, or death. Sameer smiled. Before long, we had to move on from Sameer's house, and to this day I don't know how long he lived. What I do know is that God used this man with a missing eye to transform my own sight that day.

For when I looked at Sameer, I saw what happens when severe poverty turns simple illness into almost certain death. As we walked through the rest of Sameer's village and more villages after that, we met similar people and heard similar stories of men, women, and children who had died or were dying of preventable diseases. One village we passed had recently experienced a cholera outbreak. Up to sixty people had died in a matter of weeks because of a simple stomach infection due to impure water and poor hygiene. In case you read quickly over that last sentence, that's a huge portion of an entire community who died of diarrhea. Only half the children in these villages survive to see their eighth birthday.

On the same day I walked through Sameer's village, I read in Luke 10 Jesus' summary of all God's commandments to his people: "You shall love the Lord your God with all your heart and with all your soul and with all your strength and with all your mind, and your neighbor as yourself" (Luke 10:27). That last phrase jumped off the page in light of the picture I was seeing. "Love your neighbor as yourself."

As myself?

I wondered what I would want someone to do for me if I lived in one of these villages. What if I were Sameer? Wouldn't I want somebody to help me? Or what if it were my kids or the children in my church dying of preventable diseases? What if *half* your children or my children were dying before they turned eight? If this were us, or if these were our kids, or if these were the children in our churches, we would do something. Ignoring such urgent needs simply would not be an option.

Yet this is exactly what so many of us in the Western church have done. We have retreated. We have insulated and isolated ourselves from the massive material poverty that surrounds us in the world. We have filled our lives and our churches with more comforts for us, all while turning a blind eye and a deaf ear to abject poverty in others. We have a gaping hole in the way we see the world, and we need new sight. We need our eyes opened to the implications of the gospel for how we live in a world of massive poverty.

THE WEALTHY ARISTOCRACY

Such new sight needs to start by seeing how rich we are. Obviously, first and foremost, we are spiritually rich, for all who have turned from their sin and trusted in Christ have been raised to new life. Remember the words of Ephesians 2:

> Because of his great love for us, God, who is rich in mercy, made us alive with Christ even when we were

dead in transgressions—it is by grace you have been saved. And God raised us up with Christ and seated us with him in the heavenly realms in Christ Jesus, in order that in the coming ages he might show the incomparable riches of his grace, expressed in his kindness to us in Christ Jesus. EPHESIANS 2:4-7, NIV

What a passage! And all of this is possible because of "the grace of our Lord Jesus Christ," who "though he was rich, yet for your sake he became poor, so that you by his poverty might become rich" (2 Corinthians 8:9). Without question, our greatest wealth is found in the gospel itself, for God has saved us from our sins and has given us new life with him.

Yet readers of this book are almost inevitably materially rich as well. I realize that we may not always *feel* rich. That is likely because whenever we hear the word *rich*, we immediately think of the kind of people who have far more than we do, and consequently we rarely perceive ourselves as rich. But we need a new perspective. For if we have clean water, sufficient food and clothes, a roof over our heads at night, access to medicine, a mode of transportation (even if it's public), and the ability to read a book, then relative to billions of people in the world, we are incredibly wealthy. Economics professors Steve Corbett and Brian Fikkert observe how the standard of living essentially common among us is extremely uncommon in human history. They write, "At no time in history has there ever been greater economic disparity in the world than at present." Speaking specifically about present-day Americans, they conclude, "By any measure, we are the richest people ever to walk on planet Earth."[1]

We need to open our eyes, then, to the reality that when most people in the world hear the word *rich*, they picture us. Indeed, average, ordinary, middle-class, working Americans are an extremely wealthy aristocracy in a world surrounded by billions of extremely poor neighbors. And Jesus has called us to love these neighbors—as ourselves.

Christ's command, coupled with the depth of poverty in the world and the reality of wealth in our lives, has huge implications for the way we live. For when our eyes have been opened to conditions in the world around us, our ears must be open to the question God's Word asks us: "If anyone has the world's goods and sees his brother in need, yet closes his heart against him, how does God's love abide in him?" (1 John 3:17). To be clear, this is a specific reference to followers of Christ caring for other Christians in need (a priority I will address later in this chapter). However, the command of Christ in Luke 10 to love our neighbors as ourselves surely includes care not just for the believing poor but also for the unbelieving poor. Such neighborly love is the natural overflow of men and women who know God. If the love of God is in our hearts, then it is not possible for us to ignore the poor in the world. The gospel compels Christians in a wealthy culture to action—selfless, sacrificial, costly, counter-cultural action—on behalf of the poor. For if we don't act in this way, then it may become clear that we were never Christians in the first place.

THE CONVICTING REALITY

Statements like that have gotten me into some trouble in the church. In my previous book *Radical*, I wrote about conviction in my own heart regarding materialism in my own life. My wife, Heather, and I were living in New Orleans when Hurricane Katrina sent our house underwater. Having lost almost every possession we had, we started over, and I told Heather, "We have an opportunity to rebuild our lives from the ground up, not filling our lives with things we don't need, but focusing our lives on living simply." She agreed, and we set out to do exactly that.

But in the coming months, I received a call from a large church in the South, asking me to become their pastor. Believing that the Lord was leading us there, we soon found ourselves in Birmingham, Alabama, where only one short year after Katrina, we bought a larger house than we had ever lived in with far more stuff than we had ever had. In the eyes of the world (even the church world), we were living the dream. But deep down I had this sinking feeling that we were missing the point.

Conviction came to a head when our friends John and Abigail visited us in Birmingham. Years before, they had sold everything they had and moved their family (with four young girls) to a North African country to declare and demonstrate God's love in the midst of massive poverty. They were back in the United States for a few months, and during that time they spent a couple of days with us. They shared stories of how God was providing for their needs and the needs of the people they were working among. They spoke with such joy, even as they shared about the suffering they had seen and the struggles they had experienced. As I listened to them in my large house, surrounded by all the comforts I had acquired, I knew that my friend possessed a faith with which I was unfamiliar. Neither he nor his wife ever made a comment about the extravagance in which we were living, but I was cut to the core by a sacrificial compassion I saw in him that I didn't see in me.

Conviction from God's Spirit drove me back to God's Word, where I began seeing God's heart for the poor in a way I never had before. It didn't take long for that conviction to rise to an entirely new level as I read verses like the ones below:

- Proverbs 21:13—Whoever closes his ear to the cry of the poor will himself call out and not be answered.

- Proverbs 28:27—Whoever gives to the poor will not want, but he who hides his eyes will get many a curse.
- James 2:14-17—What good is it, my brothers, if someone says he has faith but does not have works? Can that faith save him? If a brother or sister is poorly clothed and lacking in daily food, and one of you says to them, "Go in peace, be warmed and filled," without giving them the things needed for the body, what good is that? So also faith by itself, if it does not have works, is dead.
- 1 John 3:16-18—By this we know love, that [Jesus] laid down his life for us, and we ought to lay down our lives for the brothers. But if anyone has the world's goods and sees his brother in need, yet closes his heart against him, how does God's love abide in him? Little children, let us not love in word or talk but in deed and in truth.

Reading these verses, I came face-to-face with the fact that I had shut my ears to the cries of the poor and closed my eyes to their plight. I was living like they didn't exist. I was a pastor (and a successful one by all the standards of church culture) who read, studied, and preached God's Word. But when it came to the poor, I was word and talk, devoid of deed and truth.

James was right: my lack of concern for the poor was a clear sign of a fundamental problem with my faith. And James was only writing what Jesus had already said, that faith in our hearts will be evident in the fruit of our lives. Jesus taught, "You will recognize [people] by their fruits" (Matthew 7:16). He later describes the separation of Christians from non-Christians at the final judgment in terms of those who have helped impoverished followers of Christ and those who haven't (see Matthew 25:31-46). Concerning those who haven't given food, water, and clothes to brothers and sisters in need, Jesus says, "These will go away into eternal punishment" (Matthew 25:46). The more I listened to Jesus, James, and the rest of Scripture, the more it became clear: those who claim to be Christians but refuse to help poverty-stricken people are simply not children of God. This reality rocked my soul.

FREE TO WORK

Now I know (and want to be careful to communicate) that neither Jesus, James, nor any other writer in Scripture was teaching that care for the poor is a means to salvation. The Bible is clear from cover to cover that humble faith in divine grace is the only means to eternal salvation. Paul expresses this truth with utmost clarity: "By grace you have been saved through faith. And this is not your own doing; it is the gift of God, not a result of works, so that no one may boast" (Ephesians 2:8-9). The only basis for salvation is the work of Jesus in and through his life, death, and resurrection, and the only means to salvation is trust in him. The good news of the gospel is that based on nothing we have done and everything Jesus has done—by his grace alone, through faith alone in him—God will declare us right before him. In this way, the gospel frees us from any and every attempt to earn God's acceptance through our work.

But that is not the end of the story. For the more I have studied God's Word, the more I have realized that this same gospel that frees me *from* work also frees me *to* work. That may sound confusing or even contradictory, but I'm using *work* here in two different senses, much as Scripture does. Sometimes *work* in the Bible refers to actions done in the flesh in order to earn God's favor, and as we've seen, such work is completely insufficient. All our best, most radical works will never be enough to merit salvation before a holy God.

However, the Bible also talks about *work* in terms of actions fueled by faith in order to bring glory to God, and the Bible celebrates this kind of work. This is the kind of work James talks about when he speaks of loving the needy, showing mercy to the poor, and caring for the suffering. Similarly, Paul speaks of "work produced by faith" (1 Thessalonians 1:3, NIV), "every act prompted by your faith" (2 Thessalonians 1:11, NIV), and "faith working through love" (Galatians 5:6). In fact, right after the verses in Ephesians about how we are saved by grace alone through faith alone in Christ alone, Paul writes, "We are [God's] workmanship, created in Christ Jesus for good works, which God prepared beforehand, that we should walk in them" (Ephesians 2:10). Did you catch that? God has created us for good works. If you are a follower of Christ, then you are free to rest in his finished work on your behalf, and at the same time you are free to do good works according to his will.

And his will is clear. He wants to make his glory—the completeness of his character—known to all peoples everywhere in the world. He wills to show the world that he is "merciful and gracious, slow to anger, and abounding in steadfast love" (Exodus 34:6); that he "raises up the poor from the dust" and "lifts the needy from the ash heap" (1 Samuel 2:8); that he "executes justice for the oppressed" and "gives food to the hungry" (Psalm 146:7); that he is a "defense for the helpless" and "the needy in his distress" (Isaiah 25:4, NASB). These characteristics of God are ultimately revealed in Christ, who came "to proclaim good news to the poor" and "to set at liberty those who are oppressed" (Luke 4:18).

Once we see this portrait of God in Christ, we realize that caring for the poor is not only necessary evidence of faith in him; it's the natural (or supernatural) overflow of faith in him. Doesn't it make sense that those of us who love God as our Father would subsequently live as "imitators of God, as beloved children," walking "in love, as Christ loved us and gave himself up for us" (Ephesians 5:1-2)? As people whom Christ has cared for sacrificially in our poverty, aren't we compelled to care for others selflessly in their poverty? Even more, as materially wealthy men and women in a world of urgent spiritual and physical need, don't we want to reflect the majesty of our God in mercy toward the poor?

"WANT TO"

This "want to" is especially significant because it crystallizes Christians' motivation to care for the poor. We don't care for the poor because of some superficial sense that we *have to* but because of a supernatural compulsion that causes us to *want to*.

Christians in our culture shouldn't care for the poor merely because we're constrained by a low-grade sense of guilt. Sure, when we realize that nearly nineteen thousand children are dying every day of preventable diseases and recognize that we are some of the most affluent people to ever walk the planet, our eyes are opened.[2] But simple guilt in the face of global statistics doesn't produce sustainable obedience to God's commands. We may change our ways for a short time based upon guilt, but it won't last.

Instead, real, authentic, sustainable care for the poor will only happen when any low-grade sense of guilt is conquered by a high-grade sense of gospel. For through the gospel—the good news of God's great love in Christ—Christians are compelled to willing, joyful, urgent, faith-driven, grace-saturated, God-glorifying work on behalf of the poor.

Now to be clear, reaching the point where we *want to* obey the commands of Christ doesn't necessarily happen overnight.

Growth in the Christian life often begins with obedience even when acute desire is not present. However, over the course of obedience, followers of Christ learn to trust that his ways are indeed good. As a pastor, I have loved watching people take small steps to care for the poor in our community and around the world, only to realize how rewarding this is—not just for others but also for themselves. As we care for the poor over time, what may have initially been duty ("have to") inevitably becomes delight ("want to").

Even while we care for the poor, we will be tempted to forget the gospel at every turn. Christian history is unfortunately littered with stories of people who passionately worked on behalf of the poor but subtly loosened their grip on the gospel. The so-called "social gospel" of the twentieth century stripped Christianity of its core truths and set many churches on a course toward theological compromise and biblical heresy. As a result, many Christians who believe the Bible are cautious about care for the poor.

But we mustn't be cautious with something about which God is so clear. From cover to cover in Scripture, we do not read of a God who is tentative toward the poor. Instead, God is extravagant in his eagerness to hear, help, defend, and demonstrate his compassion to them. Therefore, God's people must be nothing less than these things. Yes, we must guard the truths of the gospel, but we must also obey God.

If this is an area of your life where you have been disobedient to the commands of God's Word by neglecting the poor, the gospel is still good news. God forgives this sin too, and by his Spirit he can and will enable you to walk a new path of sacrificial love for your neighbor.

What does such sacrificial love look like? I'd like to focus on five simple but significant implications of the gospel for our lives in a world of urgent spiritual and physical poverty. In a culture that places great emphasis on leisure, luxury, financial gain, self-improvement, and material possessions, it will be increasingly countercultural for Christians to work diligently, live simply, give sacrificially, help constructively, and invest eternally. Yet this is what we must do.[3]

WORK DILIGENTLY

First, the gospel compels us to work diligently. As one who himself delights in work, God has designed us to work. When God created man, he "put him in the garden of Eden to work it" (Genesis 2:15). When we remember that this was *before* sin's entrance into the world, we realize that work is a good gift of God's grace.

We often view work as a necessary evil, something we have to endure in order to make money, but this is not how the Bible views work. From the beginning, work has been a mark of human dignity, a fundamental part of God's plan for people to steward the creation entrusted to them and to develop the culture around them for the common good. Tim Keller summarizes this well:

Farming takes the physical material of soil and seed and produces food. Music takes the physics of sound and rearranges it into something beautiful and thrilling that brings meaning to life. When we take fabric and make a piece of clothing, when we push a broom and clean up a room, when we use technology to harness the forces of electricity, when we take an unformed, naive human mind and teach it a subject, when we teach a couple how to resolve their relational disputes, when we take simple

materials and turn them into a poignant work of art—
we are continuing God's work of forming, filling, and
subduing . . . [and] we are following God's pattern of
creative cultural development.[4]

As we produce goods and provide services through all sorts
of jobs, we are contributing to our culture in a way that serves
people and honors God.

And all sorts of jobs are important in society. If everyone were
a pastor or church staff member, it would be disastrous. Sure,
we'd know how to teach the Bible and shepherd the church, but
we wouldn't have any food to eat. Likewise, if everyone were a
salesperson, we wouldn't have any products to buy. If everyone
were a police officer, we'd all be safe, but we'd also be homeless. If
everyone were a lawyer . . . well, we'd all be in trouble. As Lester
DeKoster observes:

> [Work] yields far more in return on our efforts than our
> particular jobs put in. . . . That chair you are lounging
> in? Could you have made it for yourself? . . . How do
> [you] get, say, the wood? Go and fell a tree? But only
> after first making the tools for that, and putting together
> some kind of vehicle to haul the wood, and constructing
> a mill to do the lumber, and roads to drive on from
> place to place? In short, a lifetime or two to make one
> chair! . . .
>
>   If we . . . worked not only forty but, say, one hundred
> and forty hours a week, we ourselves couldn't make from
> scratch even a fraction of all the goods and services that
> we [now] call our own. . . . [Our] paycheck turns out to
> buy us the use of far more than we could possibly make
> for ourselves in the time it takes us to earn the check.[5]

He concludes:

Imagine that everyone quits working, right now! What happens? Civilized life quickly melts away. Food vanishes from the store shelves, gas pumps dry up, streets are no longer patrolled, and fires burn themselves out. Communication and transportation services end and utilities go dead. Those who survive at all are soon huddled around campfires, sleeping in caves, and clothed in rags. The difference between [a wilderness] and culture is simply, work.[6]

All sorts of human work are significant, designed by God for the good of the world.

I stress this point because work is one of the most obvious, but often overlooked, ways we provide for the poor. Sometimes people hear pleas to help the poor and immediately think, *Maybe I should quit my menial job in order to give more meaningful time to the poor.* I'm not saying that God won't lead some people to leave their professions for a particular purpose, but I do wonder if this pattern of thinking exposes a fundamental flaw in our understanding of work. For in working on a daily basis, we are lending our help to the development of a society that is able to sustain human life.

I hear this sometimes from college students who are convicted about a certain area of need in the world and decide that the obvious course of action is for them to stop wasting time in school and start doing something significant in the world. Again, I'm not saying that God is leading every single person to go to (or stay in) college, but could it be that God has actually led many to college for a reason? Could it be that rather than being a waste of time, college is a wise use of time to receive training in skills for a job that God will use in the future to accomplish his purpose in the world?

In addition, work is how we make money. Various people who have read previous books I've written or heard me talk about possessions will ask, "David, are you saying it's wrong to make a lot of money?" My answer is always and unequivocally "No. Make as much money as you can. Be a millionaire, if the Lord provides you that opportunity!" People will look surprised, and I will follow up by saying, "What matters most is not how much you earn, but what you do with what you earn."

This is not my own philosophy; it's God's prescription. Hear his Word in 1 Timothy:

> As for the rich in this present age, charge them not to be haughty, nor to set their hopes on the uncertainty of riches, but on God, who richly provides us with everything to enjoy. They are to do good, to be rich in good works, to be generous and ready to share, thus storing up treasure for themselves as a good foundation for the future, so that they may take hold of that which is truly life.   1 TIMOTHY 6:17-19

God doesn't command the rich to stop making money; instead, he commands the rich to use their money on earth to store up treasure in eternity.

We have more money than most because we have the ability to work in our culture. We have opportunities to learn in schools, to go to colleges and universities, and to get jobs and make money. When we maximize our abilities and take advantage of these opportunities, we bring honor to God and cultivate society's good. In the process, we acquire skills, attain positions, gain platforms, and obtain resources that can (and must) then be leveraged for the care of the poor.

All of this means that as long as we are able, the gospel compels us to be countercultural in the way we work. We live in a culture that doesn't view work as God's good gift, whether as young adults or older adults in retirement. So many young people are prolonging adolescence into adulthood. Scores of males in their twenties and thirties, for example, are refusing to become men, settling for playing video games instead of getting an education or a job, working part-time while leaning on their parents to pay their bills. Worst of all, some couch their laziness in spiritual language, saying they're waiting to figure out what God wants them to do, all the while ignoring the glaring biblical reality that God wants them to work for others' good and his glory.

This trend should not surprise us in a culture that minimizes the value of work by magnifying the goal of retirement. Success, according to the standards of our society, is arriving at the place where you no longer work. I just returned from speaking at a conference in South Florida, where I found myself surrounded by men and women who are spending their final years on earth resting amid the pleasures of this culture. But Christ never called us to this sort of retirement. In no way does Scripture ever speak about God calling healthy people to stop working. Nowhere do we see that God's design for productive minds and bodies is to perpetually lie on a beach, ride on a golf course, or sit in a fishing boat. The entire concept of saving money so that we can live a life of ease and self-indulgence has no biblical foundation whatsoever.

Now to be clear, I'm not speaking here of men and women who are physically unable to work. Nor am I speaking of men and women who retire from a job in order to work in ways that don't require a salary. I know many men and women who are past a certain age and are no longer employed, but they are working for God in our city and around the world in all kinds of different ways.

I think of Jack, a friend of mine in his sixties who, when he was baptized, said plainly, "My plan was to retire, buy a German sports car, and play tennis." But then he shared, "By God's grace, before I could put my plan into action, God intervened." Jack shared how God had worked in his life, not just saving him from his sin but saving him from himself. Jack now uses his previous job skills to serve the church and the needy in our community, and he leads a ministry to orphans in Cameroon. "What a joy," he told the church, "to see the smiles of children as they push to get a seat on your lap and hold your hand because they have no earthly father and you are telling them about their heavenly Father." Then he concluded, "This is the plan God had for me, and the thrill and excitement of it far exceeds retirement or any sports car."

One of the primary ways we help the poor is through diligent work.

LIVE SIMPLY

Then, just as we work diligently, the gospel compels us to live simply. The only caveat I give when I encourage people to make as much money as possible is to be extremely careful in the process. Again, this is God's Word, especially to the rich. Just before the previous passage in 1 Timothy, Paul writes, "Those who desire to be rich fall into temptation, into a snare, into many senseless and harmful desires that plunge people into ruin and destruction. For the love of money is a root of all kinds of evils. It is through this craving that some have wandered away from the faith and pierced themselves with many pangs" (1 Timothy 6:9-10).

To be sure, money is not evil by nature. However, money in the hands of sinful people—all of us—can be dangerous, deadly, or even damning. Jesus himself says, "How hard it is for the rich to enter the kingdom of God!" (Mark 10:23, NIV). Once you and I realize that we are "the rich," these words should shock our systems.

But most of us just don't believe Jesus on this one. Most people in our culture—and in the church—believe wealth is always a sign of blessing from God, and we have almost no category for understanding wealth as a barrier to God.

We are so easily deceived. Just as 1 Timothy says, money can be a powerful snare. It's like seawater. If you're thirsty out on the ocean, you look around at all the water and think, *I should drink this.* But little do you realize that because of seawater's high salt concentration, the more you drink it, the thirstier you will become. As you continue drinking to quench your thirst, you will eventually dehydrate, leading to headaches, dry mouth, low blood pressure, and an increased heart rate. Eventually, you will become delirious, lose consciousness, and die. The irony is astonishing. In drinking what you think is a source of life, you unknowingly plunge yourself into death.

This is what we do when we let money seduce us. We think, *I want more,* but we don't realize that the desire for more is a trap. The "more" that we want will never satisfy because it will never be enough. As we indulge this desire, it destroys our soul bit by bit. And it may destroy us forever. Just in case you missed the Word of God earlier, hear it again: the desire for riches "plunge[s] people into ruin and destruction."

Thankfully, Scripture gives us a remedy to the allure of money. Right before these warnings in 1 Timothy, the Bible says, "Godliness with contentment is great gain, for we brought nothing into the world, and we cannot take anything out of the world. But if we have food and clothing, with these we will be content" (6:6-8). In these words, Scripture prescribes the antidote: a simple life of contentment that prioritizes necessities and minimizes luxuries. Paul says the same thing in 2 Corinthians 8–9, where we learn that God provides enough for us (see 2 Corinthians 9:8) and excess for others (see 2 Corinthians 9:11). The gospel compels us to humbly identify what is enough for us in order to freely give away our excess to others. By voluntarily surrendering our riches for others' good, we avoid the snare and enjoy the contentment that Paul describes.

Action like this goes completely against the grain of our culture, for we are bombarded by the lie that says a higher salary requires a higher standard of living. If we have more money, we should spend more money on ourselves. We are now entitled to more things, nicer possessions, and greater luxuries. And if we're honest, most of us think this way, even if we claim to follow Christ. After all, God has blessed us with it, right? Yet this attitude doesn't square with Scripture. For the Bible teaches that God gives us more not so that we can *have* more but so that we can *give* more. God has not given us excess money to indulge in earthly pleasures that will fade away; he has given us money to invest in eternal treasure that will last forever.

For this reason, you and I must relentlessly resist the bumper sticker idea that "whoever dies with the most toys wins." Such a view of life is not only dangerous; it's demonic. God is our greatest treasure, and our lives will count on earth only when we invest them in his Kingdom for eternity.

When we really grasp this, it will change the way we live. Practically, we set a cap on our lifestyle, determining a level of "enough" beyond which we are free to use the excess for the sake of others. Much like Paul, we prayerfully look at our possessions and say, "With this we will be content." Then, if or when we receive additional money, instead of that money increasing our standard of living, it only increases our standard of giving.

But even as we do this, we soon realize that there aren't easy answers regarding how this should look in each of our lives. God has not given us laws or lists in Scripture by which to measure what kind of food we should eat, how much clothing we need, or what kind of house we should live in. Instead, God has given us something better. He has given us his Spirit to lead and guide our every decision as we surrender to him our every dollar.

I remember when Heather and I began looking for a new house in response to conviction from God's Word. Convinced that we needed to downsize, the questions started coming. What size house should we live in? What kind of neighborhood should we look in? These questions were challenging because we knew that almost every house and neighborhood in our community would be considered luxurious in comparison with the rest of the world. So we asked, how can we best prioritize necessities while minimizing excesses? Yet this question was difficult because we knew that almost everything in any house we found would be filled with things that many people in the world would consider luxuries.

Moreover, in the midst of asking these questions, it quickly became clear that Heather and I had different answers in our minds. Downsizing our home would require the Spirit to bring us together in our decisions. And I must say that my wife was incredibly patient with me.

My plan at first was to give her a list of homes that I wanted us to visit, but that plan didn't work particularly well. I remember walking into one that had no floors, cabinets, or plumbing. I remember another that was visibly old and wildly unkempt, stinking of extreme must and mold. As soon as Heather walked in, she had to run out, where she threw up in the front yard. As I watched her puke, I knew we needed another plan.

So my next idea was to ask her to write down her top ten

priorities in a house. I told her I would do the same, and then we could share our priorities with each other. She gladly agreed, and when we sat down together, she went first.

"At the top of my list," she said, "is a place for our kids to be able to play outside. In some way, I would like for them to be able to be outdoors."

I looked at her and realized our lists were going to look very different. "What's wrong?" she asked. "What's first on your list?"

I paused. "Water."

"Water?" she asked, as if to say, *"Really?"*

And just as soon as I started to explain how water was not a given in the world (as if she didn't know that), I realized that in my efforts at simplicity, I had left the realm of the spiritual and moved into the realm of the absurd. That night and in the days to come, I began to think much more reasonably, and we agreed more consistently on how and where God was leading us to live. Looking back, I am so thankful for the process the Lord took us through to bring us to the house in which we now live—a house that, I assure you, is extravagant when compared to places like Sameer's village but that we hope is a responsible use of the resources God has entrusted to us.

Downsizing our house is just one of many decisions we made in the past and of a myriad of decisions we find ourselves making in the present in a materialistic culture that constantly contradicts the Word of God. I don't presume to be a perfect model of living simply, but I do press on, alongside my family and church, in a perpetual battle against the desire for riches.

I invite you to engage in that battle, both in your heart and in our culture. As you work diligently, how can you live simply? How might you draw the line of "enough" in your own life, knowing that this will inevitably lead you to counter the culture around you? Simple living is a constant challenge, and I am convinced that the only weapon able to win this war on a daily basis is the gospel of Jesus Christ.

GIVE SACRIFICIALLY

Beyond living simply, the gospel compels us to give sacrificially. In 2 Corinthians 8, Paul uses the example of churches in Macedonia who "in a severe test of affliction [and] extreme poverty . . . over-flowed in a wealth of generosity" by giving to starving saints in Jerusalem in the first century. They gave "beyond their means, of their own accord, begging . . . earnestly for the favor of taking part in the relief of the saints" (verses 2-4). I love that picture of men and women living in extreme poverty yet *begging* to give an offering to a needy church elsewhere.

I have seen this kind of generosity personally. Not long after Hurricane Katrina hit New Orleans, I was preaching and serving among impoverished churches in East Asia. These were the sorts of underground churches that met in secret late at night, knowing that if they were caught worshiping Christ, they could lose their land, freedom, family, or lives. Most of the members of these churches were poor farmers, working long hours every day in their fields simply to survive.

I spent a couple of weeks with them, teaching God's Word about what it means to make disciples, and somewhere along the way the man who was hosting me shared with these churches how a recent hurricane had ravaged my city, scattered our church, and destroyed my home along with many others. We came to the last night that I would spend with these churches, and when we finished, Liang, one of the leaders, came up to me with an envelope in his hand. He looked at me and said, "We have taken up an offering for you and your church back in New Orleans."

Immediately I said, "Oh no, Liang, I cannot take this from

you. I appreciate your generosity, but you and your church need this money far more than I do."

Yet Liang persisted. "No," he said. "We want to give this to you."

I responded again, "No, I can't take this."

This dialogue continued until Liang finally insisted. "We want the joy of serving you and your church," he said. "Please take this."

With that, I took the envelope and thanked Liang and the church profusely. I opened it later to find a relatively meager sum of money in it. Yet that minimal amount was nothing short of a sacrificial gift, for it cost the members of that church much to give it.

With that picture in mind, I can't help but wonder what it might look like for Christians and churches in our culture to give like that. Not just to give in a way that is comfortable to us, but to give in a way that really costs us. And what would it look like for us to give like that with eagerness and enthusiasm, insisting on the opportunity to truly sacrifice for our impoverished brothers and sisters around the world?

This is the clear pattern of giving in the New Testament church, yet it is unfortunately a far cry from common practice in the contemporary American church. We have brothers and sisters in Christ with urgent needs around the world. They don't have clean water to drink, they don't have sufficient food to eat, and they can't provide essential nutrients for their babies to live. All of this raises the question for us: Are we going to overflow in sacrificial generosity for their sake?

I know that many people protest that we have a primary responsibility to care for people in our own families and our own local churches. Without question, this is biblically true, for if we don't care for the people in our own households, we are worse than unbelievers (see 1 Timothy 5:8), and Scripture clearly emphasizes caring for our neighbors who are right next to us (see Luke 10:25-37). At the same time, there is also scriptural precedent for helping impoverished brothers and sisters in other churches. The primary example of this is the offering we've already referenced from 2 Corinthians 8–9 for the church at Jerusalem. In a similar context, Paul describes in Romans 15:26 how these churches in Macedonia made a "contribution" to the poor in Jerusalem, and the word he uses for "contribution" is *koinonia*, which is the Greek word for "fellowship." The word picture here is wonderful, for the fellowship fostered by this offering was a beautiful portrait of one part of the body of Christ saying to another, "We are with you. You are not alone in your need."

It is at this point that I fear we have missed the pattern of the New Testament church in a dangerous way. We as American Christians have become incredibly wealthy compared to the body of Christ around the world. If all we do is provide for one another's needs here in the name of proximity to one another, it is as if we're saying to our desperately poor brothers and sisters around the world, "We are not with you, and you are alone in your need." Brothers and sisters, this should not be. Physical distance from the impoverished church should not create spiritual isolation from them.

Even as I say that, I immediately want to offer a variety of other qualifications. I am not trying to put an unsustainable burden upon any person or church to care for every other needy church in the world. Nor am I trying to oversimplify the complex problems that lie behind impoverished peoples in various countries and contexts. Without question, our brothers and sisters are suffering due to a variety of factors, many of which we are limited in our ability to address. But the logic that says, "I can't do everything, so I won't do anything" is straight from the pit of hell. I am simply wondering: What would happen if we let the sacrificial love of Christ for us in the gospel create in our lives, families, and churches a sacrificial generosity toward Christian brothers and sisters who are in dire need around the world?

As with living simply, there are no specific answers here regarding what that should look like in each of our lives, families, or churches. But here I offer some of the most helpful advice I have received concerning how much we ought to give. It comes from C. S. Lewis:

> I do not believe one can settle how much we ought
> to give. I am afraid the only safe rule is to give more
> than we can spare. In other words, if our expenditure
> on comforts, luxuries, amusements, etc., is up to the
> standard common among those with the same income
> as our own, we are probably giving away too little. If
> our charities do not at all pinch or hamper us, I should
> say they are too small. There ought to be things we
> should like to do and cannot do because our charities
> expenditure excludes them.[7]

Without question, the love of Christ leads us to do nothing less than this.

HELP CONSTRUCTIVELY

Even as we give sacrificially, we want to be careful to help constructively. I quoted earlier from Steven Corbett and Brian Fikkert's book *When Helping Hurts: How to Alleviate Poverty without Hurting the Poor . . . and Yourself.* I recently wrote the foreword to a revised edition of this book, and I highly recommend it for leaders and members in the church. We must be careful in our giving to the poor to do so in a way that is good for them (and us).

This means helping the poor wisely, being careful to supplement the responsible instead of subsidizing the irresponsible. The worst thing we can do for the needy is neglect them. The second worst thing we can do is subsidize them, helping people get through a day while ignoring how we can help people get through their lives. Scripture does not call us to rescue lazy people from poverty. Instead, Scripture calls us to serve and supplement the responsible. Even in 1 Timothy 5, where Paul commands the church to care for widows, he specifies "the widow who is really in need" (verse 5, NIV) and then goes on to say that not every widow qualifies for church support. Consequently, we need to consider how to help those in need in ways that empower them to fulfill the purpose for which God created them instead of enabling them to miss that purpose.

Helping like this requires personal attention, consistent accountability, and long-term commitment. Giving to those in need is not about sharing handouts; it's about sharing life. Helping those in need doesn't consist of throwing our money at something; it involves investing our lives in someone, which is much, much harder to do. We must give personal attention to the people we are helping, providing accountability in the context of a personal relationship backed up by long-term commitment, and never looking at people as temporary projects to be played with.

In all of this, we must acknowledge diversity, realizing that people are poor for different reasons, so we must help the poor in different ways. There is no one-size-fits-all approach to poverty. That would be equivalent to saying, "*This* is how we should cure sickness," as if all sickness were the same. Many factors lie behind poverty: sinful personal choices, unbiblical worldviews, natural disasters, moral disasters, lack of technological development, inequality of power, corrupt laws and leaders, and so on. What this means, then, is that we must take the time to figure out how to help those in need in ways that reflect their situations.

Several years ago, as God began convicting me regarding a lack of care for the poor in my life, God convicted our church along similar lines. We began a process of slicing budgets, trimming programs, and removing projects to free up as much as possible for urgent spiritual and physical need around the world. In the process, we adopted a local and a global focus for our giving.

Locally, we homed in on a high-crime, low-income area of our city. Some of our church members sold their homes in suburbia and moved into this community. Our church leaders began exploring ways that we could work and serve alongside churches and ministries in or near these neighborhoods. In the process, we learned much about the causes of poverty in these communities: drug lords, slumlords, all sorts of predators, urban flight, racism, transportation challenges, fractured families, inferior education systems, bad social policies, and sinful personal choices, to name a few. Simultaneously, we began studying various ministries and churches in urban centers around our country, learning what seemed to be the most helpful ways to address these needs.

In the end, we decided that given what some other ministries were already doing, the best avenue for us to take in light of the needs in our city was to establish a job preparation and placement program that revolves around gospel-saturated relationships. Our jobs initiative helps unemployed adults to get and keep jobs, to develop a biblical work ethic alongside a biblical worldview, and to move toward becoming homeowners and stakeholders in their community, all while someone who knows and cares about their deepest need (their need for the gospel) mentors them.

Not long ago, we had our first graduation of men and women from this program. It was powerful to see, among other people, a woman named Jennifer walk to the front and receive her certificate of completion. Jennifer dropped out of school when she was in the eighth grade, and years later she found herself hopelessly addicted to illegal drugs. Jennifer's downward spiral intensified as she found a boyfriend who was also a heavy user. Together they had a son. She had no way to provide for her baby, and any job she could get she would lose due to her drug abuse. She found another boyfriend, again a heavy user, and together they had a daughter. Jennifer then got another job to provide for her now two young children, but when she began stealing from her employer to support her drug habit, that was the end of the line. At twenty-two years old, Jennifer found herself in handcuffs, charged with four felony counts. She was sentenced to six years in prison, and she lost custody of both her children.

Six years later, Jennifer found herself out of prison and living at a transitional facility that our church partners with. Surrounded by the love of women who wanted to serve her, Jennifer discovered the God who wanted to save her. She believed the gospel, turning from her sin and herself and trusting in Jesus as Savior and Lord over her life. Not long after that, she connected with our job-training ministry, where she learned how to deal honestly and ethically with potential employers about her past while working humbly and diligently to alter her future. She completed the workshop and began applying for jobs with a newfound awareness of her worth in Christ and a fresh confidence in his plans for her life. Two days after receiving her certificate of completion, Jennifer received the call she had been waiting years to hear. She had a new job, and more than that, a huge first step in restoring her life and hopefully reuniting with her children.

At the same time our church began making changes for the

good of our city, we began to focus globally on needs in northern India. Among the many partnerships we've begun and the many relationships we've formed in addressing urgent need there, one that sticks out in my mind involves a few members in our church whose eyes were opened to the realities we're discussing in this chapter. Three men, all successful in their respective vocations, realized that God had not given them success simply for their own sakes. The excellent opportunities and excess income he had given them in this world were not intended to be used to buy bigger houses and nicer cars in the pursuit of greater comfort in this world.

So they began looking at their lives and businesses, considering how all that God had given them could be leveraged for the spread of the gospel amid urgent need. As they prayed and researched needs in the world and avenues for meeting those needs, they sensed the Spirit of God leading them to address the need for water. In light of a billion people in the world lacking access to clean water,[8] many of whom are in India, they formed a ministry called Neverthirst, with an aim to provide clean and living water to the poor through the local church.

From the beginning, these guys knew they wanted to do water projects in partnership with local churches who could best communicate the gospel in a local community. In addition, they knew that for a well or water filtration device to succeed, they needed the community's ownership and participation in the project, so they established safeguards to ensure this was the case. Moreover, they wanted to make sure that the local church and community were both adequately trained on how to best maintain and use the new water source for the flourishing of the community. All of these things combined to create significant challenges as well as setbacks, but these brothers in Christ who previously knew nothing about water ministry in third world contexts persevered through it all.

The result? In only a few years, the ministry they began has been able to complete over two thousand water projects, providing clean water to over three hundred thousand people, all through local churches that are proclaiming the good news of living water that is found in Christ alone.

What I appreciate most about these guys who started Neverthirst, as well as the men and women who are leading in our local jobs initiative, is that none of them see themselves as wealthy saviors coming into impoverished communities or countries to help poor sinners in need. Instead, these men and women know that they (and we) are all poor sinners in need. We may try to mask that reality with middle-class lives and material possessions, but at the core, we all need God to reach down his hand of hope into our impoverished hearts. By his grace, he has done that in Christ, so now it just makes sense for men and women whom Christ has met in their need to serve others in their need, spending time, sacrificing money, taking risks, and giving their lives pointing them to the only Savior who is fully able not just to meet someone's needs on earth but to satisfy their souls in eternity.

INVEST ETERNALLY

So much more could be said about how the gospel leads the wealthy to live in a world of desperate poverty, but I'll close with one final exhortation. God's grace in saving and caring for us compels us to invest eternally. Jesus' words about riches resound from the Sermon on the Mount: "Do not lay up for yourselves treasures on earth, where moth and rust destroy and where thieves break in and steal, but lay up for yourselves treasures in heaven, where neither moth nor rust destroys and where thieves do not break in and steal. For where your treasure is, there your heart will be also" (Matthew 6:19-21). Clearly, Jesus has put before us a choice: we can spend our resources on short-term pleasures that we cannot keep, or we can sacrifice our resources for long-term treasure that we'll never lose.

These words to the crowds remind me of my favorite part of Jesus' conversation with the rich young man. Jesus said to this wealthy ruler, "Go, sell all that you have and give to the poor, and you will have treasure in heaven" (Mark 10:21). At first this sounds like a call to sacrifice, and in one sense it is. Indeed, in this man's heart the price proved too high for him to pay—he rejected Jesus' invitation.

But upon closer examination, Jesus' words are not a call to sacrifice as much as they are a call to satisfaction. Sure, Jesus beckons the man to sell everything he has on earth, but in the next breath he promises the man everlasting treasure in eternity. When you think about it, there's a tinge (or maybe much more than a tinge!) of self-serving motivation for this man to care for the poor. It's as if Jesus is saying to him, "Give what you have to the poor; I'll give you something better." In the end, Jesus is not calling this man *away from* treasure; he's calling him *to* treasure. When we understand the passage in this way, we begin to realize that materialism is not just sinful; it's stupid. Why would we forsake eternal treasure in favor of earthly trinkets?

Where, then, are we going to invest our lives and specifically our money and our possessions? No doubt some might say in response to this chapter that I haven't accounted for the importance of saving and investing money, particularly when you consider the possibilities that exist to expand wealth for Kingdom purposes. Put your excess $10,000 in the bank, the thinking goes, let it grow, and twenty years from now you'll have $100,000 to give to the poor. Without question, that is one way to approach investment, and it may be what the Lord leads you to do.

But don't forget that there's another way. Imagine you take that excess $10,000 and invest it in a church planter who will work alongside the new medical facility being built near Sameer's village. Imagine that medical facility flourishing, meeting basic medical needs for men, women, and children in the surrounding community, dramatically reducing the death rate due to preventable disease. And imagine that church planter preaching the gospel in those same villages, telling them that God not only hears their cries in material poverty but that he will save their souls from spiritual poverty. Imagine those villages twenty years later with hundreds if not thousands of Christians singing and shouting the praises of God while spreading the good news of the gospel. Certainly that's an investment worth considering, isn't it?

Remember what Jesus said to his disciples after the rich man left: "Truly, I say to you, there is no one who has left house or brothers or sisters or mother or father or children or lands, for my sake and for the gospel, who will not receive a hundredfold now in this time, houses and brothers and sisters and mothers and children and lands, with persecutions, and in the age to come eternal life" (Mark 10:29-30). Reading those verses, we can recognize a wise investment strategy. Anyone who can guarantee 10,000 percent interest is a good investor to work with.

Yet investing eternally, despite the promise of a good return, is countercultural. Be sure that if you start putting your money in eternal investments instead of an earthly market, you will likely hear all kinds of questions and objections. Some of them may be valid and should be listened to, but never forget that you are not ultimately living for twenty years from now. You are living for twenty billion years from now, and that changes everything.

We must remember that this world with both its pleasures and its poverty is not our final home. We're living for another land, one where pleasures never fade and the poor are poor no more. Consequently, we would be wise to open our eyes now to the spiritual and material wealth God has entrusted to us on this earth and to open our hearts wide to the myriad ways that God may be calling us to use that wealth for others' good, for our own good, and ultimately for his glory in all of eternity.

FIRST STEPS TO COUNTER CULTURE

Pray

Ask God to:

- Intervene on behalf of the poor, both close to home and around the world.
- Soften your heart to identify with the poor and work for their good.
- Reveal ways that you can live on less in order to give more to those who need it.

Participate

Prayerfully consider taking these steps:

- Investigate local ministries that are involved in serving the poor in your community, and ask how you or your church body can partner with them.
- Look at your budget. Are there any luxuries you can sacrifice in order to have more resources to give to those in need?
- Make a list of your talents and assets, and consider some of the global needs mentioned in this chapter. Is there any place where your resources and the world's needs intersect?

Proclaim

Consider the following truths from Scripture:

- Acts 20:35: "In everything I did, I showed you that by this kind of hard work we must help the weak, remembering the words the Lord Jesus himself said: 'It is more blessed to give than to receive.'"
- 2 Corinthians 8:9: "You know the grace of our Lord Jesus Christ, that though he was rich, yet for your sake he became poor, so that you by his poverty might become rich."
- 1 John 3:17: "If anyone has the world's goods and sees his brother in need, yet closes his heart against him, how does God's love abide in him?"

For more (and more specific) suggestions,
visit CounterCultureBook.com/Topics/Poverty

MODERN HOLOCAUST:
THE GOSPEL
AND ABORTION

Shamefully silent and appallingly passive.

These are the words that come to mind when I consider my approach to the issue of abortion for the majority of my life as a Christian and my ministry in the church. Until a few years ago, I barely talked about it. I viewed abortion as a political issue about which I had no need to be personally concerned. I failed to realize that abortion is a biblical issue about which I had great need to be deeply concerned. For of all the pressing social issues addressed in this book, abortion poses the most clear and present danger to the most people on a daily basis.

Across the world, more than forty-two million abortions occur every year.[1] That's 115,000 abortions every single day. I find it hard to fathom that number when I look at the faces of my four children each night as I put them to bed. I find it hard to imagine 115,000 other children who that day were introduced to the world with a tool or pill aimed at taking their lives. And I find it hardest to comprehend how I, for so long, could show no concern for this gruesome global reality.

The worldwide practice of abortion is why I do not believe it is anywhere close to an overstatement to call abortion a modern holocaust. My intention in saying this is in no way to downplay the horror of the Holocaust in the mass murder of six million Jewish men, women, and children over a few short years. But we're talking here about the massacre of forty-two million unborn children every single year. And just as German Christians should not have ignored the reality of what was happening in concentration camps across their country, I should not have ignored—and American Christians must not ignore—the reality of what is happening in abortion clinics across our country and around the world. As multitudes of babies are dismembered and destroyed daily, this is clearly an issue where the gospel requires us to counter culture.

FOR ALL OF US

Abby was in her early twenties. She had grown up in a Christian home, attended a Christian school, and had even joined a church. But a relationship with Christ was far from a reality in Abby's life. Instead, she was consumed with her work and caught up in the pleasures and pursuits of the world. She met a man who captivated her thoughts and quickened her emotions, and before long they had given themselves to each other. Everything was going great.

Until Abby discovered that she was pregnant and he was gone.

In an instant, it seemed as though the world had come crashing down around her. *This can't be*, she thought. *I can't have a baby. My reputation will be ruined, my family will be shamed, and my career will be over.* Enveloped by panic and gripped with fear, Abby saw a lone solution to her problem—only one way out of her predicament.

One Friday afternoon, Abby walked into an abortion clinic. Within a couple of hours, her problem was solved and her predicament taken care of (or so she thought). The following Monday morning, she returned to business as usual and life as normal, hiding the secret of what she'd done as if nothing had ever happened.

Abby is not alone when it comes to abortion in America. Conservative estimates reveal that approximately one-third of American women have had (or will have) an abortion at some point in their lives. In light of this, I realize that various Abbys with abortions in their past are likely reading this book right now. Some of these women have never shared that secret with anyone else. Abortion has been called a silent killer—not only of babies but of moms who possess deep wounds and dark scars from past history.

So I want to be sensitive to women who have had abortions. I do not presume to know all that may go through your mind and your heart as you read what I'm writing. I lean on good friends who have had abortions and who have shared with me that their deepest comfort has come not in minimizing the severity of abortion before God but in magnifying the reality of grace from God. That, more than anything, is what I want to do. I want to be clear about how a holy God views abortion, but I want to be equally clear about how a loving God views you in the gospel.

Moreover, my aim in this chapter is not simply to write for women who have had abortions. I hope also to speak to women who have thought about aborting a baby in the past, who may be thinking about aborting a baby in the present, or who might ever think about aborting a baby in the future. In addition, this chapter is not only for women who are able to bear children; it is for every Christian who lives in a culture marked by abortion. My hope in the pages ahead is that every follower of Christ might see how the gospel informs our thinking on abortion, and that in so doing, we might be compelled not by way of party politics but by way of gospel passion to speak clearly and stand boldly against abortion in the church, in our country, and around the world.

GOD AND THE UNBORN

As you read through the Bible, you won't find the word *abortion* anywhere. But that doesn't mean Scripture is silent about it, for the core truths we've already seen in the gospel concerning who God is, who we are, and what Christ has done speak directly to the issue of abortion.

Consider the way the Bible describes the relationship between God and an unborn baby. The psalmist writes to God:

> You formed my inward parts;
>   you knitted me together in my mother's womb.
> I praise you, for I am fearfully and wonderfully made.
> Wonderful are your works;
>   my soul knows it very well.
> My frame was not hidden from you,
> when I was being made in secret,
>   intricately woven in the depths of the earth.
> Your eyes saw my unformed substance;
> in your book were written, every one of them,
>   the days that were formed for me,
>   when as yet there was none of them.

PSALM 139:13-16

As we read these words, we're reminded of the core gospel truth that God is the Creator. He alone has the power and authority to give life. Elsewhere in the Bible, Job says, "The Spirit of God has made me, and the breath of the Almighty gives me life" (Job 33:4). He also says, "In his hand is the life of every living thing and the breath of all mankind" (Job 12:10).

God is not only the Giver of life; he is also the Taker of life. Again, Job confesses, "Naked I came from my mother's womb, and naked shall I return. The LORD gave, and the LORD has taken away" (Job 1:21). God himself declares, "I put to death and I bring to life" (Deuteronomy 32:39, NIV). This is why murder and suicide are both sins. It is God's prerogative alone, as Creator, to give and take innocent life.

In light of these biblical realities, it becomes abundantly clear that abortion is an affront to God's sole and sovereign authority as the Giver and Taker of life. Abortion, like murder or suicide, asserts human beings as the ones who control life and death. But God the Creator alone has the right to determine when someone lives and dies, and abortion flies directly in the face of his authority.

Abortion is not only an affront to God's authority as Creator; it is also an assault on his work in creation. Did you hear the psalmist describe the beauty of the way God forms the "inward parts" of a baby in a "mother's womb"? As the psalmist reflects on God's work in the womb, he responds in an outburst of worship: "I praise you! I am fearfully and wonderfully made!" The way God creates people compels praise.

These verses are all the more stunning when we realize that the psalmist came to his conclusions without knowing so many of the details that we know today concerning a baby's development. The psalmist didn't necessarily know how God takes an egg and a sperm and brings them together. How a few weeks later, often before a woman even realizes she is pregnant, a human heart is beating and circulating its own blood. Within a few more weeks, fingers are forming on hands and brain waves are detectable. Before long, these "inward parts" are moving. Kidneys are forming and functioning, followed by a gall bladder, and then by the twelfth week, all the organs of a baby boy or girl are functional, and he or she can cry. All of this occurs within three short months—only the first trimester! A heart, a brain, organs, sexuality, movement, reaction—and the Creator of the universe is orchestrating all of it! This work of creation evokes awe and amazement.

So then, imagine in this moment of creation inserting a tool, taking a pill, or undergoing an operation that takes the very life God is developing and destroys it. Most abortions occur between ten and fourteen weeks of gestation—what is described as the "optimal time" for dismemberment and removal. Abortion is without question an assault on God's grand creation of a human life. There is no way around it.

Our lives and language testify to this. When I think about the journey my wife, Heather, and I have walked, including years of physical infertility, I remember the pure joy that filled our hearts when we found out that she was pregnant. Finally, a baby was living inside of her—the beginning of life for a boy who now reads every book put in front of him and runs around my house doing tae kwon do moves on me and the rest of our family. From the very beginning, we talked about our son like he was a person. He was never a clump of tissue that could become our son if we chose to have him. He was our child from the start, and we loved him as such.

Similarly, I think about Chris and Melody, two close friends whose two kids are the joy of their lives. One is entering college, and the other is just starting elementary school. Between the births of these two children, Melody miscarried four times. Chris and Melody don't speak in terms of losing tissue. Instead, they speak at their most vulnerable moments, through many tears, of losing treasured babies whom they loved and longed to raise.

Chris, Melody, my wife, and I are not alone in the way we think and speak about what is happening in the womb. Even abortion advocates join with us, albeit unintentionally, in talking about unborn babies as exactly that: *babies*. I remember when reports announced that Princess Kate of England was pregnant. Even the most secular news outlets immediately began talking about the child in the womb as an heir to the throne. They made much of the significance of this baby, and no one spoke in terms of a "blastocyst" or "blob of cells." We would loathe the journalist who dared to use such language. But doesn't the dignity we conferred on a "royal" baby apply also to countless other "ordinary" babies whose lives are no less significant?[2]

THE KEY QUESTION

The key question that we all must answer—and the question that determines how we view abortion—is this: What is contained in the womb? Is it a person? Or is it merely an embryo, a fetus? Virtually every other question and every single argument in the abortion controversy comes back to this question: What, or who, is in the womb? And once this question is answered, everything else comes into perspective.[3]

Think about it. As Gregory Koukl points out, "If the unborn is not a human person, no justification for abortion is necessary."[4] And some people contend this. They will say that the unborn is not a person or that the unborn is merely a person who has the potential to become human (whatever that means).

Again, if this is true, the argument is over; no justification for abortion is necessary.

However, as Koukl writes, "If the unborn is a human person, then no justification for abortion is adequate."[5] Many people say, "Abortion is such a complex issue, and there just aren't any easy answers." But if what is in the womb is a person, then even if someone is proabortion or pro-choice for any number of reasons, all of their reasoning falls apart. Regardless of where you currently stand on the abortion issue, imagine for a moment that the unborn *is* a person formed and created by God himself. If this is true, then think through the primary arguments for abortion.

"Women have a right to privacy with their doctors." Without question, we all have a right to some measure of privacy. Yet our laws regularly override people's privacy when another person's life is in question. No woman or man has a right to a private conversation with a doctor to conspire how to end someone else's life. If the unborn are people, then we must protect them, regardless of what that means for someone's privacy.

"Women should have the right to choose." Yet we all agree that no one should have unlimited rights to make choices. If toddlers or teenagers become burdensome or expensive, parents don't have the right to eliminate them. Similarly, then, when it comes to abortion, the real question is not whether a woman has a choice, but whether that woman actually has a human being that God recognizes as a valuable person in her womb. If so, then a moral duty to honor life supersedes the personal hardship that might come due to pregnancy. Choosing to terminate innocent life is by definition choosing to murder.

Indeed, the primary issue in the debate over abortion is the identity of the unborn. Listen to Gregory Koukl describe a little girl named Rachel, a daughter of a family friend:

Rachel is two months old, but she is still six weeks away from being a full-term baby. She was born prematurely at 24 weeks, in the middle of her mother's second trimester. On the day of her birth Rachel weighed one pound, nine ounces, but dropped to just under a pound soon after. She was so small she could rest in the palm of her daddy's hand. She was a tiny, living, human person. Heroic measures were taken to save this child's life. Why? Because we have an obligation to protect, nurture, and care for other humans who would die without our help—especially little children. Rachel was a vulnerable and valuable human being. But get this . . . if a doctor came into the hospital room and, instead of caring for Rachel, took the life of this little girl as she lay quietly nursing at her mother's breast, it would be homicide. However, if this same little girl—the very same Rachel— was inches away resting inside her mother's womb, she could be legally killed by abortion.[6]

To any reasonable person, this makes absolutely no sense. Abortion is utterly ludicrous *if* this is a child in the womb.

Everything—everything!—revolves around what is happening in a mother's womb, and Scripture is clear: that womb contains a person being formed in the image of God. Any distinction between the unborn and a person (or a human and a person, for that matter) is both artificial and unbiblical. God recognizes the unborn as a person and designs the unborn for life from the moment of conception. While our culture is continually pushing against this idea, it is not possible to believe the Bible and deny that the unborn are persons. And once followers of Christ accept this, we can no longer sit idly by while people are mercilessly murdered in their mothers' wombs.

WONDERFUL WORKS

Abortion not only assaults God's work in creation, it also attacks God's relationship with the unborn. One of the wonderful things about Psalm 139 is the glimpse we get into how God relates to a child in the womb. He is intimately involved in the life of that baby from the moment of conception—and even before that! God tells Jeremiah, "Before I formed you in the womb, I knew you; before you were born I sanctified you" (Jeremiah 1:5, NKJV). The psalmist says to God, "You are He who took Me out of the womb . . . from My mother's womb You have been My God" (Psalm 22:9-10, NKJV). Scripture speaks about how God calls, names, and blesses children while they are still in the womb (see Galatians 1:15; Isaiah 49:1; Luke 1:15). The Bible even describes a baby leaping with joy in the womb (see Luke 1:39-44)! God reminds us in his Word that though an unborn baby is visibly hidden from us, he or she is not hidden from him. God sees children in wombs all across the world right now, and he is personally forming, fashioning, knitting, creating, nurturing, shaping, and crafting them in wonderful ways (see Job 31:15; 10:8-12).

Unfortunately, this biblical view of God's relationship with the unborn is more and more at odds with what our culture believes to be true. Much of the contemporary defense for abortion denies that these works of God in the womb are all that wonderful. Abortions in America often occur because children are seen as inconvenient. Childbearing and child rearing are too costly. It's too much for women in certain situations to handle. It's inadvisable for women in other situations to undertake.

With the advancement of medical technology that enables us to detect gender before birth, people in countries around the world now have the choice to abort children based on this revelation. China, for example, limits the number of children each family can have, and it's advantageous to have boys, which subsequently leads to the abortion of many girls. In India, it's much more expensive to have a girl (because a family will lose money on her dowry), so families who find out the child in the womb is a girl will often choose to discard her.

Do we believe this is right? Aren't all children, regardless of gender, wonderfully made in God's image? And if it's not right for people to discard girls in China or India for the sake of their convenience, then why is it right for us to discard children in America for the sake of ours?

This is not only an issue when it comes to the sex of a child but also when it comes to disability in children. It is possible for us to determine whether a baby in the womb is at risk for Down syndrome or other disabilities that will affect his or her life. So should abortion be permissible in such circumstances? Again, not if we actually believe all of God's works are wonderful.

Consider the man born blind in John 9. Most of the Jews who knew this man would have considered his disability a sure sign of sin in either his life or his parents' lives. So the disciples ask Jesus, "Whose fault is this?" Jesus answers them, "This is not his or his parents' fault, but this happened so that the wonderful works of God might be revealed to and through him." Jesus reveals that this man was born blind so that one day he might see, know, declare, and delight in the glory of Christ.

I in no way claim to know all the difficulties associated with disabilities. My wife and I have invested time and resources in a special-needs orphanage in China, where we have seen and served boys and girls with severe disabilities. Closer to home, we have walked alongside various families in our church who have taken heart-wrenching journeys with children with disabilities. I think of Thomas, a teenage boy with Down syndrome who for years has come up to me almost every Sunday, shaken my hand, given me a hug, and told me all about his week. And I just can't get Thomas out of my mind when I hear a pediatric geneticist at Boston Children's Hospital report that "an estimated 92 percent of all women who receive a prenatal diagnosis of Down syndrome choose to terminate their pregnancies."[7] We're killing 90 percent of the Thomases in our culture.

Based on Scripture, I beg us not to deny the wonderful work of God even (or especially) in disability. Even when we don't understand it, God has a design and a desire to use everything for our good and his glory (see Romans 8:28), and it is not only wrong but also foolish to play god in such situations by essentially saying that we know better than he does.

Likewise, God's works are wonderful even (or especially) in the midst of difficulty. People ask, "Well, what about cases of incest or rape? Is abortion justifiable then?" Once again, I don't claim to know what it is like to be in such a situation. I shudder at the horror of rape happening to my wife or to any other woman, for that matter. I cannot imagine the physical and emotional toll such a situation brings upon a woman and her family.

Yet we come back to the fundamental question: Is the baby in the womb a person? If so, then our entire perspective changes. Would we murder a child *outside* the womb because he or she was conceived by rape? Of course we wouldn't. Then why would we murder a child *inside* the womb? Why should we punish a child for the father's crime (see Deuteronomy 24:16)?

How, after all, should we treat an innocent child who reminds us of a terrible experience? The answer is clear: with love and mercy.

But people will say, "Have you no care for the emotions of the woman?" Again, I cannot imagine what that woman has gone through emotionally. Without question that precious woman needs compassionate women and men around her to love her, support her, and serve her in every way possible. But think about it this way. If the rapist were caught, would we encourage this woman to murder him in order to get emotional relief? Surely not. Then why would we encourage her to murder an innocent child in the name of emotional relief?[8]

On this question, I find myself particularly going against the culture, for even the most socially conservative politicians today would never say that abortion should be illegal in cases of rape or incest. But I am not a politician. I am a follower of Christ, and I am confident of this: the God of the gospel has a proven track record of working all things, including evil things, for his good purposes. He took Joseph's brothers' attempt to murder him and turned it into the preservation of multitudes of people. He used incest to eventually bring about the very birth of Jesus Christ (see Matthew 1:3). Ultimately, God took the murder of his Son and turned it into the means of our salvation.

The gospel proves that we can trust God. All of his works, even those we least understand, are wonderful, and he has the power, love, goodness, and grace to give you and me all that we need to persevere through difficulty. And in the end, he promises to turn all of our mourning into dancing and all of our suffering into joy.

GOD THE JUDGE

Abortion is an affront to God's authority as Creator, an assault on God's work in creation, and an attack on God's relationship with the unborn. Once we realize the severity of abortion before God, the implications of the gospel for abortion become clear.

Remember God's character. He is the holy and righteous Judge of all, and he hates injustice. He detests the taking of innocent life, and he is the Judge of all who participate in it. God is the Judge of mothers who have aborted babies, fathers who have encouraged abortion, grandparents who have supported abortion, and friends who have advised abortion. God is the Judge of doctors who have performed abortions, leaders who have permitted abortions, pastors who have counseled people to have abortions, and legislators who have worked to make abortion possible.

This includes President Barack Obama and an ever-increasing host of other leading politicians in my country who are proactively and aggressively working to keep the murder of innocent children legal. I venture cautiously into the political arena with no desire to support a party line. Rather, I want to speak biblical truth, for Scripture is not silent on abortion, and it is not silent on government's role in it.

In Romans 13, the Bible addresses the role of civil authorities and our responsibility to them:

> Let every person be subject to the governing authorities. For there is no authority except from God, and those that exist have been instituted by God. Therefore whoever resists the authorities resists what God has appointed, and those who resist will incur judgment. For rulers are not a terror to good conduct, but to bad. Would you have no fear of the one who is in authority? Then do what is good, and you will receive his approval, for he is God's servant for your good. ROMANS 13:1-4

The Bible teaches that God has given us government for our good. Government exists under God's authority. According to God's design, government is to reflect the morality of God, who cares for the weak, the poor, the oppressed, and the vulnerable who are least able to protect themselves. The fundamental purpose of government under God is to promote the good of all its people.

Government does this by making and enforcing laws that reward good and punish evil. Many people today say, "It's not the government's job to legislate morality." This is a sham argument, though, and we all know it. The state not only has the right but also the responsibility to legislate morality. The state should most definitely say that stealing, lying, murder, and a host of other things are wrong. This is foundational to its purpose. Government imposes morality on people every day, and this is a good thing.

Other people say, "It's not the role of government to take away people's right to choose." But this is absolutely the role of government. You cannot choose to steal: if you do, there will be consequences. You cannot choose to do a whole host of things there are laws against, and it is good that government has made those laws. If everyone chose to do whatever they wanted, the inevitable result would be anarchy. It's moral silliness and cultural suicide to say that government shouldn't take away people's right to choose.

What matters is what we're choosing. Someone should have the right to choose Mexican or Chinese food for dinner, or where to live, or what kind of car to drive. Of course we are pro-choice on these and thousands of other things. But we aren't pro-choice about rape. And we aren't pro-choice about burglary. We aren't pro-choice about kidnapping children. So why should we be pro-choice about killing them?

If you are a Christian, I plead for you to step out of a muddled middle road that says, "I may not choose abortion, but I don't think we should take away others' right to choose it," and to realize how inconceivable it is for us to stay silent while millions of children—individuals made in the image of God—are dismembered and destroyed around us in the world. Such thinking is not enlightened tolerance; it is sinful indifference. Moral and political neutrality here is not an option for us. Randy Alcorn put it best when he said, "To endorse or even to be neutral about killing innocent children created in God's image is unthinkable in the Scriptures, was unthinkable to Christians in church history, and should be unthinkable to Christians today."[9]

As I said earlier in the book, we cannot pick and choose which issues we will address and which we will be silent on. If we believe the gospel, then we must speak out against the injustice of abortion. For God is not only the Judge of parents who have abortions, doctors who perform abortions, and politicians who permit abortions, but he is also the Judge of church members and leaders who do nothing about abortion. And as I mentioned at the beginning of this chapter, I am the chief of sinners on this issue. For far too long, I have been guilty of selective injustice when it comes to abortion, and I desperately need God's grace.

REDEEMED AND RESTORED

Thankfully, God has given such grace—to me, to you, to all of us—in the gospel.

Remember: God is not only the Judge of sin, but he is also the Savior of sinners. God is the Judge who loathes abortion and the King who loves even those who participate in it, so hear this good news. To anyone and everyone who has ever aborted a child, supported abortion, encouraged abortion, performed abortion, permitted abortion, or done nothing about abortion, may the following realities lodge deep within your soul.

God forgives entirely. "As the heavens are high above the earth, so great is [God's] mercy toward those who fear Him; as far as the east is from the west, so far has He removed our transgressions from us" (Psalm 103:11-12, NKJV). God says, "I am he who blots out your transgressions for my own sake, and I will not remember your sins" (Isaiah 43:25). "If we confess our sins, he is faithful and just to forgive us our sins and to cleanse us from all unrighteousness" (1 John 1:9). The good news of the gospel is that when we turn from our sin and trust in Christ, we find that he has paid the price for any part we have ever played in abortion, and because of his cross, we are entirely forgiven.

God not only forgives entirely, but he also heals deeply. God does not desire for you or anyone else to live with the pain of regret. It is altogether right to hate sin in your history. The pain of past sin is often a powerful deterrent to future sin, but don't let it rob you of the peace God has designed for you in the present. Remember what Jesus said to a woman who had lived an immoral lifestyle: "Your sins are forgiven. . . . Your faith has saved you; go in peace" (Luke 7:48-50). God desires that peace to be yours today.

He forgives entirely, he heals deeply, and he restores completely. To all who trust in Christ, remember this: in Christ you are not guilty, and there is no condemnation for you. This is true whether you have had one abortion or five. This is true whether you have medically performed thousands of abortions or legally permitted millions. You do not walk around with a scarlet *A* on your chest, for God does not look at you and see the guilt of abortion. Instead, he looks at you and sees the righteousness of Christ. God restores, and he redeems. Even as we saw earlier, God has a track record of working all things, including evil things, ultimately for good.

Remember Abby, whom I mentioned at the beginning of this chapter? For years she kept the secret of her abortion to herself. But on the weekend that her husband proposed to her, she decided she needed to tell him what she had done years before they met. He listened graciously, and they chose to keep it a secret between them for the next eight years. No one else knew.

Until one day Abby and her husband were talking with some friends who told them about the freedom and forgiveness found in the gospel. Abby knew about Christ and had grown up in church, but the words of Isaiah 61 had never clicked in her mind and heart. In a passage that Jesus would later quote in reference to himself, the Bible says, "The LORD . . . has sent me to bind up the brokenhearted, to proclaim liberty to the captives, and the opening of the prison to those who are bound . . . to comfort all who mourn . . . to give them a beautiful headdress instead of ashes, the oil of gladness instead of mourning, the garment of praise instead of a faint spirit" (Isaiah 61:1-3).

For the first time, Abby realized why Christ came and died on the cross. He came to heal the broken hearts of people just like her by freeing them from their bondage to sin and shame. For fifteen years Abby had done all she could to cover her past in order to have others' approval. Now, for the first time, she knew that in Christ she had God's approval, regardless of her past.

The freedom Abby has experienced now propels her to lead a ministry in the church that reaches out to women who have had abortions. She has received training on how to wisely, carefully, and compassionately come alongside these women to serve and support them. She puts this training into practice on a regular basis with groups of women in the city. In addition to leading other women in the church, Abby is actively involved in public efforts to minimize abortions in the city, specifically counseling pregnant women who are considering abortions, sharing her own story, and telling them there is another way to solve their "problem." She does all of this together with her husband and two children—a beautiful daughter, who runs up to me with a huge smile to hug me every time I see her, and a wonderful son, whom I had the opportunity to help coach in basketball. It is a priceless picture to see this woman who once thought abortion had permanently stained her past and forever stolen her peace now transformed by the gospel, and to watch God use her quite literally to save countless children's—and women's—lives.

EVERY ONE WORTH IT

As I bring this chapter to a close, I think about a mom who lives in one of those countries of the world where baby girls are not favorably looked upon. Over thirty-five thousand children are ripped from wombs every day in China, and over half of the women there have had at least one abortion.[10] Some of these abortions are voluntary; others are mandatory. Government officials enforce abortion to ensure population control. Women in rural villages are routinely checked to make sure they neither are pregnant nor have given birth recently.

I don't know all the details about this particular mom, but I do know that when she became pregnant, she believed she was not able to take care of her child. Yet she refused to have an abortion. Instead, she brought her child to term and gave birth to a precious little girl on her own.

Then she took that newborn baby girl, wrapped her in a light-blue cloth, placed her in a brown paper box, and in the middle of the night laid her in front of an orphanage for children with special needs. The orphanage found this baby girl the next morning and conducted a search for her mother, only to come up empty.

Though I don't know who that mom is, I thank God for her. Because of her courage to refuse abortion, and because of her compassion for the unborn, a little girl was able to live. And every day when I come home from work, that little girl comes running up to me with a smile spread across her face, jumps into my arms, yells, "Daddy!" and gives me the biggest bear hug you can imagine.

Every one of these children is worth it. May we have the conviction, compassion, and courage to do everything we can to stop the modern holocaust around us.

FIRST STEPS TO COUNTER CULTURE

Pray
Ask God to:
- End the injustice of abortion in our country and around the world.
- Forgive you for whatever part you have played in abortion.
- Convict those in positions of power to use their influence to end abortion.

Participate
Prayerfully consider taking these steps:
- Write to your representatives in Congress and clearly and respectfully lay out why abortion in this country must stop.
- Work with ministries or participate in events (e.g., Sanctity of Human Life Sunday, 40 Days for Life, prayer walks) that seek to uphold the value of unborn human life.
- Volunteer with a crisis pregnancy center in your city to aid in their work of showing women in desperate situations that there are options other than abortion.

Proclaim
Consider the following truths from Scripture:
- Psalm 139:15-16: "My frame was not hidden from you, when I was being made in secret, intricately woven in the

depths of the earth. Your eyes saw my unformed substance; in your book were written, every one of them, the days that were formed for me, when as yet there was none of them."

- Proverbs 24:10-12: "If you faint in the day of adversity, your strength is small. Rescue those who are being taken away to death; hold back those who are stumbling to the slaughter. If you say, 'Behold, we did not know this,' does not he who weighs the heart perceive it? Does not he who keeps watch over your soul know it, and will he not repay man according to his work?"

- Matthew 19:14: "Jesus said, 'Let the little children come to me and do not hinder them, for to such belongs the kingdom of heaven.'"

For more (and more specific) suggestions,
visit CounterCultureBook.com/Topics/Abortion

THE LONELY IN FAMILIES: THE GOSPEL AND ORPHANS AND WIDOWS

As soon as we found out who our daughter would be, we knew exactly what we would name her.

Years before, Heather and I had inadvertently backed into adoption. Month after month for five years, we had prayed, longed, and tried to have children, but God had not provided in the way we had hoped. Unsure whether we would ever be able to conceive, we finally considered adoption. "I guess this is second best," we said to each other. "Since we can't have children biologically, at least we can adopt."

It didn't take long for us to understand that adoption was just as "best." God used infertility to open our eyes to the orphan crisis around the world. And it *is* a crisis. Approximately 153 million children live as orphans, meaning they have lost at least one parent. Included in that number are about eighteen million children who have lost both parents. Not included in that number, though, are the millions of effectively orphaned children who live in institutions or on the streets, in addition to vast multitudes who live as "social orphans," meaning that even if a parent is alive, the children rarely, if ever, see that parent or experience life as part of a family.[1]

But I had heard these statistics before. As you may be prone to do, I could read a paragraph like the one above and move on without a second thought. But everything changed when we opened our lives to the possibility of adoption. Everything changed when we first saw the face of a precious ten-month-old boy in Kazakhstan who was in need of a mom and a dad. Everything changed when we visited his orphanage, saw children playing outside, and saw their crib-filled rooms inside. Everything changed when we realized that the statistics represent individual children just like our soon-to-be son. We learned pretty quickly that orphans are easier to forget if you don't see their faces. They're easier to ignore if you don't know their names. They're easier to overlook if you don't hold them in your arms. But once you do, everything changes.

As soon as God provided our first son through adoption, God surprised us with a second son the more natural way. About two weeks after we came home from Kazakhstan with Caleb, Heather was pregnant, and Joshua came along nine months later. When I tell that story, people often try to offer a physical or emotional explanation for how my wife could get pregnant after adoption when she couldn't before adoption. While I in no way want to argue the physiology of procreation, I have no doubt that divine prerogative is the only explanation behind why Heather got pregnant when she did. God clearly had something more glorious in mind as he used this hardship in our lives to lead us to adopt a precious little boy in an obscure city of northwestern Kazakhstan whom we would never have met otherwise. We are forever grateful for the five long years of infertility that God led us through.

But even with the awareness that we could conceive, Heather and I knew that we wanted to adopt again. God had opened our eyes to the needs of the orphan, and an adoption process that began as a desire to fill a void in our hearts became a desire to reflect a reality in God's.

When you read the Bible, you see over and over God's passion to demonstrate his power and love in the life of the orphan. "For the LORD your God is God of gods and Lord of lords, the great, the mighty, and the awesome God, who is not partial and takes no bribe. He executes justice for the fatherless and the widow" (Deuteronomy 10:17-18). "A father to the fatherless; a defender of widows, is God in his holy dwelling" (Psalm 68:5, NIV). In the initial giving of his law, God commands his people, "You shall not mistreat any widow or fatherless child" (Exodus 22:22). Then continually throughout their history, God exhorts his people, "Learn to do good; seek justice, correct oppression; bring justice to the fatherless, plead the widow's cause" (Isaiah 1:17).

When we read these verses, we quickly notice that God's heart is not just for the orphan but also for the widow. In each of the verses above (and in many others), God groups these two classes of people together. It's no surprise, then, to come to this breathtaking verse later in the Bible: "Religion that is pure and undefiled before God, the Father, is this: to visit orphans and widows in their affliction, and to keep oneself unstained from the world" (James 1:27).

What an astounding statement. This is God's definition of pure religion: "to visit orphans and widows in their affliction." True religion apparently doesn't consist of monotonous participation in superficial pious activity. True religion consists of just and consistent demonstrations of supernatural, selfless love.

When the Bible describes "visiting" orphans and widows here, it means more than simply saying hello to them every once in a while. This same word for "visit" in James 1:27 is used in different places in the New Testament to describe how God himself visits his people to help them, strengthen them, and encourage them.[2] To visit orphans and widows means to seek them out with a deep concern for their well-being and a clear commitment to care for their needs.

Why, we might wonder, would God define "pure religion" in this particular way—in terms of care for orphans and widows? The answer to that question is found in the second half of James 1:27, when James describes "[keeping] oneself unstained from the world." It's at this point that many people think, *Okay, if I'm going to have true religion, then that means I need to care for orphans and widows, and then I need to avoid immorality in the world.* Of course it's true that we are to avoid immorality, and the rest of James elaborates on this theme in different ways, but we need to be careful not to disconnect "[keeping] oneself unstained from the world" from "visiting orphans and widows." For in the verses right after James 1:27, James chides the church for catering to a world system that prioritizes the wealthy and neglects the needy. People who live according to the ways of the world, James says, give attention and honor to the kind of people who can benefit them the most, who have the most to offer them in return for their kindness. True religion, however, doesn't cater to culture; it is unstained from this worldly way of thinking and living. True religion counters culture and results in sacrificially caring for people who can benefit you the least, who have the least to offer you in return for your kindness.

Enter the orphan and the widow—children and women who have lost a significant member of their family on whom they depended for physical, emotional, relational, and spiritual sustenance. Consequently, they desperately need someone to step in and provide physical, emotional, relational, and spiritual sustenance to them. True religion, according to God, is to love people like that. True religion is to be family to those who have lost family.

So what does this mean for followers of Christ in a world of 153 million orphans? Moreover, what shall we do in a world filled with 245 million widows, 115 million of whom live in poverty and suffer from social isolation and economic deprivation as a result of losing their husbands?[3] Knowing that each one of these millions represents a unique child or woman for whom God possesses divine compassion, it's not a question of what we should do. The only question is whether we'll do it.

A STORY OF REDEMPTION

God has not only shouted throughout Scripture his passionate concern for the fatherless and the widow; he has also given us an entire book that illustrates his care for those who lose family like this. Ruth is one of my favorite books of the Bible. It is a love story for the ages that contains all the requisite components of a romance: tragedy, loss, despair, triumph, hope, and loyalty, all wrapped into one. But it's not merely a love story. It's a story within a story, and it's about far more than a Moabite woman named Ruth. It's a story about you and me and every other person who stands on the stage of human history. If you'll permit me a bit of time to tell it, I promise it will prove helpful in seeing how we fit into the narrative God is weaving together in the world on behalf of orphans and widows everywhere.

The setting of Ruth is the time of the judges, a period when "there was no king in Israel" and "everyone did what was right in his own eyes" (Judges 21:25). The story begins in Bethlehem, a town known as "the house of bread," but to its citizens' dread and dismay, there is no bread. Instead, a famine has left families starving and in desperate need of food. So a man named Elimelech packs up his wife and two sons and moves to Moab.

Moab was far from Bethlehem, and its culture was foreign in every way. Generations before, the Moabites had come into being when Lot, Abraham's nephew, had an incestuous relationship with his daughter (see Genesis 19). The Moabites were a scandalous people. On one occasion, some Moabite women seduced the Israelites into sexual sin, leading to the eventual death of twenty-four thousand Israelite men (see Numbers 25:1-10). The Moabites were known for their immorality and idolatry, and God declared that no Moabite should enter the assembly of his people down to the tenth generation (see Deuteronomy 23:3). Needless to say, for a Jewish man to travel to Moab was not only a sign of desperation but also an act sure to bring shame upon him.

But what starts as shame turns to pain in what seems to the reader like an instant. After describing Elimelech's journey with his family to Moab, the story's narrator uses a mere three verses to describe ten years of tragedy. First, Elimelech dies, leaving his wife, Naomi, a widow. Next, her two sons, Mahlon and Chilion, take Moabite wives named Ruth and Orpah, respectively. Then, ten years after Elimelech's death, Mahlon and Chilion die, placing Naomi in the nexus of a nightmare. She has no husband. She has no children. She is destitute, her only family two daughters-in-law from a despised people. This is the curse of curses for an Israelite woman. She now has no physical descendants to carry on her family line, no promise of future provision, and no idea what to do next.

Until, the narrator tells us, Naomi hears in Moab that God has "visited" his people in Bethlehem (Ruth 1:6), providing food to the people and ending famine in the land. Naomi tells Orpah and Ruth of her plans to return to Bethlehem. She urges both of them to stay in Moab. Certainly it will not be good for them to go with her to a land where they will be seen as strangers and will have no hope of a husband or a future heir. Besides, Naomi concludes, it is clear that God's hand is against her. They will be wise to stay away from her.

Orpah obliges, but not Ruth. In one of the most momentous speeches in all of Scripture, Ruth tells Naomi, "Where you go I will go, and where you lodge I will lodge. Your people shall be my people, and your God my God. Where you die I will die, and there will I be buried. May the LORD do so to me and more also if anything but death parts me from you" (Ruth 1:16-17). These unforgettable words are often spoken between a husband and wife at weddings (and if you used them at your wedding, that's wonderful), but we need to remember that these words are from a daughter-in-law to a mother-in-law. I've performed a lot of weddings, but I've never heard in-laws talk to each other like this!

Naomi concedes, and the two women journey to Bethlehem. One can only imagine all the thoughts running through Naomi's mind as she approaches the land that years before she had left with her husband and two sons. They had left the Promised Land for a pagan land. She had left as a blessed wife, but she now returns a bitter woman. When the women of Bethlehem see her in the distance, they run out to her, eagerly asking, "Is that you, Naomi?" Naomi's response tells all. "Do not call me Naomi," she says. "Call me Mara, for the Almighty has dealt very bitterly with me" (*Naomi* means "pleasant"; *Mara* means "bitter"). She continues, "I went away full, and the LORD has brought me back empty. Why call me Naomi, when the LORD has testified against me and the Almighty has brought calamity upon me?" (Ruth 1:20-21).

What a welcome! The women of Bethlehem greet Naomi in excitement after a decade away, and she responds tersely, "Did you call me pleasant? Nothing could be further from the truth. My name is bitter!"

Now imagine you are Ruth. The women of Bethlehem stand there shocked as they listen to Naomi, and as soon as they hear Naomi say, "I have come back with nothing but calamity," immediately they turn to look at you. Your eyes drop. For you are a portrait of the Lord's affliction. You are a picture of the misfortune the Almighty brings.

Little do Naomi or Ruth know in the somber silence of that moment what God has in store for them. They stand in desperate need of two things: food to fill their stomachs and family to provide them shelter. And this is when the narrator tells us that waiting behind the curtain is a generous and wealthy relative of Elimelech named Boaz.

The next day, Ruth tells Naomi that she will find a field where she can harvest some food for them to eat. One of the ways God had provided for the poor was by mandating that landowners leave grain for the poor and the destitute to glean from their land. So the writer tells us that Ruth "happened to come to the part of the field belonging to Boaz, who was of the clan of Elimelech" (Ruth 2:3). As she started working, "behold, Boaz came from Bethlehem" (Ruth 2:4).

The way the writer tells the story here drips with dramatic coincidence. Ruth *just so happens* to come to Boaz's field. At that moment, Boaz *just so happens* to arrive, and Boaz *just so happens* to be from the clan of Elimelech.

When I read this Bible story, I can't help but think about the romance movies Heather loves to watch, in which multiple factors suddenly come together to create an unexpected meeting between a man and a woman. If I'm watching with her, I'll often start to roll my eyes and say, "This is absurd—things never happen that way!" But just before I speak, I will inevitably look over at Heather, who will have tears in her eyes, engrossed in the movie and enthralled by every detail. At this point, I'll catch my tongue and think, *She's actually buying this!* before returning my attention to the movie in frustrated silence.

But the book of Ruth is no fairy tale. This is the God of the universe divinely scripting a drama for the provision of the poor. Boaz notices Ruth and asks a worker in the field, "Who is that woman?" The man responds, "She is the young Moabite woman, who came back with Naomi from the country of Moab" (Ruth 2:6).

This news leads Boaz on a beeline across the field to the outcast Ruth. He walks past all the other workers right up to her, addresses her with a term of endearment ("my daughter"), and then assures her that she will be well provided for in his field. She will be safe and satisfied as long as she stays with him. Ruth is in awe, wondering aloud why he has shown such favor to her, a despised woman at the bottom rung of the social ladder. Boaz responds by pronouncing God's blessing on her: "A full reward be given you by the LORD, the God of Israel, under whose wings you have come to take refuge!" (Ruth 2:12).

This conversation sets the stage for what we in our culture might call the "first date" in the book of Ruth, when Boaz invites Ruth to a meal at his table. "Come here and eat some bread and dip your morsel in the wine," he says to her. The narrator writes, "So she sat beside the reapers, and he passed to her roasted grain. And she ate until she was satisfied" (Ruth 2:14).

After the meal, Boaz instructs his men to make sure she leaves with a lot of grain, and they obey by giving her "about an ephah of barley" (Ruth 2:17). To put this amount in perspective, an average worker in that day would harvest a couple of pounds of barley per day. At the end of this day, though, Ruth leaves the field with somewhere between thirty to fifty pounds of barley. This is how we know that Ruth did CrossFit regularly, for she hoists the grain over her shoulders and carries it all the way back into the city.

When she arrives home, Naomi is grateful, to say the least. "Where did you glean today?" she asks. "And where have you worked? Blessed be the man who took notice of you." Keep in mind at this point that Naomi has no idea where Ruth has worked all day long. Imagine her amazement, then, when Ruth responds, "The man's name with whom I worked today is Boaz." Upon hearing this, Naomi no doubt goes from grateful to giddy. She exclaims, "May he be blessed by the LORD, whose kindness has not forsaken the living or the dead! . . . The man is a close relative of ours, one of our redeemers" (Ruth 2:19-20).

Naomi's declaration introduces us to the most important word in the book of Ruth: *redeemer*. God, in his mercy, had set up a system by which near relatives would care for one another when they faced desperate need, including the death of a husband. In such a case, a kinsman-redeemer would act on behalf of an afflicted relative. He would take ownership of the relative's land and subsequent responsibility for the relative's life.

Old Testament passages like Leviticus 25, Deuteronomy 25, and Jeremiah 32 outline three basic requirements for someone to be a kinsman-redeemer. First, a man must have the *right* to redeem. Basically, he had to be first in the family line of potential providers for the afflicted relative. Possessing this right implied a responsibility—a duty to care for a relative in need. Next, a man needed the *resources* to redeem. In order to help someone in need, a potential redeemer needed the ability and capacity to provide for that person as part of his own family. Finally, a man had to have the *resolve* to redeem. In other words, he had to be willing. It was possible for a man to be first in the family line and fully able to provide yet lack the resolve to take a family member into his care.

With that understanding, the story of Ruth continues as day after day she works in the fields of Boaz, a potential redeemer for Naomi and her family. And day after day, Ruth brings food home, but Boaz seems slow in moving toward redeeming them as part of his family. Naomi, by now an impatient mother-in-law, decides to prod Boaz, and she contrives a plan for Ruth to approach him in the middle of the night and request that he redeem them. Ruth complies, which leads to a curious encounter with Boaz on the threshing floor in which he tells Ruth, "It is true that I am a redeemer. Yet there is a redeemer nearer than I. Remain tonight, and in the morning, if he will redeem you, good; let him do it. But if he is not willing to redeem you, then, as the LORD lives, I will redeem you" (Ruth 3:12-13).

The next morning Boaz approaches the man who has the first right to redeem Naomi's land. The suspense in the story builds as this other potential redeemer initially declares, "I will redeem it." But Boaz gently informs him that redeeming Naomi and her land also means acquiring Ruth the Moabite in order to preserve the relative's inheritance. This significant bit of information results in the man's refusal to redeem. "I cannot redeem it because I might endanger my own estate," he says (Ruth 4:6, NIV). Having the resources to redeem, this man lacks the resolve to do so, and he yields the right to Boaz.

With the other guy now out of the way, Boaz states his resolve to redeem: "Today you are witnesses that I have bought from Naomi all the property of Elimelech, [Chilion,] and Mahlon. I have also acquired Ruth the Moabitess, Mahlon's widow, as my wife, in order to maintain the name of the dead with his property, so that his name will not disappear from among his family or from the town records" (Ruth 4:9-10, NIV). With these words, Naomi and Ruth are brought into Boaz's family, and Ruth becomes his wife.

A verse after redemption is announced, Ruth and Boaz are married, and Ruth bears a son. The final scene then ensues as Naomi holds the child in her arms, and the women of Bethlehem pronounce, "Praise be to the LORD, who this day has not left you without a kinsman-redeemer. May he become famous through-out Israel! He will renew your life and sustain you in your old age. For your daughter-in-law, who loves you and who is better to you than seven sons, has given him birth" (Ruth 4:14-15, NIV).

But that's not where the story ends. The book of Ruth is like a movie in which you've watched the final scene come to a close, you've seen the screen go dark, and you think it's over until that same screen lights back up with a postscript describing what happened in subsequent days. The book of Ruth contains what must be one of the most powerful postscripts to any story, for the narrator writes concerning Ruth and Boaz's son, "They named him Obed. He was the father of Jesse, the father of David" (Ruth 4:17).

To Jewish men and women who first heard this story, this postscript was nothing short of jaw-dropping. This story just rose from the tale of a kinsman-redeemer during a time when there was no king in Israel to the genealogy of the man who would become Israel's most famous king. The genealogy included in the closing verses of the book of Ruth spans ten generations, a symbolic yet sure nod to ten years of death and barrenness in Moab and the ten generations of curse upon the Moabite people. Thus concludes the story of how God, in his mercy, saved a despised Moabite woman in an otherwise hopeless Israelite family by way of a resolute kinsman-redeemer.

MIRROR OF GOD

I mentioned earlier that the book of Ruth is not intended simply to be a story of love; it is a story within a story, intended to point us ultimately to the God over history and his heart for the afflicted. Boaz is onstage in this story not as a model of goodwill but as a mirror of God. He illustrates God's gracious design to provide for those with no family through the broader family of men and women who have put their faith in him.

This is where you and I come in. Sure, we may not live in the time of the judges, centuries before the coming of Christ, but this doesn't mean we should be any less compelled to reflect God's character in our culture today. For in a culture that increasingly views the orphan and the widow as liabilities, countercultural opportunities for Boaz-like generosity abound all around us.

In preparation for preaching on James 1:27 one Sunday, I called the Department of Human Resources (DHR) in our county. I wanted to find out if they had any needs in orphan or foster care.

When I put my question to the DHR director, she laughed. "Yes!" she exclaimed. "We have tons of needs!"

Well, I wanted to know, how many families would DHR need in order to take care of all the foster and adoption needs that we have in our county?

More laughter.

"No, really," I said. "If a miracle were to take place, how many families would be sufficient to cover all the different needs you have?"

She collected herself for a minute, then answered, "It would be a miracle if we had 150 more families."

The day came when I preached from James 1:27. At the close, I gave our church an unusual invitation: "If Christ in you is compelling you to be a part of serving children in our county in this way, then please come to a meeting two weeks from today."

When the meeting time came, people poured into the auditorium. That night, more than 160 families signed up to help with foster care and adoption in our county. As a family of faith in Christ we said, "We want to make sure, as best we are able, that every child in our county has loving arms around him or her at night. We want to point every one of these children to the Father of the fatherless and Defender of the weak who cares for them."

The church is now filled with children from all over the city. Men and women are working together not only to provide for these children, but to work with their parents toward reunification in their families. The immense joy of foster care has invaded the church, and our families will never be the same.

Looking back at that initial informational meeting, I'll never forget one particular conversation with a DHR worker. As members of the church streamed into the meeting, one of the DHR workers pulled me aside with tears in her eyes and said, "What made you decide to do this? And how did you get all these people to participate?"

I smiled. "*I* didn't decide to do this," I said. "*God* did. These men and women are a mirror of God's love for these kids and their families that you serve every single day."

A CULTURE OF ORPHANS AND WIDOWS

The more our church became involved in foster and adoptive care in the city, the more we realized that orphans and widows often live in the same home. A few years ago, some church members intentionally began moving into impoverished areas of the city. In learning about these specific areas, we found that over 60 percent of the children in one community lived with a grandparent instead of a mom or dad. For most of those children, both mom and dad were virtually absent from their lives. Moreover, most of those grandparents were single grandmothers due to abandonment, divorce, or the death of their husbands. When we put all this together, we realized that the majority of homes in that community had both orphans and widows living under the same roof. Needless to say, in a culture like this, the opportunities for ministry are many.

Such opportunities are only multiplied across our culture with the increase of children living in single-parent homes. When Scripture speaks of the orphan and the widow, doubtless it refers primarily to those who were orphaned or widowed due to a parent's or husband's death. But at the present time, well over a third of children in the United States are living in a home with only one parent, and nearly half of the births are to unmarried women[4]—both inevitable realities in a culture that minimizes the priority and permanence of marriage (which we'll explore later). The result is a growing number of children and women who lack a parent or husband in the home.

The implications of this are mammoth for the church in contemporary culture. Now, possibly more than at any other point in history, the church has an opportunity to rise up and show God's love not just to children and women whose parents or husbands have died, but also to children and women whose parents or husbands have disappeared from their lives. Christ compels us to counter culture by stepping in to care for orphans and widows when significant people have stepped out of their lives. Indeed, the Father to the fatherless and the Defender of the widow is calling his people to care for these children and women as our own families.

I think about Frank, a retiree in the church who serves on the parking team every Sunday. A couple of years ago, Frank was in a conversation with a hospice nurse who told him of all the needs she had seen in her patients' homes. The nurse described how many widows, in particular, live imprisoned in their homes with no family or friends to care for them. As he listened, Frank said, "It was like God was saying, 'Are you going to do something about this?'"

Frank decided to act. He realized that "pure religion" involves more than helping people find a spot for their cars at a Sunday-morning service. It also involves helping widows find a place in a family that loves and cares for them. Immediately Frank began visiting various widows' homes. He met women whose trash hadn't been emptied in months and whose bedsheets hadn't been changed in just as long. He met others who needed wheelchair ramps because they couldn't walk down the three simple stairs outside their mobile homes, leaving them insulated and isolated for weeks at a time. He met others whose holed roofs allowed flooding in the house every time it rained. True to James 1:27, Frank not only visited these widows, he began mobilizing teams from the church to take responsibility for their care.

Together they began serving women like Mrs. Maureen, a precious sister in Christ on the verge of widowhood with the responsibility of caring for her two granddaughters. Mrs. Maureen's husband was dying of cirrhosis of the liver due to alcoholism. She had previously committed to care for her two granddaughters while their mother was in prison, only to see the mother abandon her children the moment she was released from custody.

When Frank visited Mrs. Maureen's home, he discovered that it had been built more than fifty years prior with untreated lumber, and it was infested with termites. The one toilet in the home had sunk completely through the floor, and the cast-iron tub was collapsing into the ground. One of Mrs. Maureen's petite granddaughters had been standing on the front porch one day when it collapsed underneath her.

Frank and a group of men and women, including Frank's own granddaughter, started spending time at Mrs. Maureen's house, eventually performing a virtual makeover of it. Along the way, they had numerous opportunities to encourage and pray for one another. Frank recalls standing by Mrs. Maureen's husband's bedside one day when Mrs. Maureen said her husband wanted to pray. "He woke up and was reaching out and crying," Frank said. "He couldn't talk because he'd had multiple strokes, but my granddaughter held his hand as together we prayed."

I wish you could see Frank's face light up when he talks about the reward of obedience to James 1:27. "This is something I never in my wildest dreams thought I would do," Frank remarked one day. And then he said, "You know when you see this person smiling at you, and they haven't smiled in six months, they're smiling because they see God in you, and that's what we're supposed to be."[5] Sounds a lot like what we see in Boaz, doesn't it?

THE RIGHT TO REDEEM

So what is preventing more churches from coming together in concentrated efforts on behalf of orphans and widows? What is keeping more Christians from countering the cultural tide of neglect and abandonment in homes here and around the world? Certainly such work is not limited only to the church, for a person doesn't need to be a Christian in order to care for an orphan or a widow. Yet I would maintain that men and women who believe the gospel have more motivation than any other people in the world to carry out this work. Just consider the requirements of a redeemer and how they parallel the reasons why those who have been grafted into the family of God are compelled to come alongside orphans and widows.

First, a redeemer must have the right to redeem. In the Old Testament, we saw that this dealt primarily with family lineage. This right implied responsibility, for close ancestors were obligated to care for near relatives in need. This is obviously reflected in the New Testament as well, where Christians are commanded to care for their near relatives. In the words of Paul, "If anyone does not provide for his relatives, and especially for members of his household, he has denied the faith and is worse than an unbeliever" (1 Timothy 5:8).

However, the New Testament goes much further than simply calling Christians to care for members of their own physical families. For in Christ, Christians have been adopted into an entirely new family that rises far above physical lineage. We no longer think only in terms of biological bloodline, for we have been united by an entirely different bloodline. In Christ, because of his shed blood for our sins, we have been brought together as brothers and sisters. Addressing Jews and Gentiles in the first century, Paul tells the Gentiles:

> Now in Christ Jesus you who once were far off have
> been brought near by the blood of Christ. For he . . .
> has made us both one and has broken down in his flesh
> the dividing wall of hostility . . . that he might create
> in himself one new man in place of the two, so making
> peace, and might reconcile us both to God in one body
> through the cross, thereby killing the hostility. . . . For
> through him we both have access in one Spirit to the
> Father. So then you are no longer strangers and aliens,
> but you are fellow citizens with the saints and members
> of the household of God. EPHESIANS 2:13-16, 18-19

This gospel truth has huge implications for the way followers of Christ think and speak about family. We must be finished and done with talk in our homes of "not wanting to adopt until we have children of our own" or of "wondering whether we could love a foster child as much as we love our own child." Such conversations show a lack of understanding regarding what it means to "visit orphans"—to take responsibility for their care just as we do our own family. We have not been put on this earth simply to preserve our genetic material. We have been put on this earth to portray a gospel message, and that gospel message crosses physical barriers and transcends biological bloodlines.

I was preaching not long ago to a large church in an Asian country. As I was introducing myself to the people, I told them the story of how God had led my wife and me to adopt two of our children. Later in the day, a church leader came up to me and said, "David, your story of adopting children was very unfamiliar to our church. In our country, preserving one's bloodline is of supreme importance. We just don't have a category in our culture for thinking about family in a way that doesn't involve a shared bloodline."

Immediately I asked the question, "What does that mean for orphans in this culture?"

He responded, "We don't adopt. Orphans are placed in homes under the supervision of caregivers, and they are provided for there. But there is a stigma of shame over them because they have no family. Furthermore," he said, "anyone who adopts an orphan would then bring a stigma of shame over their family."

"Why is that?" I asked.

He answered, "Because the consistency of the bloodline in the family would be compromised."

This comment led me down a totally different track than I had planned for my preaching that week. The more I talked with this church leader about adoption, the more he realized that this was an issue that needed to be addressed in his church. He not only allowed but encouraged me to preach on the gospel and adoption, so I walked through Scripture over the next couple of days, showing God's clear commands to care for the orphan and the gospel's clear portrayal of adoption as integral to understanding what it means for any of us to be a child of God.

"I know physical bloodline is important to you in your

culture," I said. "But when you come to Christ, another blood-line becomes far more important to you. The blood of Christ on a cross makes you who you are, unites you as a church, and compels you to risk shame and ridicule in your culture to show that Christ cares for those who have no family."

As I preached, it was as though I could see hearts opening across the room. By the end of the conference, a station had been set up outside the main meeting room where members of this church were signing up to begin the adoption process. The call of Christ to counter culture in this way had become clear, and the members of this church were joyfully putting it into practice.

THE RESOURCES TO REDEEM

The church not only has the *right* (and responsibility) to reach across physical family lines to care for those with no family, but the church also has the *resources* to accomplish this work. We have seen in the book of Ruth and throughout the Bible that God has purposefully designed his people for the care of the orphan and the widow. And I have seen this firsthand in my life.

I will never forget the day I flew home from preaching at a conference in the western United States. When I arrived home to my wife in New Orleans, I began unpacking my things, and not long thereafter I received a call from my younger brother in Atlanta, where my parents lived. His voice was shaking, and he said, "David, it's Dad. You need to pray for Dad." All my attention was now fixed on the stammering voice of my brother on the other end of the phone. My dad was my best friend and biggest fan, I guess you could say, and my mind was now racing as my brother continued speaking.

"David, I don't know what's wrong. The ambulance is here, and the doctors are putting him on the stretcher. I don't know what's going on. You just need to pray." I said I would, and my brother hung up the phone.

Immediately, I fell to my knees and cried out to God with greater intensity and urgency than I had ever prayed for anything before. Tears now flowing from my eyes, I pleaded with God for my dad's life. As far as I knew, he was in the best health he had been in for years, and this was totally unexpected. Not knowing or understanding what was going on, I begged God to heal whatever was wrong in my dad.

The next half hour felt like half a day as I waited, praying with the phone in my hand. Finally, it rang, and this time it was my older brother on the line. He was at the hospital, and I can still hear the sound of his voice. "David," he said.

"Yes," I quickly responded. "How's Dad?"

After a long pause, my strong big brother spoke with a soft, trembling cry. "He's dead."

Even as I write this, I can't keep back the tears or hold back the hurt in my heart. I wept uncontrollably. My brother explained to me that while Dad was lying on the couch that night, he suddenly started gasping for breath, and by the time the ambulance arrived just a few moments later, he had died of a severe heart attack.

I can still remember the pain I had that night and how it progressed in the days to come, a pain that still comes back periodically in a way that I'm not sure I'll ever shake. Yet amid the somber severity of grief's pain in those moments, I also experienced the calming comfort of God's presence. For the people of God immediately surrounded my brothers, my sister, and my mom in poignant and powerful ways. I can still remember specific people who hugged me, prayed for me, drove me to Atlanta, came to visit my family, and went out of their way to be at the funeral. Even today, years later, I still receive texts, e-mails, and calls from people who take the time to pray for and encourage me in ways my dad would have. My family and I have continually commented, "I can't imagine going through this grief without the church around us." This is part of God's design for the care of the widow and orphan through the church, and I am deeply grateful for it.

I have seen this same reality on display in the church as I watch members serve orphans around them. While some have adopted and fostered children in our community and among the nations, I have seen others rise up not just around these kids but around the adoptive and fostering families, supporting and serving them in countless ways. While God has called certain families to adopt and foster, he has called other families to give foster children rides to and from various places, other families to cook meals for foster families, and still other families to watch adopted children so that adoptive parents can have some time alone. In all these ways and more, I have observed how the church has the unique resources to care for both the widow and the orphan, and how the Christian has a variety of avenues to explore in considering what such care might look like in his or her life.

In my own journey, as I mentioned, when my wife and I returned from Kazakhstan, we knew we wanted to adopt again. So we started asking all the questions. Domestic or international? If international, which country? Which adoption agency should we work through? How will we finance everything? As we asked all these questions, we sensed the Lord was leading us to adopt internationally, and specifically from Nepal.

The infant mortality rate in Nepal is alarming, the prevalence of poverty is overwhelming, and the number of young girls who are trafficked for sex is devastating. After years of being closed to adoption, Nepal was reopening with some unique regulations. For example, in order to adopt from Nepal, either a family had to have no children or their children must all be the same gender, in which case a family could adopt a Nepali child of the opposite gender. So, because we had two boys, we were eligible to adopt a little girl from Nepal. We were told that the whole process would take about a year, and we began immediately.

After a year of paperwork, fingerprints, physicals, home studies, moving homes, and more paperwork, we had finally completed everything that was necessary on our end to adopt a little girl from Nepal. Our next step was to be matched with a little girl.

Meanwhile, due to a variety of factors associated with a relatively unstable and constantly shifting government, soon Nepal was shut down for adoptions. I was preaching at an adoption conference about two years after our process had begun, and I met an official from the US State Department who, when he found out we were adopting from Nepal, immediately told us to get out of that process. He said to my wife and me, "There is no hope for you to adopt from Nepal."

Our hearts were crushed. I remember praying in tears with Heather at that conference, wondering what to do next. We had prayed with our boys almost nightly over the previous two years for "their little sister in Nepal." We knew that there are innumerable Nepali children without a mother or father to care for them, so why was God, the Father to the fatherless, closing this door?

Little did we know, however, that while God was closing the door of adoption from Nepal, he was opening a door of adoption from China. As we eagerly turned all our energies in this new direction, neither Heather nor I could deny that a piece of our hearts remained in Nepal. We knew that God had put orphans in that country on our minds for a reason, so even as we began praying for a little brother- or sister-to-be in China, we continued praying for a little girl in Nepal.

Not long thereafter, I met a man named Jack who leads a ministry to children in the mountains of Nepal. I had heard reports about the powerful ways Jack and the ministry he leads were addressing issues of health, education, and trafficking among mountain children, all with gospel preaching and church planting at the center of what they do. So I sat down with him and shared my family's particular burden for Nepal. That conversation opened the door for what is now a close friendship and partnership that my family has with the ministry Jack leads. By God's grace, we are now involved in giving to and serving alongside not just one precious little girl in Nepal, but multitudes of little girls and boys in Nepal who have needs far beyond what I ever could have imagined.

I share this simply to remind you that adoption is one route God may lead you to take, but there are scores of other routes through which you might put God's priority for the orphan into practice in your life. Similarly, God may call you to start a ministry to widows like Frank leads, or there are numerous other avenues through which you might serve the widows in your church, in your community, and around the world. The bottom line, however, is that God is calling *every* child of his to look after the orphan and the widow in some way. Regardless of what this means for each of our lives, as a people captivated by the love of the Father in heaven, we are compelled to show his love to those without family on earth.

THE RESOLVE TO REDEEM

That leads to the last requirement of an Old Testament redeemer. A redeemer could have the *right* and the *resources*—the responsibility and ability—to care for the destitute, but in the end a redeemer also needed the *resolve* to do something for them. Such resolve cannot be manufactured by mere numbers, statistics, or stories of need. The only reservoir from which such resolve flows is the fountain of God's love revealed in the gospel.

Remember that the story of Ruth is really *our* story. We were once wayward in our sin, wandering in the field with nothing to draw the Lord of the harvest to us. In fact, everything was against us. We were outcast sinners, rebels far from God and in desperate need of his favor. Yet he sought us out as his family. He picked us out and made a beeline toward us, becoming human and shedding his blood on our behalf. Paul writes in Ephesians:

> Praise be to the God and Father of our Lord Jesus Christ, who has blessed us in the heavenly realms with every spiritual blessing in Christ. For he chose us in him before the creation of the world to be holy and blameless in his sight. In love he predestined us to be adopted as his sons through Jesus Christ, in accordance with his pleasure and will—to the praise of his glorious grace, which he has freely given us in the One he loves. In him we have redemption through his blood. EPHESIANS 1:3-7, NIV

What good news—that the God of the universe left his throne to pursue us by his grace! It was his love that led him to adopt us as his children.

Not only has he sought us as his family, but he has saved us from all harm. He has drawn us to himself, nestling us under the shadow of his wings, so that even when storms rage around us and difficulties befall us, he is "our refuge and strength, an ever-present help in trouble" (Psalm 46:1, NIV).

Moreover, the Lord of the harvest has invited us to eat with him at his table. Not only that, he has even stooped to serve us there. Shocking us with his mercy, he has spoken to our hearts and satisfied our desires such that we have no need to run to any other field for fulfillment.

Ultimately, the Lord of the harvest has showered us with his grace. Jesus is our kinsman-redeemer with the *right* to redeem us—made like us in every way, yet without sin (see Hebrews 4:15). He has the *resources* to redeem us—possessing all authority over nature and nations, disease and demons, sin and Satan, suffering and death. Finally, he has the *resolve* to redeem us. His resolve drove him to take responsibility for our sin, enduring the wrath of God that we deserve, so that through faith in him, we might no longer be outcasts separated from God, but instead we might be called sons and daughters of God.

When we realize what God has done for us as revealed in the gospel, we recognize that God desires this same action from us on behalf of orphans and widows. For we are not *rescuers* giving our lives and families to save orphans and widows in need; instead, we are the *rescued* whose lives have been transformed at our deepest point of need. So now it just makes sense that men and women who have been captivated by the mystery of God's mercy might be compelled to give themselves to the ministry of God's mercy. Compelled to care for the orphan and the widow in our churches and around our world through a variety of different means. And just as readers of the book of Ruth had no idea how God was using this story in Israel's history, you and I may never imagine the immeasurable ways God might use our care for orphans and widows in his overarching redemptive plan.

MARA RUTH

Almost seven months after we began the adoption process in China, we were matched with a precious baby girl. As soon as we heard her story, we knew exactly what we would name her.

Mara Ruth.

Mara. Not because we figured she'd be a bitter little baby but because from the first moments of her life, she seemed to have tragedy written all over her. As I wrote earlier, she was abandoned and left in a brown paper box outside an orphanage. Even for my wife and me, after years of infertility in our marriage, we at one point seemed to have barrenness written all over us. But the Father in heaven knows exactly what he's doing on earth. And just as Naomi had no idea how God would use *Ruth* to turn her tale of sorrowful tragedy into surprising triumph, our daughter, my wife, and I had no idea how God would bring our stories together according to his sovereign design. For God would take this abandoned girl and make her into an adopted daughter, and at the same time he would take a barren woman and make her into a blessed mother.

At the end of the day, God delights in displaying his mercy in seemingly desperate situations to seemingly destitute people. Who can measure the massive postscript that might be written upon the pages of human history when all the stories have been told of how God's people showed God's compassion to the orphan and the widow in the world? And who can imagine the myriad ways he might use you and me to write it?

FIRST STEPS TO COUNTER CULTURE

Pray
Ask God to:
- Open your eyes to see the orphans and widows around you and to open your heart to care for them.
- Empower Christians around the world to protect the most vulnerable.
- Remind you of the way he has adopted you as his child in Christ.

Participate

Prayerfully consider taking these steps:

- Start the process of foster care or adoption, or find tangible ways to support families who are fostering or adopting children.
- Either on your own or with your family, consider reaching out to, spending time with, and serving a specific orphan or widow in your church or neighborhood.
- Sponsor an orphan or widow in another country through a gospel-driven Christian ministry, and maintain contact with the person you are sponsoring.

Proclaim

Consider the following truths from Scripture:

- Psalm 68:5-6, NIV: "A father to the fatherless; a defender of widows, is God in his holy dwelling. God set the lonely in families."
- Galatians 4:4-5: "When the fullness of time had come, God sent forth his Son, born of woman, born under the law, to redeem those who were under the law, so that we might receive adoption as sons."
- James 1:27: "Religion that is pure and undefiled before God the Father is this: to visit orphans and widows in their affliction, and to keep oneself unstained from the world."

For more (and more specific) suggestions,
visit CounterCultureBook.com/Topics/Orphans-Widows

A WAR ON WOMEN:
THE GOSPEL
AND SEX SLAVERY

Meet Maliha.

Maliha's name means "beautiful." She was born in northern Nepal, high among the Himalayan mountains. From the moment she entered the world, Maliha and her family struggled to survive, lacking clean water, sufficient food, and basic medical care.

Imagine her mother's hope, then, when a young man came through the village and saw Maliha outside washing the family's clothes in the local water tap. She was nine years old, though she looked even younger than that. The man knew where Maliha lived, so he went to her home and introduced himself to her mother.

"*Tashi delek*," he said as he bowed with his hands clasped. It's a Tibetan Buddhist greeting that means "Blessings and good favor upon you."

Her mother, startled, replied in kind to the man. "*Tashi delek*."

Then the man began to speak in Nupri, the local language in this region of Nepal. "I have noticed that your daughter is very beautiful," he said.

"She is," the proud mom responded. "And she is a hard worker, too. She takes care of her younger siblings, and she helps me with whatever I need."

Maliha had never been to school. Besides the fact that no school existed within a day's walk, even if one did, Maliha would not have been able to attend. Her father had left her mother years prior, and Maliha had a younger sister and brother to care for. This didn't bother Maliha, for she loved her family deeply and prided herself in helping provide for them. A year before, Maliha's younger brother became severely sick from a simple stomach infection due to dirty drinking water. Maliha's mom had traveled down the mountain that week, and it fell upon Maliha to nurse her brother back to health, which she did successfully. As long as her mom and siblings were healthy, Maliha was happy.

"Yes," the man said, "I've noticed that your husband is gone, and you have three kids to take care of by yourself. I would like to help provide for your family."

Maliha's mother was intrigued. "What can you do?" she asked.

The man said, "There is opportunity for work down in Kathmandu, the large city at the base of these mountains. So many jobs exist that can provide so much money for families like yours in these mountains."

Maliha's mother leaned in, now listening intently, and the man said, "I know that you need to stay here in order to provide for your children and tend your land. But I would be willing to take your daughter with me down to the city. There she could do some of the same jobs that she does around the village here, but she could make much more money. She could then send that money back to support you and her brother and sister. At the same time," the man continued, "she would be well taken care of with plenty of water and food in a nice home along with other girls her age."

Without question the man had Maliha's mom's attention. As she listened, she thought, *Could this really be true? Could this be the answer to what my family most needs? For me and my little boy and little girl to be provided for, all while my oldest daughter is cared for by this kind man in the city?* Yet as these questions swirled in her mind, she immediately thought, *No. I cannot be separated from my precious daughter. She means so much to me.*

When the man finished his proposal, Maliha's mom looked back at him and said, "Thank you so much for your kind offer to help our family. However, I am not able to receive it. My daughter needs to stay with me."

The man was clearly disappointed, but he said, "I really want to help you and your family, and I would take good care of your daughter. Why don't you think about it some more, and I may come back another day to talk about it again."

Maliha's mom, hesitant to acquiesce even to this request but not wanting to shame this man, politely said that would be fine, and she sent him on his way.

In the days to come, as hard as Maliha's mom tried, she couldn't get the man's offer out of her mind. She would look at beautiful, hardworking Maliha and think, *I suspect Maliha would want to go with that man, knowing that she could provide even more for our family. And the man seems so nice. I bet Maliha would enjoy his company. Maybe someone like him would even marry her one day.* But she still couldn't bear the thought of sending her daughter away while she was so young.

Until one day the man returned to Maliha's home, again while Maliha was away doing chores. He approached Maliha's mom with a smile and greeted her. Then he said, "I have been thinking more about our conversation a few weeks ago, and I understand that you are hesitant to send your daughter to the city with me. But I have come today with a pledge to you that I hope will demonstrate my desire to provide for you."

Maliha's mom sat down across from the man. "As a pledge of my promise to provide for your family here and your daughter in the city," the man said, "I want to give you ten thousand rupees." Maliha's mom's eyes immediately widened. Ten thousand rupees is the equivalent of about one hundred dollars and amounts to approximately half a year's wages for Maliha's mom. *This man is more generous than any man I've met in my entire life!* she thought.

"In addition," the man said, "I promise to bring your daughter back up these mountains with me once a year to see you and spend time with her brother and sister. I know this is important to her and to you."

About this time, Maliha returned home and saw the man conversing with her mom. Maliha's mom looked over at her, and after a long pause, she asked Maliha to come sit on her lap. She said, "Maliha, this man has come to offer help to you and to our family."

Maliha smiled hesitantly as her mother continued. "He is willing to take you to Kathmandu, the great city at the bottom of these mountains. There, you can live and work with some other girls your age. You will have all the food and water you want, and you will live in a nice place, where this man will take care of you. You will do the same kind of work that you do here, but the difference is that you will be able to make a lot of money that you can send back to help your sister and brother and me. And then, after you have worked for a while, this man will bring you back up the mountain so you can visit us and see all the ways you have helped us."

As her mother spoke, Maliha's eyes welled up with tears. She immediately thought, *No, I can't leave my family.* But the more her mother talked, the more she realized this was a wonderful opportunity to help the people she loved most. Sure, there was risk. Maliha had never been out of these mountains before. But even if things didn't go well, she would be able to come back to her village soon and live with her family again.

Maliha's mom gazed at her daughter, both of them now crying, and she said, "I believe it would be best for you and for our family for you to go with this kind man."

Maliha looked up into her mom's eyes, believing that her mom loved her and knew what was best. She said, "I will do whatever you want to provide for you and my sister and brother."

The man put his arm on Maliha's shoulder, smiled, and said, "I promise to take good care of you."

Arrangements were made over the next couple of days, and the man returned with his ten-thousand-rupee pledge. A tearful departure ensued as Maliha hugged her mom, her little sister, and her brother, and then she set off down the trail with the man.

As they walked together over the next few days, the man gave Maliha instructions on what would happen as they approached the city. "There will be places where police are looking for identification," he said. "We don't want to get stopped by the police, so you will need to hide yourself in a group of people as best as you can. This will help us get to the city faster."

So that's what Maliha did. At every checkpoint, she innocently wandered into a pack of people where she could slip by officials who weren't very diligent in their jobs in the first place. It was easy, which was no surprise to the man who was escorting Maliha. He had done this with other girls in the past, and he knew most of the police officers anyway.

It was evening when they arrived, and they immediately went

to a restaurant to get something to eat. But this restaurant was different from other restaurants. It was called a cabin restaurant. It sat alongside a row of restaurants where families would come and eat, but the booths in this restaurant were unique. They were more like cubicles. Wood frames starting at the floor and reaching all the way to the ceiling divided each booth from the next so that no one could see into or out of the booth. A small table sat in the middle of each booth with a bench wrapped around it. Other girls, all of them older than Maliha, sat at the front of the restaurant. She assumed they were resting after a long day of work, and she smiled as she walked past them.

The man led Maliha into one of the booths, where she sat down, and soon a large plate of food was placed before her. Famished from the journey, and quite honestly never having seen this much food on one plate before, she ate it all, and then the man escorted her to her room upstairs. It was a small room with a cot-like bed in the corner. A dirty, stained sheet covered the thin mattress, and the man said, "You can give me your bag. I'll get you some brand-new clothes that you can wear tomorrow. In the meantime, you sleep well tonight, and I'll see you in the morning."

Maliha obliged. She was tired, to say the least, and though she missed her family, she was thankful that she had finally arrived at the place where she would live and provide for them. She thought, *I need to get a good night's rest so that I can work hard tomorrow, like those other girls, before coming back here for dinner.* With this, she fell quietly asleep, never dreaming that this would be her last quiet night for years to come.

The next morning Maliha awoke to the man's voice. He came into her room, his hands full of nice, new, and tight clothes for her to wear. He encouraged her to clean up and get dressed and then come downstairs in the restaurant, where they would talk about the work she was to do. She promptly obeyed and came down again to one of the booths, where the man sat waiting for her. Maliha sat across the table from him, and he began to give her instructions.

"Now in order to provide for your mom, your sister, and your brother back home, all you need to do is what I say. I have already paid your family a lot of money, so you are going to need to start working today to pay that back. Then, once you make more money, I can send it to your family," he said.

Maliha nodded her head and asked, "What would you like me to do?" In asking that question, Maliha never could have imagined what the man's answer would entail. It would start that evening during dinner with the man, who gave her alcohol to drink with her meal. Then he escorted this nine-year-old girl upstairs, her senses now impaired, where he took off her pretty clothes, took away her innocence, and raped her in her room.

He left her there for the night, arriving again the next morning to ask Maliha if she would like some breakfast. Now frightened and still unsure of what exactly had happened the previous day, but knowing that her body had been hurt badly in ways she had never experienced before, she followed the man downstairs to eat. He told her that she had done a good job making money the night before, but that she needed to do more work if her family was going to have what they needed to survive. Maliha cried because she didn't want to do more work like she had done the previous night. But the man threatened her and said, "You better not cry, or you won't make the money you need to make. If you want to provide for your family, you do what I say, and you don't cry."

In the days that followed, the man repeatedly raped Maliha, sometimes more than once a day. Each episode was accompanied by drinking, and in the weeks that followed, drugs were added as well. At first, Maliha tried to fight. She didn't want to do what the man wanted her to do; she just wanted to go home. But the sheer force of the man overpowered the fragility of her body as day after day, week after week, she was beaten into submission. It didn't take long—only a couple of months—before her spirit was completely broken.

The stage was now set for other men to get involved. They would walk into the restaurant, where they would find Maliha, this beautiful young girl, sitting at the entrance, looking down at the floor with a string of condoms hanging from the ceiling above her head. A man would grab her by the hand, and she would quietly follow him into one of the booths. There, he would eat and drink and then either take Maliha upstairs to her room or stay right there in the booth and force her to do whatever he told her to do. After he was finished, she would go out and wait for another man, and then another man, and then another man. Sometimes, on a busy night, fifteen or twenty different customers would have their way with Maliha however they desired.

This was Maliha's life, and there was no way out. The man who first smiled at her back in her village months before had gone back to find other girls, and Maliha now worked for other men. They told her that if she tried to stop working at the restaurant, they would go back to the village and bring her little sister there to take her place. They assured her that her work was providing for her family back home. Little did she know that her mom never received another rupee. Meanwhile, for all her mom, little brother, and little sister knew, Maliha had completely forgotten about them when she got to the big city.

Even if Maliha could have escaped, where would she go? She had no clue where she was and no idea how to get home. She knew no one but the men who owned her. She had nothing to her name. The only thing she had was her shame; she was clearly a cursed woman in a culture that believes your present place in life is what you deserve based on your behavior in a past life. *Ke garne,* she would think to herself on many days, a common Nepali phrase that simply means, "Life is what it is, and you deal with it." So she dealt with it, eventually becoming a teenager, now successful at her trade but stripped of all her hope.

CLOSER TO HOME

Maliha's story can seem worlds away until you meet Hannah, whose experience may hit much closer to home. Hannah is in her early twenties now, but she was born into an environment much different from Maliha's. Hannah was born in the buckle of America's Bible Belt, in Birmingham, Alabama. Her family was far from poor. Instead, her parents were able to provide all that Hannah needed—and wanted. On Hannah's sixteenth birthday, her mom and dad got her a car, and along with that car came newfound freedom and opportunity. She could go out with her friends whenever she wanted.

Or so she thought. Over the next year, Hannah's parents saw their daughter misusing the trust they had put in her, and before long they tightened down on where she could go and when she could go there. Along the way, they also developed stricter rules regarding what Hannah wore. Her skirts had been getting shorter and her neckline lower, and her parents decided that the clothes she had picked out were no longer permissible.

That's when Hannah met Molly, a new friend at school. Unlike Hannah, Molly had no boundaries on what she could wear, where she could go, and who she could be around. Hannah wanted to be like Molly, and they became close friends quickly. Along the way, Hannah confided in Molly that she was struggling to make enough money to pay for her car insurance, and she really wanted more money to buy clothes that she could change into at school once she was out of her parents' seemingly over-attentive gaze.

Molly was happy to help Hannah. She introduced Hannah to Mark, who introduced Hannah to a whole new world. Hannah went out on a date with Mark, and he treated her like a queen. Mark told Hannah how beautiful she was, flattering her with conversations about how she should be a model. Hannah felt like a million dollars, and it seemed Mark had that much to give her. He showered her with nice, new clothes, perfume, and jewelry— anything she wanted. Before long, Hannah had fallen in love. She knew that Mark was the one for her. When Mark encouraged her to live with him outside of the city, it just made sense. She was now old enough to make that kind of decision on her own, so a couple of weeks later, in the middle of the night, Hannah left home, her parents having no idea where she had gone.

Soon Mark started talking about his desire to take Hannah away to a city like Los Angeles, where they could live together and she could be a model. *Could I really be a model in California?* Hannah would ask herself, idealizing what that life might be like. All she needed to do, Mark said, was to sell her car and do a few photo shoots with some of his friends in Birmingham. This would help them save enough money to get to LA, and it would also help Hannah to build her modeling portfolio.

Hannah agreed. She started modeling and enjoyed it until one day Mark suggested that she pose nude for some of the pictures. Hannah was initially hesitant, but Mark affirmed how beautiful she was and guaranteed that this would help her make a lot more money so they could get to California. Hannah reluctantly agreed.

It didn't take long, however, for these photo shoots to become far more than what Hannah had envisioned. Mark would drop her off for a photo shoot with his friends, and when he had left, Mark's friends would ask her not only to pose naked, but to perform sexual acts in front of the camera. When Mark returned and brought her home, Hannah told him that she didn't want to do that anymore. Mark got angry and insisted that if she loved him, she would do these shoots. He reminded her of all the things he had given her and insisted that she start making more money for the two of them.

Hannah acquiesced, and the photo shoots in the days ahead only got worse. The more she resisted the acts that Mark and his friends wanted her to do in front of the camera, the more Mark insisted that she do them. He began beating her and eventually took away all of her identification. He told her that she needed to make more money, and that's when the photo shoots by day led to personal engagements by night. Mark would pick Hannah up from a photo shoot at his friends' house and drive her to a rest stop along Interstate 20. There they would get something to eat, and then they would sit outside in the car until truckers came along. Mark would send Hannah out to a semitruck, where she would offer the driver an assortment of sexual pleasures. The trucker would pay her in return for her services, and she would bring the money back to Mark. Within a matter of months, Hannah's promising boyfriend had become her pimp.

MODERN SLAVERY

I am ashamed to confess that it wasn't until recently that I realized the severity of sex trafficking in the world around me. For a long time, the idea of slavery seemed to me a relic of a bygone era centuries before my time. I never could have imagined that there are more slaves today than were seized from Africa in four centuries of the transatlantic slave trade.[1] I never could have comprehended that twenty-seven million people live in slavery today—more than at any other time in history.[2] I never could have fathomed that many of these millions are being bought, sold, and exploited for sex in what has become one of the fastest-growing industries on earth.[3]

But even when I heard these numbers, they still seemed distant to me. As long as they were mere numbers on a page, I could insulate and isolate myself from them. Quite honestly, I could live as if they didn't exist—both the numbers and the individuals they represent.

That all changed when I walked through Maliha's village in the Nupri valley of Nepal. For the first time in my life, I came face-to-face with the horrifying reality of what happens in those mountains. I heard story after story of girl after girl, and when I got back to the big city of Kathmandu, I walked past restaurant after restaurant with slaves waiting outside to provide services in cubicles inside. I saw where Maliha once lived, and I saw where Maliha now works, and no matter how hard I try, I can't get these sights out of my mind.

When I flew back from Nepal, I landed in Atlanta and drove to my home in Birmingham. On Interstate 20. I have grown up going up and down this interstate that spans all the way to west Texas, and I had no idea that it is the "sex trafficking superhighway" of the United States. This same road that represents freedom for ten million travelers every year reflects the reality of slavery for countless girls every night.[4] It changes your perspective to realize that the man and young woman at the table next to you at the rest stop may not be what you once thought.

Slavery still exists. And now that I know it does, I have no choice but to do something about it. Further, now that *you* know it does, you have no choice but to do something about it.

CREATED EQUAL

But how do we fight slavery? Much could be (and has been) written in response to that question from a variety of perspectives. I in no way claim to be an expert on how to stop slavery in the world around us. The more I become involved in this issue, the more complex I realize it is. Even this chapter is limited in its focus on female sex trafficking, not exploring the ways this unspeakable horror also affects boys or the various other forms of slavery in the world. There are no easy answers to questions about slavery, and there are no simple solutions to this epidemic problem.

However, I am deeply convinced that the gospel alone provides the depth of perspective alteration and heart transformation needed to eradicate slavery. I know that is a bold statement, but I make it with humble confidence in the truth of the gospel to change minds and the power of God's Spirit to change hearts. Let me explain.

The gospel begins with God—the God who alone has authority to rule and reign as Master and Lord in the universe. He alone owns us all (see Psalm 24:1). This does not preclude relationships between people marked by loving authority and glad submission, such as we see in God's design for a good father who loves and cares for his young children. But even here, a dad does not *own* his children, nor do those children ultimately belong to their dad. Ultimate ownership and ultimate belonging are reserved for the ultimate Owner, the God to whom we belong. When Scripture specifically addresses first-century slavery, it reminds those who would call themselves "master" that *their* Master is in heaven (see Ephesians 6:9), and he alone rules over them.

This leads to a second and fundamental component of the gospel: that God, the Owner of all things, has created all people everywhere in his image. As such, all people everywhere possess equal value before him and each other. No man or woman is superior to another man or woman, and no man or woman is inferior to another man or woman. "Four score and seven years ago our fathers brought forth, upon this continent, a new nation, conceived in liberty, and dedicated to the proposition that 'all men are created equal.'"[5] These words begin one of the most famous speeches in all of American history, the Gettysburg Address, delivered on November 19, 1863, by then-president Abraham Lincoln. But Lincoln didn't come up with the idea that all men are created equal; God did.

The first chapter of the Bible tells us that "God created man in his own image, in the image of God he created him; male and female he created them" (Genesis 1:27). Job implies this when he talks about why he refuses to mistreat his servants. He asks, "Did not the One who made me in the womb also make them? Did not the same God form us both in the womb?" (Job 31:15, HCSB). Such equal dignity before God is also evident in the New Testament, where Paul writes, "There is neither Jew nor Greek, slave nor free, male nor female, for you are all one in Christ Jesus" (Galatians 3:28, NIV). In other words, even though we have differences, we all have equal dignity before God, and specifically all followers of Christ have an equal position in Christ. This equal dignity is the basis James uses for arguing against favoritism in the church (see James 2:1-9).

In light of equal dignity shared by all people, God denounces physical abuse specifically as it relates to slavery (see Exodus 21:20-27). In addition, God condemns any type of human trafficking. Kidnapping another person is punishable by death, a penalty that applies both to the one selling the slave and the one buying the slave (see Exodus 21:16). Paul decries the sin of trafficking in the same breath in which he speaks about murder and sexual immorality. The word translated "enslavers" in 1 Timothy 1:10 literally means a "man-stealer" or a "slave-dealer."[6] Anyone who kidnaps people in order to sell them as slaves is "lawless and rebellious . . . ungodly and sinful . . . unholy and irreverent" (1 Timothy 1:9, HCSB).[7]

Needless to say (but important to note), if this biblical truth had been embraced and obeyed by Christians in the eighteenth and nineteenth centuries, the African slave trade across Europe and America never would have existed as it did. Millions of men and women were transported in cruel, grueling conditions that left many of them dead before arriving at their destination. Upon being sold, slaves were subjected to harsh working conditions as well as physical abuse, sexual abuse, and torture. Frederick Douglass, a leader of the abolitionist movement in the 1800s, wrote the following about his first slave master, Captain Anthony:

> He was a cruel man, hardened by a long life of
> slaveholding. He would at times seem to take great
> pleasure in whipping a slave. I have often been awakened
> at the dawn of day by the most heart-rending shrieks of
> an own aunt of mine, whom he used to tie up to a joist,
> and whip . . . till she was literally covered with blood.
> No words, no tears, no prayer, from his gory victim,
> seemed to move his iron heart from its bloody purpose.[8]

Accounts like this remind us of the horrors of slavery, horrors that God explicitly condemns. Clearly, pastors and church members in the pre–Civil War United States who used God's Word to justify the practice of slavery were living in sin. For whether then or today, Scripture clearly considers any slavery that undercuts the value or dignity of any person as rebellion against God's lordship, a violation of God's law, and a denial of God's love for every single person made in his image.

Many cultures in the world, however, do not believe God created all people with equal dignity. For example, a variety of Muslim, Hindu, Buddhist, animistic, and atheistic cultures around the world deny the value of women in a diverse array of ways. And just as the oppression of women in the Middle East or the abortion of baby girls across Asia begins with the devaluation of a woman's life, so sex slavery starts at the same place. Once a woman is seen as less important, less dignified, or less worthy than a man, she is more easily discarded as an object to be used or abused, and her plight is more practically disregarded by a country's officials.

I think about walking down a city street in South Asia, swarmed by thousands of Hindu worshipers who had gathered to celebrate the supreme Hindu god Shiva, who had sex with multiple women. For some followers of Hinduism, sex itself is a form of Shiva worship, even a requirement in order to please and appease this and other gods. Some of these families give their daughters to the temple at age twelve as an offering to the gods to be used for sex. It is no wonder, then, that this worldview might lead to hundreds of thousands of girls working in the brothels of Indian megacities like Mumbai, Delhi, and Calcutta.

SLAVERY AND PORNOGRAPHY

American culture is certainly not immune to such a worldview, for our culture's worship of sex has led to the devaluation of women. This is apparent in the prostitution and pornography industries, and it is evident not only in the culture around us but even in the church among us, where instead of countering culture, Christians are imitating culture. Surveys consistently show that over half of men and increasing numbers of women in churches are actively viewing pornography. Remarkably (but when you think about it, not necessarily surprisingly), statistics are similar for the pastors who lead these churches.[9]

Such pornography is a severe problem on a number of levels, but don't miss its connection to sex trafficking. Research continually demonstrates a clear link between sex trafficking and the production of pornography.[10] Federal legislation has acknowledged this,[11] participants in the production of pornography have confirmed this,[12] and while exact figures are hard to pin down, one anti-trafficking center reports that at least a third of victims trafficked for sex are used in the production of pornography.[13] Another study on the relationship between prostitution, pornography, and trafficking found that one half of nearly nine hundred prostitutes in nine different countries reported pornography being made of them while in prostitution.[14] When we hear such research, we mustn't miss the connection. Men and women who indulge in pornography are creating the demand for more prostitutes, and in turn they are fueling the sex-trafficking industry.

Yet the cycle is even more vicious than that. For the more people watch pornography, the more they desire sexual fulfillment through prostitution.[15] Such desire drives men (and women) to engage in physical prostitution or even virtual prostitution as "every home computer [becomes] a potential red light district."[16] Pornography thus feeds prostitution, again increasing the demand for sex trafficking.

Do we realize what we're doing? Every time a man or woman views pornography online, we are contributing to a cycle of sex slavery from the privacy of our own computers. We are fueling an industry that enslaves people for sex in order to satisfy selfish pleasure in our living rooms, our offices, and on our mobile phones.

Do we see the depth of irony here? A quick survey of the

college landscape in our culture reveals zealous activism on behalf of slaves around the world. Students watch documentaries, listen to speakers, hold charity walks and runs, and raise money to help trafficking victims. Meanwhile, almost 90 percent of college males and over 30 percent of college females are viewing porn in their dorms, apartments, and on their phones.[17] And this is not limited to secular campuses or non-Christian activists. According to a recent study of evangelical Christian colleges, nearly 80 percent of male undergraduate students at these colleges have viewed Internet pornography in the last year, and over 60 percent view it every week.[18] The hypocrisy is staggering, and the conclusion is clear. No matter how many red *X*s we write on our hands to end slavery, as long as these same hands are clicking on pornographic websites and scrolling through sexual pictures and videos, we are frauds to the core.

Any and every time we indulge in pornography, we deny the precious gospel truth that every man and woman possesses inherent dignity, not to be solicited and sold for sex, but to be valued and treasured as excellent in the eyes of God. People are not inferior objects to be used and abused for selfish, sexual, sensual pleasure; they are equal image bearers of the God who loves and cares for them. We may scoff at how pre–Civil War churchgoers justified slaves in their backyards, but aren't we dangerously like them when we participate in pornography (and promote the sex slavery to which it is inextricably tied) in our own homes?

FIGHTING WITH THE GOSPEL

Fighting slavery begins with believing the gospel—with seeing that the good, holy, and loving Creator God alone is the Owner of all people. Fighting slavery continues with applying the gospel—with living the truth that all people have been made in God's image and thus are to be esteemed and never enslaved. And fighting slavery requires that we proclaim the gospel—that we do all that we can to tell the utterly hopeless that ultimate hope is found in Jesus Christ.

This leads us to the shocking reality of the way the gospel addresses slavery. For in Scripture, God takes slavery, a clear product of sin in the world, and turns it into a powerful image of his salvation for the world. The very center of the gospel is the person of Jesus Christ, who though he is fully divine, "emptied Himself by assuming *the form of a slave*, taking on the likeness of men" (Philippians 2:7, HCSB, emphasis mine). The word *slave* here—*doulos*—comes from the same root as words used in other New Testament texts to talk about slaves who had masters. Quite literally, the Bible says, Jesus became a slave of humanity in order to save humanity. When you read these words, you can't help but picture Jesus, just before going to the cross, wrapping a garment around his waist, kneeling down, and washing his disciples' feet (see John 13). His earlier words to his disciples almost certainly echoed in their minds: "Even the Son of Man came not to be served but to serve, and to give his life as a ransom for many" (Mark 10:45).

This is the essence of the gospel. The climax of the Christian message is that the Master over the world has become a servant for the world. God has come to us in the flesh, as a man, made like us in every way (except without sin). He has walked among us in this world of sin and suffering, and he has suffered for us. He has died on the cross in our place and for our sin, and he has risen from the dead with an offer of eternal life to all who confess him as Lord.

The Christian gospel does not depict God as a Master doling out a list of demands for men and women to do as slaves in order to please or appease him. Rather, the gospel depicts God as a Master who says, "I will meet you where you are, in the depth of your sin and suffering, and I will save you. I will restore you. I will redeem you—I will purchase you by the sacrifice of my life—so that you will one day be free from all sin and all suffering."

This gospel reveals what (or rather *who*) Maliha and Hannah most need. In that cabin restaurant or on the side of the interstate, Maliha and Hannah do not need news of gods who condemn them in their sin and provide requirements for their salvation. They and other girls like them, by the time they become adults, will have been raped literally thousands of times. They don't need a Savior who waits for them to come to him. They need a Savior who comes to them, like a shepherd who leaves ninety-nine sheep to search for the one, like a woman who turns her house upside down looking for a lost coin, and like a father who goes sprinting after a wayward son (see Luke 15). In their endless feelings of filth, they need a Savior who will look at them with compassionate eyes and say, "I will make you clean" (see Luke 5:12-14). With hopeless feelings of shame, they need a Savior who will restore their honor on this earth and renew their hope for all eternity.

This is the same Savior traffickers need as well. The men and women behind the trafficking industry need to see the severe nature of their sin and God's coming judgment upon that sin. At the same time, they need to see the gracious sacrifice of God to ransom their souls. They need a Savior who will forgive their sins and transform their lives, that they might no longer take advantage of these girls but might advocate for them instead. Only the power of the gospel can effect this kind of change in these evil hearts. And the same can be said for the men and women who use these girls in prostitution and watch these girls in pornography.

When it comes down to it, you and I and all of us need this Savior. We need God, in his mercy, to serve us with his salvation and to change us from the inside out, that we might follow him as the only Lord over all and that we might love the people around us, recognizing the dignity he has bestowed upon them. When this gospel changes our lives, it changes the way we encounter our culture. In this way, as scholar Murray J. Harris puts it, the gospel lays "the explosive charge . . . that . . . ultimately . . . lead[s] to detonation, and the destruction of slavery" altogether.[19]

HOPE AND HEALING

I have referenced Nepal numerous times already in this book, and in the last chapter I mentioned Jack, a friend of mine who lives and leads a ministry there. Jack first traveled to Nepal on a trekking expedition. He was looking forward to hiking in the Himalayas and had spent much time and money preparing for the adventure. As he began his ascension into the mountains, the first rest stop he came to brought him in contact with a variety of travelers going up and down the mountains. He noticed a couple of men who were traveling with a group of young girls. As Jack conversed with these men, they willingly told him what they were doing. They were taking these girls to the border, where they would hand them over to be sold in one of India's megacities for sexual prostitution.

Jack was stunned. As he looked at the faces of these girls, he didn't know what to do. He just started crying. In his words, "It wasn't a shallow type of cry. This was deep, real deep, like a well that frankly I haven't found the bottom of yet." In that moment, he felt more helpless than he had ever felt before. He realized there was nothing he could do for these girls, but there was something he could do for others like them. In his words, "I decided to turn the tears into tactics."

Jack immediately packed his bag and went back down the mountain. That was over ten years ago, and in the time since that day, Jack has given his life to carrying the hope of the gospel into those Himalayan mountains. Among other things, the ministry he leads hosts a coalition of over forty different gospel-centered organizations that are working together in Nepal to fight sex trafficking in multifaceted ways including education, prevention, rescue, and restoration. The war against sex trafficking is extremely complex and overwhelmingly difficult, but it is undoubtedly worth it for the sake of seemingly countless Malihas in need of gospel hope.

This war is also being waged on behalf of countless Hannahs in the so-called Bible belt of the United States. I think of Tajuan, a woman who was sexually exploited when she was fifteen years old by her boyfriend-turned-pimp. She was trafficked so many times to Birmingham, Alabama, that it became her home. But by God's grace, she was delivered out of the sex-trafficking industry. Now, because of her transformation in the gospel, Tajuan provides housing and help for sexually exploited women in Birmingham who not only are being rescued from sex trafficking but also are experiencing restoration through the hope and healing found in Christ alone.

For Christians, it is the portrait of Christ in the gospel that compels us to fight for the detonation and destruction of slavery in the world. He is the pursuing Savior, and as men and women who are identified with him, we must pursue the enslaved. We cannot be silent, and we must not be still. We do not have that choice. We are compelled to pray, to give, and to work to see sex slaves released from their captors and restored to new life. In the midst of our praying, giving, and working, we are compelled to proclaim Christ, who alone has the ability to bring complete freedom. We are compelled to fight in all these ways with the truth of the gospel on our minds, the power of the gospel in our hearts, and the love of the gospel in our hands.

FIRST STEPS TO COUNTER CULTURE

Pray

Ask God to:

- Intervene and rescue individuals around the world who are being used as sex slaves.
- Open the eyes of Christians and churches to the plight of sexual slavery.
- Redeem the perpetrators of sex slavery or otherwise execute justice in light of their sin.

Participate

Prayerfully consider taking these steps:

- Support a ministry that addresses the problem of sex slavery and consider ways you can be involved in their work.
- Make fellow church members or church leaders aware of this issue so that you can pray for the victims of sex slavery and strategize how to help them.
- Call and write to your government representatives, urging them to oppose sex trafficking as well as the pornography industry.

Proclaim

Consider the following truths from Scripture:

- Psalm 24:1 (NIV): "The earth is the LORD's, and everything in it, the world, and all who live in it."

- Psalm 82:4: "Rescue the weak and the needy; deliver them from the hand of the wicked."
- Psalm 7:11: "God is a righteous judge, and a God who feels indignation every day."

For more (and more specific) suggestions,
visit CounterCultureBook.com/Topics/Sex-Trafficking

A PROFOUND MYSTERY:
THE GOSPEL
AND MARRIAGE

Definitions of terms are extremely important.

I was preaching in Germany one day, and a group of new friends asked me, "Do you want to play football with us this afternoon?"

I enjoy football—both watching it and playing it. In high school and college, my friends and I used to spend our weekends throwing the ball outside and playing pickup games. "Count me in!" I told them excitedly.

To my surprise, when I got down to the field, I didn't find tall goalposts and a brown ball with pointy ends. Instead, I saw two goals with nets on them and a round, black-and-white ball. That's when I remembered: football in Europe (and most of the rest of the world) is a lot different from my American understanding of football. I call their kind of football *soccer*.

Football. Same term, different definitions. And definitions of terms affect the decisions we make. Football is a simple, relatively inconsequential, example of this (though had I known I'd agreed to play soccer with a group of European friends who are experts in the sport, I may have come to the field with a little less enthusiasm!). But there are other more significant, extremely consequential examples of this as well. As we considered in chapter 3, one's definition of a *human* has huge ramifications for one's view of abortion. How terms like this are defined by a culture determines much about how people not only make decisions but also lead their lives in that culture.

So how does one define *marriage*?

This question lies at the heart of a moral revolution in our time and culture. For millennia, civilizations have defined marriage as an exclusive, permanent union of a man and a woman. Two decades ago politicians in our country voted across party lines to defend this definition of marriage in what was called the Defense of Marriage Act. Yet in June 2013 the Supreme Court of the United States struck down key provisions of that Act, paving the way for the complete redefinition of marriage across our culture. In the days that followed, states began officially defining marriage according to different terms, now notably allowing same-sex relationships to be classified as so-called marriages. Such state decisions were then confirmed in June 2015, when the Supreme Court officially legalized so-called same-sex marriage across the United States, requiring all states to issue and recognize marriage licenses for same-sex couples.

As if these Supreme Court rulings were not enough of a paradigm shift, the majority opinion written in one case by Justice Anthony Kennedy asserted that the men and women who originally voted for the Defense of Marriage Act were acting with the intent to harm. In their minority opinions, Justices John Roberts and Antonin Scalia both acknowledged how the majority court was painting supporters of marriage as it has been defined for millennia as "bigots" who sought to "demean," "disparage," "humiliate," and "injure" same-sex couples. In a sweeping decision, the Supreme Court of our country thus redefined "an aspect of marriage that had been unquestioned in our society for most of its existence—indeed, had been unquestioned in virtually all societies for virtually all of human history" while simultaneously defining proponents of traditional marriage as "enemies of the human race."[1]

The court's decisions in 2013 and 2015 represent only one part of a much larger trend away from traditional marriage across our culture that has taken place over many years. Though it's difficult to obtain precise data, census figures project that nearly half of all first marriages will end in divorce.[2] And that's if men and women even decide to marry. The number of cohabiting couples in our culture has nearly quadrupled over the last thirty years as more and more singles postpone or put aside marriage altogether.[3] Lifelong marriage between a man and a woman is clearly on the decline. According to Mark Regnerus, over the past forty years, "the number of independent female households in the U.S. has grown by 65 percent, while the share of independent male households has skyrocketed, leaping 120 percent. As a result, fewer than half of all American households today are made up of married couples."[4]

All of these realities cause us to wonder, *Is marriage really that important in the first place? And what's the problem with redefining it? Are we really going to say it's wrong for two men or two women to marry each other? Isn't it more wrong (maybe even hateful) to deny two men or two women the right to love one another like this?* In the words of one "Christian" leader who advocates the redefinition of marriage, "God [is] pulling us all forward into a greater realization that we need more love. . . . We need more people who are committed to each other. It's not good for us to be alone. So this is a huge moment when I think lots of us are realizing the old way of seeing things doesn't work."[5]

So is the discussion of marriage in our culture simply a matter of moving on from an "old way of seeing things" to a new way of seeing things? Is marriage merely a tradition that is open to changing with the times? Or is marriage an institution that was ordained to be consistent through all time?

More foundational than each of these questions is how the gospel applies to marriage. What has the Creator God said about marriage? Have we turned aside from what he has said? Does Christ's death on the cross have anything to do with how we define marriage? And what does it mean for followers of Christ to live in a culture that often defines marriage differently than the Bible does? If we're willing to ask these questions honestly, we need to be ready for surprising answers. More important, we need to be prepared to counter the culture around us in significant ways.

MALE AND FEMALE HE CREATED THEM

Our understanding of marriage is built upon our understanding of sexuality. According to our culture, sexual differences are merely social constructions. Sure, men and women have physical distinctions, but even these can be altered or disregarded, if we prefer. Even if we maintain an understanding of human beings as distinctly male and female, we view them as equal—and by equal, we mean identical. Consequently, it makes complete sense for a man to marry a man or a woman to marry a woman, just as it makes sense for a man to marry a woman. There is no difference since we are identical—so our culture says.

But what does God say?

The first two chapters of Genesis record complementary accounts of human creation. Genesis 1 tells us, "God created man in his own image, in the image of God he created him; male and female he created them" (verse 27). The dignity of men and women is on display from the start. Nothing else in all creation, not even the most majestic angel, is portrayed "in the image of God." Men and women alone are like God, but not in the sense that we share all of his qualities. He is infinite; we are finite. He is divine; we are human. He is spirit; we are flesh. Yet in a way that nothing else in all creation can, men and women share certain moral, intellectual, and relational capacities with God. We have the power to reason, the desire to love, the ability to speak, and the facility to make moral decisions. Most important of all, men and women have the opportunity to relate to God in a way that dogs and cats, mountains and seas, and even angels and demons can't. As soon as God creates man and woman, he immediately blesses them, beginning a relationship with the only beings in all the created order who resemble him.

This is where any Bible-informed conversation about men and women must begin: with men and women *both* created with equal dignity before God and each other. We previously explored what this reality means for slavery in chapter 5, but we must also consider what equal dignity means for how we understand sexuality. Men and women *both* share in the inexpressible worth of creatures formed in the image of God himself. In this way, God speaks loudly from the start of Scripture against any sort of male or female superiority or dominance. Near the end of Scripture, God refers to men and women as fellow "heirs . . . of the grace of life" (1 Peter 3:7). According to God's design, men are never to be perceived as better than women, and women are never to be perceived as better than men. God abhors any treatment of men or women as inferior objects to be used or abused.

For all of eternity, no gender will be greater than the other. No one should feel superior or inferior by nature of being a man or a woman. Both are beautifully—and equally—created in the image of God.

But not *identically*. Equal dignity does not eliminate distinction. Genesis 1 makes clear that God creates humans uniquely male and female, and he does it for a reason. Right after he blesses them, he commands them, "Be fruitful and multiply and fill the earth" (Genesis 1:28). This command is only possible by virtue of the peculiarity of male and female. Multiplication would have been impossible if God had created humans male and male or female and female. God's unique design enables them to carry out his command.

Moreover, this divine design involves far more than the capacity to reproduce (as important as that is). There is something greater than mere biological accident or evolutionary adaptation going on here. God creates man and woman to cherish their shared equality while complementing their various differences.

Genesis 2 provides a more close-up picture of how God initially creates man. God forms him from the dust, breathes life into his nostrils, and places him in the Garden of Eden. God parades animals before him, tasking him with assigning names to each of them. The point of this procession is to make clear to man that he is alone—that there is no one else like him. As man looks at each animal, considering monikers that match their nature, he realizes, *None of these match my nature.* He sinks back in solitude, and for the first time in the Bible, we read, "It is not good" (Genesis 2:18).

Keep in mind that this is before sin has entered the world. Throughout Genesis 1, there is a constant interchange between earthly creation and heavenly declaration. God creates light, and he declares it good. God creates the land and the water, and he declares them good. God creates the sky and the planets, the animals and the plants, and he declares them all good. But one thing is not good. Man is alone.

So God says, "I will make him a helper fit for him." When man falls asleep, God performs the first surgery, taking a rib from man. Obviously God doesn't need to do this. Just as he has created man from dust, he can create woman the same way. But he doesn't. Instead, God takes a rib from man's side, and he forms a woman. When the man opens his eyes, he is stunned, to say the least. The first recorded human words are poetry, as the man sings,

This at last is bone of my bones
　and flesh of my flesh;
she shall be called Woman,
　　because she was taken out of Man.
GENESIS 2:23

Don't miss the magnificence of this scene. God brings man to realize that he needs someone equal to him, made with the same nature that he possesses but different from him, in order to help him do things he could never do on his own. This is precisely what God gives to man in woman, and the stage is thus set for the institution of marriage. In the very next verse, we read, "Therefore a man shall leave his father and his mother and hold fast to his wife, and they shall become one flesh" (Genesis 2:24).

Behold the beauty of God's design for man, woman, and marriage. Two dignified people, both molded in the image of their Maker. Two diverse people, uniquely designed to complement each other. A male and a female fashioned by God to form one flesh, a physical bond between two bodies where the deepest point of union is found at the greatest point of difference. A matrimony marked by unity in diversity, equality with variety, and personal satisfaction through shared consummation.

CHRIST AND THE CHURCH

None of this was haphazard. From the beginning of time, God designed marriage in this way for a purpose. That purpose was not fully revealed until Jesus died on the cross, rose from the dead, and instituted the church. After all of this, the Bible looks back to the institution of marriage and asserts, "This mystery [of marriage] is profound, and . . . it refers to Christ and the church" (Ephesians 5:32). When God made man, then woman, and then brought them together in a relationship called marriage, he wasn't simply rolling dice, drawing straws, or flipping a coin. He was painting a picture. His intent from the start was to illustrate his love for people.

This revelation stunned men and women in the first century, and it should shock us in the twenty-first century. Moreover, it is momentous for the way people understand marriage in any culture. Whether Greco-Roman citizens then or American citizens today, most people view marriage as a means of self-fulfillment accompanied by sexual satisfaction. A man or woman's aim is to find a mate who completes him or her. In this view, marriage is an end in itself, and sexual consummation is a celebration of such completion.

Yet the Bible teaches that God created marriage not as an end but as a means to an end. While personal enjoyment and sexual pleasure are part of God's good plan for marriage, God's purpose does not stop there. For God created the marriage relationship to point to a greater reality. From the moment marriage was instituted, God aimed to give the world an illustration of the gospel. Just as a photograph represents a person or an event at a particular point in history, marriage was designed by God to reflect a person and an event at the most pivotal point in history. Marriage, according to Ephesians 5, pictures Christ and the church. It is a living portrait drawn by a Divine Painter who wants the world to know that he loves his people so much that he has sent his Son to die for their sins. In the picture of marriage, God intends to portray Christ's love for the church and the church's love for Christ on the canvas of human culture.

So how is this picture portrayed? The Bible explains, saying, "The husband is the head of the wife even as Christ is the head of the church, his body, and is himself its Savior." Moreover, "as the church submits to Christ, so also wives should submit in everything to their husbands" (Ephesians 5:23-24). In other words, God designs husbands to be a reflection of Christ's love for the church in the way they relate to their wives, and God designs wives to be a reflection of the church's love for Christ in the way they relate to their husbands.

But talk about countercultural! Or maybe more aptly put, talk about politically incorrect! *The husband is the head of his wife? Wives should submit to their husbands? Are you serious?*

God is serious, and he is good. In our limited understanding, we hear words and phrases like the ones in Ephesians 5, and we recoil in disgust. But if we pause for just a moment to consider the picture of marriage from a gospel perspective, our reaction may be different.

When the Bible says that "the husband is the head of the wife even as Christ is the head of the church," we immediately need to ask the question, "What does it mean for Christ to be the head of the church?" The Bible answers that question by saying, "Christ loved the church and gave Himself for her to make her holy, cleansing her with the washing of water by the word. He did this to present the church to Himself in splendor, without spot or wrinkle or anything like that, but holy and blameless" (Ephesians 5:25-27, HCSB).

What a breathtaking picture. For Christ to be the head of the church is for Christ to give everything he has for the good of the church. Christ takes responsibility for the beauty of his bride, ready to lay aside his rights and willing to lay down his life for the sake of her splendor.

So this is who God has designed a husband to be: a man who gives everything he has for the good of his wife. A man who takes responsibility for the beauty of his bride, ready to lay aside his rights and willing to lay down his life for the sake of her splendor. God has designed a husband to be the head of his wife like this so that in a husband's love for his wife, the world might see a picture of Christ's love for his people.

I think about Don, a husband I watched serve his wife, Gwen, through terminal cancer. In the years preceding Gwen's diagnosis, it was clear that Don cherished his wife. But when Gwen began a thirteen-month journey that eventually led to her death, I watched Don lay down his life, in every way he knew how, to serve her. He walked alongside her, waited on her, took her to appointments, and attended to her every need. He put himself aside, prioritizing his wife more than his own life in a way that powerfully portrayed the way Christ put himself aside on a cross, prioritizing his church more than his own life.[6]

Likewise, "as the church submits to Christ, so also wives should submit in everything to their husbands" (Ephesians 5:24). As soon as we hear the word *submission* alongside the previous picture of *headship*, we immediately think in terms of inferiority and superiority, subordination and domination. But that's nowhere close to what the Bible means with these terms. As we've already seen, God made clear from the start that men and women are equal in dignity, value, and worth. Submission is not about denigrating the value of another's life. Instead, this biblical word means to yield to another in love.

Such submission throughout Scripture is a wonderful, if not inevitable, component of human relationships. I am a dad, for example, with four children. They are in a position of submission in their relationship to me (though they unfortunately don't always acknowledge it!). But this is a good position for them as I love, lead, serve, protect, and provide for them. Their submission to me in no way implies that I am superior to them. Instead, their submission shows that they trust my love for them.

Such submission is not limited to human relationships; it's also true of the divine. The Bible describes one God revealed in three persons: God the Father, God the Son, and God the Holy Spirit. These three persons of the Trinity are equally divine. The Father is fully God, the Son is fully God, and the Spirit is fully God. They are all equally worthy of eternal worship, with no person in the Godhead superior to another. Yet the Son submits to the Father. Jesus says, "My food is to do the will of him who sent me and to accomplish his work" (John 4:34). When facing the cross, Jesus pleads, "Father, if you are willing, remove this cup from me." But then he prays, "Nevertheless, not my will, but yours, be done" (Luke 22:42).

Not insignificantly, in another instance where the husband is described as the head of his wife, the Father is also described as the head of the Son: "The head of every man is Christ, the head of a wife is her husband, and the head of Christ is God" (1 Corinthians 11:3). Certainly this doesn't mean that God the Father is dominating and that God the Son is cruelly forced into compulsory subordination. Rather, the Son gladly submits to the Father in the context of close relationship.

This, then, is what the Bible means when it talks about

the church submitting to Christ. As followers of Christ in the church, we are in a position of submission to Christ. Is this a bad thing? Certainly not. It's a great thing! Christ loves, leads, serves, protects, and provides for us, and we gladly submit to him in the context of close relationship with him.

God has designed marriage to display this relationship. God desires people to know that following him is not a matter of begrudging subordination to a domineering deity. God longs for people to know that following him is a matter of glad submission to a loving Lord. So he calls a wife to submit to the loving leadership of a husband who lays down his life for her good. And as this portrait of marriage is portrayed all around the world, God shows men and women that he can be trusted to lead them by his love.

I think about Clint and Katie, friends of ours who recently moved their family to another city. Clint is a doctor, and an opportunity arose to join a practice with a former coworker in a completely different place. When he first mentioned the idea to Katie, she was hesitant. She had a variety of concerns and a list of questions about whether they should go. Clint listened to his wife, empathized with her concerns, and addressed her questions with wisdom and care. After many discussions and much prayer, Clint believed God was leading them to move, and Katie supported his decision. But it wasn't because Katie wanted to move. In reality, she was still hesitant with remaining concerns and questions about the unknown, and if it were up to her alone, she would not have moved. But she trusted Clint's loving leadership of her life and their family, and she gladly moved where he was leading them. Many people in our culture would call Katie weak, and some might even say that she should have stayed, with or without Clint. But Katie knows that God has designed her marriage to be a picture of what it looks like for people to trust his loving leadership and to gladly follow wherever he guides, regardless of whether they fully understand what he is doing. In turn, she knows that Clint will continue to love and serve her amidst the challenges of adjusting to a new place, and in so doing he will demonstrate the way Christ loves his people.

This is why biblical marriage is worth defending in the face of cultural redefinition, and this is why biblical marriage is worth displaying even when it may mean cultural confrontation. For God established marriage at the beginning of creation to be one of the primary means by which he illustrates the gospel before a watching world. As husbands sacrifice their lives for the sake of their wives—loving, leading, serving, protecting, and providing for them—the world will get a glimpse of God's grace. Sinners will see that Christ has gone to a cross where he has suffered, bled, and died for them, that they might experience eternal salvation through submission to him.

They will also see in a wife's relationship to her husband that such submission is not a burden to bear. Onlookers will observe a wife joyfully and continually experiencing her husband's sacrificial love for her and then gladly and spontaneously submitting in selfless love to him. In this visible representation of the gospel, the world will realize that following Christ is not a matter of duty. Instead, it is a means to full, eternal, and absolute delight.

THE DISTORTION OF GOD'S DESIGN

Unfortunately, this is not the picture of marriage that the world most often perceives. And the primary reason is not the laws in various states, or even the decisions of the Supreme Court. The primary reason the gospel is not clear in marriage across our culture is that the gospel has not been clear in marriage across the church.

I'm not talking here only about the divorce rates and cohabitation patterns among self-professing Christians. Data on these realities is hard to nail down for a variety of reasons,[7] yet numbers themselves would fail to tell the stories that lie beneath the surface—stories of how God's plan and pattern for marriage to portray the gospel have been denied, distorted, and disparaged in the lives of those who claim to follow Christ. In the words of Francis Schaeffer,

> Evangelicalism is deeply infiltrated with the world spirit of our age when it comes to marriage and sexual morality. . . . There are those who call themselves evangelicals and who are among evangelical leadership who completely deny the biblical pattern for male and female relationships in the home and church. There are many who accept the idea of equality without distinction and deliberately set aside what the Scriptures teach at this point.[8]

But even this should not be altogether surprising in light of the first few chapters of the Bible. For the first sin occurred not as a reaction to a generic temptation but as a response to a gender-specific test. The serpent's design in deceiving the couple in Genesis 3 was a deliberate subversion of God's design in creating the couple.

In Genesis 2, before God has even created the woman, God tells the man not to eat fruit from the tree of the knowledge of good and evil (see Genesis 2:16-17). God thus entrusts the man with the responsibility of carrying out the divine command. Yet in Genesis 3, the serpent approaches not the man but the woman. He converses with her while the man does nothing (see Genesis 3:1-6). Instead of taking responsibility for protecting himself and his wife from temptation, the man sits silently by—like a wimp. Then, when God confronts him in his sin, the man has the audacity to blame his wife (see Genesis 3:12). In all of this, the world witnesses the first spineless abdication of a man's responsibility to love, serve, protect, and care for his wife.

Stories of such spineless abdication are all too common among professing Christian men and their marriages today—husbands who have refused to take responsibility for loving, serving, protecting, and providing for their wives in every way possible. Sure, through a job a man may rightly and responsibly provide for the physical needs of his wife, but if he is not careful, that same job often prevents him from providing for her spiritual, emotional, and relational needs. He comes home and can't put his phone down or e-mail aside. He turns on the TV, surfs the Internet, or tinkers in the garage—whatever it is, he manages to maintain his physical presence in the house while creating emotional distance from his wife. He never asks how she feels, and he doesn't know what's going on in her heart. He may think he's a man because of his achievements at work and accomplishments in life, but in reality he's acting like a wimp who has abdicated his most important responsibility on earth: the spiritual leadership of his wife.

This is the story among many men who have decided to marry, not to mention other men who have ignored marriage altogether. I'm not talking here about those God has called to maximize singleness for the spread of the gospel (see 1 Corinthians 7), which I will address in a moment. I'm talking about men in their twenties and thirties who dwell in perpetual adolescence that revolves solely and selfishly around *them* and what *they* want to do. Maybe it's the guy who is ten years into his undergraduate studies and hasn't taken a wife because he has no idea where he would take her. Or maybe it's the guy who works part-time while he plays video games the rest of his time, leaning on his parents or others in the church to help him pay his bills. He's trying to "find himself," which means he doesn't take responsibility for himself, and he's certainly not willing to take responsibility for anyone else. Or maybe it's the guy who works hard at his job in order to advance himself in the world, but he never takes time to consider how he might deny himself in order to lay down his life for a wife. In all his attempts to be successful according to our culture, he fails to consider how God may be leading him to commit less of his time to a career and more of his time to a marriage. Such warped pictures of singleness are yet more evidence of the tendency among men to abdicate the responsibility God has given them to love a wife in a way that displays Christ's love for the church.

The pendulum can swing, though, from a man's spineless abdication of his responsibility to his wife to a selfish abuse of authority over her. One of the effects of sin in Genesis 3 is the tendency for a man to rule his wife in a forceful and oppressive way that denigrates woman's equal dignity with him. It is as if a man says, "Okay, I'm not going to be a wimp; instead, I'm going to *dominate* my marriage."

This is one of the primary reasons why *submission* and *headship* are such unpopular and uncomfortable terms for us today—because we've seen the dangerous ways these ideas have been exploited. Particularly in marriage, we think of men who mistreat their wives emotionally, verbally, and even physically in order to show they are in control, men who selfishly use their wives to get what they want when they want it, no matter how their wives feel or how their wives are affected. This, of course, is not how Christ loves the church and is nowhere close to what the Bible means by submission and headship. Yet this is exactly what many men are communicating to the world about submission and headship.

The corresponding effects in women's lives are clear, and wives find themselves susceptible to a sinful distortion of God's design for them. When the woman receives the penalty of her sin in Genesis 3:16, God tells her that as a result of sin, not only will her husband be tempted to oppress her, but she will have a tendency to oppose him—to work against him and his role in marriage. A wife will also be prone to do what she wants when she wants, regardless of what her husband says or does. *He's not in charge; I am*, she'll think, as she defies not only her husband but ultimately her God.

See how the work of Satan in Genesis 3 is a foundational attack not just upon humanity in general but specifically upon men, women, and marriage? You can almost imagine the adversary laughing as he thinks, *Now I've created confusion that will forever muddle their marriages*—a confusion that will also ruthlessly misrepresent the gospel. For husbands will waffle back and forth between abdicating their responsibility to love and abusing their authority to lead. Wives, in response, will distrust such love and defy such leadership. In the process they'll completely undercut how Christ's gracious sacrifice on the cross compels glad submission in the church.

COUNTERCULTURAL MARRIAGE

So what does it look like for Christians to counter culture in the area of marriage? Surely personal, not political, action is the primary starting point. To be sure, none of us (including me) has the perfect marriage, and all of us have distorted God's design in some way, whether in past or present marriages or sin amid singleness. But the gospel is good news for all.

I think of Bob and Margaret, who each married early, divorced quickly, and then found themselves together in a second marriage that was on the verge of collapse. Yet by God's grace, they came to understand the gospel, and they realized the role of marriage in illustrating that gospel. Forty long, hard, good years later, they're still illustrating it. I think of Andre, who loved his wife Emily even when she committed adultery; through his Christlike forgiveness and patience, they (and their children) now enjoy one another in a resentment-free family that testifies to God's glory. Though our culture neither cultivates nor encourages such grace-saturated, gospel-centered approaches to marriage, these men and women know (and show) that God is able to redeem and reconcile this most important of relationships, and he is willing to strengthen and sustain all who will trust in his ways and live according to his Word.

We have seen God's clear command to husbands: "Love your wives, as Christ loved the church and gave himself up for her" (Ephesians 5:25). This is the first of four times in the matter of nine verses that husbands are commanded to love their wives in Ephesians 5. Love them unselfishly, the Bible says. Our culture tells us to defend ourselves, assert ourselves, and draw attention to ourselves, yet Christ compels us to sacrifice ourselves for our wives. Headship is not an opportunity for us to control our wives; it is a responsibility to die for them.

This means, husbands, that you and I don't love our wives based upon what we get from them. That's how the world defines love in marriage. The world says that you love your wife because of all her attractive attributes and compelling characteristics, but this is a dangerously fickle love. For as soon as some attribute or characteristic fades, then love fails. Husbands, love your wives not because of who *they* are, but because of who *Christ* is. He loves them deeply, and our responsibility is to reflect his love.

Now obviously we don't do all that Christ has done—namely, we don't die for the sins of our wives. Yet we do live to serve them and to see them grow in Christlikeness. We are accountable for loving our wives in such a way that they grow in loveliness. Just as Christ takes responsibility for the spiritual health of his church, we have responsibility for the spiritual health of both our wives and our marriages.

Imagine the captain of a navy ship falling asleep on his watch. As he sleeps, a rebellious sailor runs that ship into the ground. Is the sailor guilty? Absolutely. Is the captain responsible? Without question. In a similar way, the Bible is not saying a wife is not guilty for sin in her own life. Yet the Bible is saying a husband is responsible for the spiritual care of his wife. When she struggles with sin, or when they struggle in marriage, he is ultimately responsible.

For this reason, God calls a man to "nourish" and "cherish" his wife, "just as Christ does the church" (Ephesians 5:29). The language of Scripture here is evocative. A husband is to treasure, encourage, build up, and comfort his wife. He is to take the initiative in tending to his wife, not waiting for her to approach him and say, "There are some problems in our marriage that we need to talk about," but going to her and saying, "How can I love you and lead our marriage better?" I regularly ask my wife that question, and she is usually able to answer without any hesitation! I share that to make clear that in all this talk about marriage, I have so much room to grow. Yet I want to grow, not only because I love my wife, but also because I want to show an accurate picture of Christ in our culture.

Husbands, realize what is at stake here: you and I are representing Christ to a watching world in the way we love our wives. If we are harsh with our wives, we will show the world that Christ is cruel with his people. If we ignore our wives, we will show the world that Christ wants nothing to do with his people. If we leave our wives, we will show the world that Christ deserts his people. What pictures are our marriages giving to our culture about Christ's relationship with his church?

Similarly, wives, revere Christ through respect for your husband. Hear God's wisdom in the final verse of Ephesians 5: "Let each one of you love his wife as himself, and let the wife see that she respects her husband" (verse 33). Notice how the husband is commanded to love his wife, yet the wife is commanded to respect her husband. Now obviously that doesn't mean that love and respect should not both be expressed by a husband and a wife, but God's Word is subtly yet clearly pointing out that God has created women with a unique need to be loved and men with a unique need to be respected.

Women often find it easier to love their husbands than to respect them. A woman can sit with other women and speak about her husband disrespectfully, but then quietly go home and care for his needs. Why? Because she loves him. But the more important question is, does she respect him? So also when a wife is trying to work on a troubled marriage, she may tell her husband that she loves him, which is what she would like to hear. But again, the more important question is, does she respect her husband, and does she tell him that she respects him?

A wife may think, *Well, my husband doesn't work hard enough or do enough to earn my respect.* Might such a wife be buying into the unbiblical lie that respect is based purely upon performance? In the same way that a husband's selfless love for his wife is based upon God's charge to him, isn't a wife's selfless respect for her husband based upon God's charge to her?

So wives, see yourselves in a complementary, not competitive, relationship with your husband. Yield to leadership in love, knowing that you are representing the church's relationship to Christ. If you disrespect your husband, you show the world that the church has no respect for Christ. If you do not pursue your husband, you show the world that Christ is not worth following. If you sleep around on your husband, you show the world that Christ is not satisfying enough for his people.

For that matter, if you are single, for the sake of the gospel, don't sleep around with any man or woman who is not your husband or wife. We will explore God's clear command for single brothers and sisters to flee sexual activity outside of marriage in the next chapter, but suffice it for now to say that it is appalling today to see young, single evangelicals, who are often most passionate about social issues like poverty and slavery, simultaneously undercutting the social fabric of marriage through sex outside of marriage. According to one "nationally representative study of young adults," close to "80 percent of unmarried, church-going, conservative Protestants who are currently dating someone are having sex of some sort."[9] If this is you, then I beg you to stop and see how God has mysteriously and gloriously designed this one-flesh union in marriage to display the love of Christ for the church. If you do not stop, even in all your action on behalf of the poor and enslaved, you will undermine the gospel you claim to believe while mocking the heart of the God you claim to worship. As we've seen throughout this book, we cannot pick and choose where to obey God.

Along these lines, Scripture speaks clearly to single men and women. For those who have a strong sexual desire for marriage, God's Word exhorts single men and women to be married (see 1 Corinthians 7:2). The onus here is particularly upon men, whom God has designed to take the initiative in the marriage relationship. Without question, this call to pursue a wife goes against the grain of current cultural trends that minimize the importance of marriage. Yet part of why God made us male and female is to pursue marriage over and above the comforts of this world and our careers in this world.

At the same time, Scripture also contains exhortations to singles who are waiting for a husband or wife as well as to men and women whom God specifically calls to singleness. The apostle Paul put himself in the latter category, even saying, "I wish that all were as I myself am" (1 Corinthians 7:7). "In view of the present distress"—the persecution and perversion that surrounded Paul in first-century culture—he advocated remaining single in favor of "undivided devotion to the Lord" (1 Corinthians 7:26, 35). Scripture thus encourages every man and woman who is single, as long as they are single, to maximize the potential of singleness through commitment to Christ and his commission in the culture around us.

All of this is good for us. It is good for husbands to lay down their lives for their wives, and in losing their lives, to find them, just as Jesus promised (see Matthew 10:38-39). Moreover, it is good for wives to receive this love and respect their husbands. I have yet to meet a wife who didn't want to follow a husband who was sacrificially loving and serving her. Finally, it is good for a single man and a single woman to join together in a supernatural union that God designed to satisfy them both. Yet as long as they remain single (which may be their entire lives, as it was for Christ and has been for many Christians throughout history), it is good to maximize such singleness through purity before God and with a passion to spread the gospel.

Ultimately, all of this is glorifying to God. He has sent his Son to die for sinners, and he has set up marriage to reflect that reality. When we understand this, we realize that marriage exists even more for God than it does for us. God has ultimately designed marriage not to satisfy our needs but to display his glory in the gospel. When we realize this, we recognize that if we want to declare the gospel, we must defend marriage.

ONCE AND FOR ALL

For these reasons, it is altogether right to be grieved about the redefinition of marriage in our culture. So-called "same-sex marriage" is now recognized as a legitimate entity in the eyes of our government. Such a designation by a government, however, does not change the definition God has established. The only true marriage in God's eyes remains the exclusive, permanent union of a man and a woman, even as our Supreme Court and state legislatures deliberately defy this reality. Without question, we are living in momentous days—momentous in devastating ways.

Yet all is most definitely not lost. The opportunity for gospel witness in contemporary culture is far greater now than it was even a couple of years ago. As spiritual darkness engulfs the biblical picture of marriage in our culture, spiritual light will stand out even more starkly in the portrait of a husband who lays down his life for his wife and a wife who joyfully follows her husband's loving leadership. Be sure of this: God's design for marriage is far more breathtaking and much more satisfying than anything we could ever create on our own. The more men and women manipulate marriage, the more we will discover that "this kind of marriage" or "that kind of marriage" will not fully gratify us, for only the King who designed marriage is able to finally (and eternally) satisfy us.

Furthermore, we have much reason to be confident in the resilience of marriage as God has defined it. After all, it has been around since the beginning of time (see Genesis 2:24-25). Jesus himself affirms the foundational reality of marriage in the fabric of God's creation (see Matthew 19:1-12). Moreover, marriage will be around at the end of time. Sure, it won't look the same as it does now, for this earthly shadow will one day give way to its eternal substance. On that day, Christ will be united completely with his church, and all of heaven will shout, "Hallelujah! For the Lord our God the Almighty reigns. Let us rejoice and exult and give him the glory, for the marriage of the Lamb has come, and his Bride has made herself ready" (Revelation 19:6-7). John writes in the book of Revelation, "The angel said to me, 'Write this: Blessed are those who are invited to the marriage supper of the Lamb.' And he said to me, 'These are the true words of God'" (verse 9).[10]

Based upon these "true words of God," we need not worry about whether marriage is going to make it. Ultimately, we do not look to any court or government to define marriage. God has already done that, and his definition cannot be eradicated by a vote of legislators or the opinions of Supreme Court justices. The Supreme Judge of creation has already defined this term once and for all. *Marriage* does not morph across cultures the same way that *football* does, for *marriage* is a term that transcends culture, representing timeless truth about who God is and how God loves. The call and challenge for us is to live according to such truth in the time and culture in which he has placed us.

FIRST STEPS TO COUNTER CULTURE

Pray

Ask God to:

- Empower you to be pure, faithful, and selfless in your own marriage or in your singleness.
- Strengthen the church's witness to the beauty of the gospel and to the biblical pattern of marriage.
- Change the hearts and minds of legislative and judicial bodies on the issue of so-called same-sex marriage.

Participate

Prayerfully consider taking these steps:

- Humbly ask the leadership of your church to address the topic of marriage through the preaching and/or teaching ministries of the church.
- Offer to talk to, pray with, or meet with individuals you know (of the same gender) who are struggling in their marriage.
- Vote for political candidates who support a biblical view of marriage and actively encourage them to continue their support.

Proclaim

Consider the following truths from Scripture:

- Genesis 2:24: "Therefore a man shall leave his father and his mother and hold fast to his wife, and they shall become one flesh."
- Ephesians 5:22, 25: "Wives, submit to your own husbands, as to the Lord. . . . Husbands, love your wives, as Christ loved the church and gave himself up for her."
- Hebrews 13:4: "Let marriage be held in honor among all, and let the marriage bed be undefiled, for God will judge the sexually immoral and adulterous."

For more (and more specific) suggestions,
visit CounterCultureBook.com/Topics/Marriage

BOUGHT WITH A PRICE:
THE GOSPEL
AND SEXUAL MORALITY

I remember the conversation like it was yesterday.

I was getting married that weekend, and many of my relatives had traveled into town for the wedding. When I was growing up, my family would spend time with our extended family every year, even though we lived in different states. We worked hard to keep geographical distance from preventing relational intimacy, and as a result, we were all pretty close to one another. But now that many of us had moved to different locations and were beginning new families, it was rare for all of us to be in the same place at the same time. So this marriage celebration served as a sort of family reunion. We talked, we ate, we played, and we laughed ourselves to tears as we recounted old stories and shared new ones.

The night before my wedding, I found myself driving a family member whom I deeply love back to his hotel. We talked about various things in our lives, and it was just plain good to catch up. As he was about to get out of the car at his hotel, he turned to me and said, "David, I want to share something with you."

"Okay," I said.

He said, "I want you to know that I'm gay."

Silence filled my seat in the car as I didn't know what to say. Thoughts swirled through my mind, and I wasn't sure what to do with them.

He continued, "I want you to know that I've had these desires for a long time, and now I'm choosing to fulfill them in a homosexual lifestyle."

Regrettably, silence continued to fill my seat. Looking back at that moment, I wish I had said so many different things. I wish I had thanked him for his honesty, transparency, and vulnerability in sharing that with me. I wish I had assured him that his revelation to me would not change my affection for him. I wish I had asked him sincere questions to understand him better: How did he come to his conclusion? Whom else had he shared this with, and how hard had those conversations been on him? What were the biggest ups and downs he had experienced as a result of his desires and this decision?

Unfortunately, I barely said a thing. He got out of the car, and I told him it was really good to see him. But our conversation went no further.

My thoughts, on the other hand, went much further. I found myself driving home on the eve of my wedding with a myriad of questions running through my mind. Why do I have sexual desire for a woman while he has sexual desire for a man? Did we learn these desires somewhere along the way, or were we born with them? Did my family member choose this, or did God make him this way? And why is it right (and celebrated) in everyone's eyes for me to fulfill my desires while it is wrong (and condemned) in so many people's eyes for him to fulfill his? Can't he love a man in the same way I love a woman?

These questions led me down a path that went far beyond that night. In the days since then, I have shared life with other family members, friends, and men and women in my church and city who are attracted to the same sex. These close relationships in my life, combined with current trends in the culture, have caused me to explore what light, if any, the gospel shines upon homosexuality. In my exploration, though, I have found that the rays of the gospel are not limited to homosexuality, for the gospel's light infuses *all* of sexuality. Who God is and what Christ did on the cross have huge implications for who we are personally and what we desire sexually. And these implications have inevitable ramifications for how we counter the culture around us.

LOVING BOUNDARIES

As we've already seen, God created us as uniquely sexual beings. We are men and women with distinct male and female bodies that have been gloriously designed in God's image. The Bible emphasizes the importance of our bodies, saying that the body is meant "for the Lord, and the Lord for the body" (1 Corinthians 6:13). That simple phrase is a substantial starting point for understanding God's design for us. Our bodies have been created not only *by* God but also *for* God.

This is a very different starting point than most people have in our culture. We are driven today by whatever can bring our bodies the most pleasure. What can we eat, touch, watch, do, listen to, or engage in to satisfy the cravings of our bodies? We are swimming in a cultural ocean that cries out with every wave, "Gratify your body!"

But what if our bodies have not ultimately been created for

self-gratification? What if our bodies have actually been created for *God*-glorification? And even better, what if God-glorification is actually the way to experience the greatest satisfaction in our bodies?

Look back at that phrase from 1 Corinthians: the body is meant "for the Lord, and the Lord for the body." Not only are our bodies designed for God, but God is devoted to our bodies. Literally, he is *for* your body. God wants you to experience the maximum joy for which your body is built, and as the Creator of our bodies, he knows what will bring them the most pleasure. This takes us back to one of the core truths of the gospel—the reality that God loves us and is for us, not against us. God desires the best for us, and he has designed our bodies not just for his glory but also for our good.

This truth is vitally important, particularly in light of discussions today about transgender identity. It is increasingly common for men, women, and even children in our culture to question whether God's design for their bodies as male and female is indeed good. Males wish they were females, and females want to be males. I don't presume to know the depth of the physical, emotional, relational, and other factors behind these desires, but I do know that God is for our bodies, and he has distinctly designed each of us as male or female for our good. Contrary to culture, the Bible equates our gender identity with our sexual identity and asserts that the way God has made each of us as a man or a woman is good.

God's design for our bodies is good, and this is why God, in his love, gives us boundaries for our bodies: he loves us and knows what is best for us. He desires to protect us from harm and provide for us something greater than we can see. Whenever God gives us a negative command, he always gives two positives to us:

he is providing us with something better while also protecting us from something worse.

Consider an example from everyday life. When I tell my kids to stay in our yard and not run into the road, I'm telling them this for their good. I know what could happen when a car comes racing down the street, so I rightly give them this restriction—because I know it is best for them. I want to protect them from harm while also providing them a safe environment in which they can flourish. In a much greater way, the God who designed our bodies knows what is best for their flourishing.

These simple truths help us to see more clearly what we are doing when we ignore God's good instructions. All throughout the Bible he gives us boundaries for how our bodies are to be used. But when we ignore these boundaries, it's as if we're saying to God, "You don't know how this body is to be used. I know better than you do." It seems a bit arrogant, doesn't it? Kind of like my four-year-old telling me I don't know what I'm talking about when it comes to cars on the road.

In his love for us, God has told us the best use of our bodies, and he has been specific when it comes to our sexuality. As we've seen from the very beginning of the Bible, God designed a man's and a woman's body to join together as "one flesh" in marriage (Genesis 2:24). The language of "one flesh" points to the personal nature of this union. Sex is not a mechanical act between two objects; it is a relational bond between two people. And not just any two people. This physical union is designed by God for a man and a woman who have committed their lives in a covenant relationship with each other (see Proverbs 5:3-20; Malachi 2:14). There is not one instance in all of God's Word where God advocates or celebrates sex outside of a marriage relationship between a husband and a wife. Not one.

According to God, then, this is the safety zone in which sex is to be enjoyed. God creates this loving boundary to maximize the sexual experience in all of its richest meanings. Moreover, this is the reason the Bible is full of prohibitions against any and all sexual activity outside of marriage between a man and a woman. For example, God prohibits sexual prostitution (see Leviticus 19:29; Deuteronomy 23:18; Proverbs 6:25-26) and sexual violence (see Deuteronomy 22:25-27). He commands us not to have sex with animals (see Leviticus 18:23; 20:15-16) or relatives (see Leviticus 18:6; 1 Corinthians 5:1-2). These are boundaries that most people agree on in our culture (at least for now), but they are not the only boundaries the Bible includes.

With the same force of command, God also prohibits sex between a man and woman who are not married to each other. The Bible calls this adultery, and it is forbidden in the Ten Commandments (see Exodus 20:14; see also Leviticus 20:10; Proverbs 6:28-32). But this isn't just an Old Testament command. Jesus and the writers of the New Testament reiterate this restriction (see Matthew 19:7-9; Romans 13:9; Hebrews 13:4). According to God, sex with anyone who is not your husband or your wife is sin, whether that happens before marriage, during marriage, or after marriage.

As we've already seen in God's complementary design of man and woman for marriage (chapter 6), this prohibition also includes sex between a man and a man or a woman and a woman. On this the Bible is explicit. Right before prohibiting sex with animals, the Old Testament reads, "Do not lie with a man as one lies with a woman; that is detestable" (Leviticus 18:22, NIV). Someone might say, "But that's just Old Testament law, which also includes prohibitions against eating pork (see Leviticus 11:7). Does that mean Southern barbecue is also sin?"

This may sound like a good argument until we realize the clear and critical distinctions between different types of laws in

Leviticus. Some of the laws are civil in nature, and they specifically pertain to the government of ancient Israel in a way that they do not necessarily pertain to governments today. Other laws are ceremonial, prescribing particular sacrifices, offerings, and festivals for God's people under the old covenant. These civil and ceremonial laws applied specifically to Jewish people in the Old Testament, and we know this because these laws are not reiterated for all people in the New Testament. However, various moral laws (such as prohibitions against stealing and lying, for example) are explicitly reiterated in the New Testament.[1] These laws, based upon God's character, clearly apply to all people for all time.[2]

We know that moral laws include prohibitions not only against stealing and lying, but also against homosexual activity because when we get to the New Testament, Jesus himself teaches that the only God-honoring alternative to marriage between a man and a woman is singleness (see Matthew 19:10-12). Moreover, the New Testament describes "dishonorable passions" with the example of women who "exchanged natural relations for those that are contrary to nature" and men who "likewise gave up natural relations with women and were consumed with passion for one another, . . . committing shameless acts with men and receiving in themselves the due penalty for their error" (Romans 1:26-27). God is clear in his Word that homosexual activity is prohibited.[3]

In many people's minds, we've already gone too far at this point, but we're actually only getting started when it comes to seeing and understanding God's protective boundaries and sexual prohibitions in Scripture. In order to protect us from lusts, greeds, desires, and temptations that give birth to sin, the Bible also prohibits all sexual looking and thinking outside of marriage between a husband and a wife. In Jesus' words, "Everyone who looks at a woman with lustful intent has already committed adultery with her in his heart" (Matthew 5:28). According to Christ, it is sinful even to *look* at someone who is not your husband or wife and entertain sexual thoughts about that person (see also 2 Peter 2:14).

Not only is it contrary to God's grand desire and therefore wrong to possess and cultivate sexual desires *for* others outside of marriage, it is also wrong to provoke sexual desires *in* others outside of marriage. God forbids immodest clothing (see 1 Timothy 2:9-10) and warns sternly against seductive speech (see Proverbs 5:1-23; 7:1-27). Even more, God prohibits *any* kind of crude speech, humor, or entertainment that remotely revolves around sexual immorality. In the words of Ephesians 5, "Sexual immorality and all impurity or covetousness must not even be named among you. . . . Let there be no filthiness nor foolish talk nor crude joking, which are out of place. . . . For you may be sure of this, that everyone who is sexually immoral or impure . . . has no inheritance in the kingdom of Christ and God" (verses 3-5). Addressing the rampant sexual immorality in the culture surrounding the church in the first century, Ephesians 5 continues, "It is shameful even to speak of the things that they do in secret" (verse 12).

These words cut to the core of the church in twenty-first-century culture because we are so often colluding in rather than countering a culture of sexual immorality. Even Christians who refuse to indulge personally in sinful sexual activity often watch movies and shows, read books and articles, and visit Internet sites that highlight, display, promote, or make light of sexual immorality. It's as if we've said to the world, "We're not going to do what you do, but we will gladly entertain ourselves by watching you."[4] It's sick, isn't it, this tendency that brings delight to us when we observe others in sexual sin?

Ultimately, God prohibits sexual worship—the idolization of sex and infatuation with sexual activity as a fundamental means to personal fulfillment. All throughout Scripture and history, people have mistakenly fallen into the trap of thinking that the God-created pleasure of sex and sexuality will bring us ultimate satisfaction (see Exodus 32:2-6; Deuteronomy 23:17; Proverbs 7:1-27; 1 Corinthians 10:8). Sadly, it seems that we are no different in our time. All across our culture, people believe, "If only I have sexual freedom in this way or that way, then I will be happy." But this is not true. Sex is good, but sex is not God. It will not ultimately fulfill. Like anything else that becomes an idol, it will always take more than it gives while diverting the human heart away from the only one who is able to give supreme joy.

Each of the Bible's sexual prohibitions is encapsulated in the all-encompassing command "Flee from sexual immorality" (1 Corinthians 6:18). These words were written to a church in the sex-crazed city of Corinth, where singles were sexually involved before marriage, husbands and wives were sexually involved outside of marriage, homosexuality was condoned, and prostitution was common. (Not much has changed in two thousand years.) So to the church in that culture and to the church in our culture, God says, "Flee from sexual immorality—any and all sexual thinking, looking, desiring, touching, speaking, and acting outside of marriage between a man and a woman. Don't rationalize it, and don't reason with it—*run from it*. Flee it as fast as you can."

God says this for his glory.

And God says this for our good.

BORN THIS WAY

But we don't believe God on this one. None of us do. By this point it should be clear that the Bible doesn't speak simply against adultery or homosexuality but against multiple manifestations of sexual immorality in every single one of our lives.

Let me confess the obvious before I go any further. I represent the class of people responsible for the vast majority of sexual immorality in the world today: male heterosexuals. It is heterosexual men who fund the pornography and prostitution industries in the world, and I'm convinced it's the lack of loving leadership and selfless sacrifice in heterosexual husbands and dads that has caused the majority of sexual confusion across our culture.

I emphasize this because when my initial questions about my gay family member drove me to the gospel, I was immediately convicted not about sexual sin in *his* life but about sexual sin in *my* life. My purpose in even addressing the issue of sexual immorality is not to rail against the dominance of sexual sin in the culture around us but to expose the depth of sexual sin that lies within us. I and every reader of this book are guilty at multiple levels of sexual thought, desire, speech, and deed outside of marriage between a husband and a wife. None of us are innocent of sexual immorality, and none of us are immune to it.

The gospel tells us why this is so. We all possess a heart of pride that is inclined to turn away from God (see Genesis 8:21). One of the most significant passages on sexual immorality in the Bible starts, "Although they knew God, they did not honor him as God or give thanks to him, but they became futile in their thinking, and their foolish hearts were darkened. . . . Therefore God gave them up in the lusts of their hearts to impurity, to the dishonoring of their bodies among themselves" (Romans 1:21, 24). These potent verses diagnose dark hearts as the root of sinful desires. In our hearts, we all have a sinful tendency to turn aside from God's ways to our wants. This tendency has an inevitable effect on our sexuality. Note the fascinating connection made by these Scriptures. When we spurn praising God in our hearts, we are prone to sexual impurity in our lives.

To make matters worse, we were born this way. Ever since Adam and Eve sinned in the Garden of Eden, every single person born of a man and a woman has inherited this sinful heart. We may all have different biological heritages, but we all share one common spiritual inheritance: sin (see Psalm 51; Romans 5:12-21). This is important to remember, because not one of us can or should say, "God wouldn't allow me (or someone else) to be born with a bent toward a particular sexual sin." Instead, the Bible is clear: every one of us is born with a bent toward sexual sin.

But just because we have that bent doesn't mean we must act upon it. We live in a culture that assumes a natural explanation implies a moral obligation. If you were born with a desire, then it's essential to your nature to carry it out.

This is one reason why our contemporary discussion of sexuality is wrongly framed as an issue of civil rights. Even in the virtual absence of scientific evidence that proves homosexual desire is linked to DNA, the emerging cultural morality is now willing to elevate personal desires to the level of highest moral authority so that people have a "right" to fulfill their sexual desires however they prefer. Furthermore, it is now argued that to deny people that "right" is akin to racism. According to popular opinion, just as we must not discriminate between black and white people, we should not differentiate between heterosexual and homosexual preferences. We live in a day when saying that heterosexual or homosexual activity is immoral is equivalent to saying a white or black person is inferior.

But this line of thought is fundamentally flawed, for it denies the obvious distinction between ethnic identity and sexual activity. Ethnic *identity* is a morally neutral attribute. Black or white is not an issue of right or wrong, and any attempt to say otherwise should be opposed (as we will explore in the next chapter). However, sexual *activity* is a morally chosen behavior. To be sure, similar to how we have different skin colors, we may possess different dispositions toward certain sexual behaviors. But where our ethnic makeup is not determined by a moral choice or contrary to a moral command, our sexual behavior is a moral decision, and just because we are inclined to certain behaviors does not make such behaviors right.

Take, for example, a report in *Time* magazine that infidelity may be in our genes.[5] Does this mean that because a married man has an innate desire for sex with a woman who is not his wife, he must fulfill that desire in order to be fully himself? Surely not. The mere presence of desire does not excuse unfaithfulness to one's wife. This is not an issue of a man's makeup; it's an issue of his morality. His disposition toward a behavior does not mean justification for that behavior. "That's the way he is" doesn't mean "that's how he should act." Adultery isn't inevitable; it's immoral.

This applies to all sexual behavior that deviates from God's design. Every single one of us has a heart that tends toward sexual sin. These tendencies produce different temptations in each of our lives. Some of us experience sexual desire for the same sex, and others of us are prone to fulfill sexual desire with the opposite sex. Even the ways we want to fulfill those sexual desires vary among us. Without question, part of the mystery of this fallen world includes why certain people have certain desires while other people have other desires. We do not always choose our temptations. But we do choose our reactions to those temptations.

"DID GOD REALLY SAY . . . ?"

That brings us back to the fundamental question of what God *has* said. And it takes us back to the first question of the Bible, when the adversary asked the woman, "Did God really say, 'You must not eat from any tree in the garden?'" (Genesis 3:1, NIV). We've already seen how sin began when God's command was reduced to a question. At that moment the most deadly spiritual force was covertly smuggled into the world: the assumption that God's Word is subject to human judgment.

This spiritual force is not only alive and active in our culture, but it also threatens to undermine the church. Take homosexual activity as just one example of sexual immorality. Let's dive a bit deeper here and honestly ask the question, what does God say in his Word about it?

The design of marriage in Genesis 2 is sufficient to establish God's prescribed pattern for sexual union between a man and a woman. But not much later, in Genesis 19, we also read about homosexual activity as a primary impetus for God's judgment on the cities of Sodom and Gomorrah. Some claim that Sodom and Gomorrah were destroyed for other reasons, such as a lack of care for the poor, which is also true (see Ezekiel 16:49). Yet in the New Testament when Jude looks back to Genesis 19, that is not what he points out. Instead, he refers to the "sexual immorality and . . . unnatural desire" that led to God's judgment (Jude 1:7).

When it is time to establish his law among his people in the Old Testament, as we've already seen, God commands, "Do not lie with a man as one lies with a woman; that is detestable" (Leviticus 18:22, NIV). Some have claimed that homosexual activity here is only condemned because of its association with idolatry in that day. But homosexual activity is addressed alongside adultery, incest, bestiality, and child sacrifice in these passages. Surely these things are not permissible as long as they are avoided in the context of idolatry.

Moreover, Paul takes the same term that's used for "homosexual activity" in Leviticus 18 to refer to homosexual activity as dishonoring to God in 1 Corinthians 6 and 1 Timothy 1.[6] He writes, "Do not be deceived: neither the sexually immoral, nor idolaters, nor adulterers, nor men who practice homosexuality, nor thieves, nor the greedy, nor drunkards, nor revilers, nor swindlers will inherit the kingdom of God" (1 Corinthians 6:9-10). Similarly, he includes "the sexually immoral" and "men who practice homosexuality" in a list of the "disobedient" that also includes "murderers, . . . enslavers, [and] liars" (1 Timothy 1:8-11). This corresponds with the words we've already read in Romans that describe "dishonorable passions" in terms of "women exchang[ing] natural relations for those that are contrary to nature" and men who "gave up natural relations with women and were consumed with passion for one another" (Romans 1:26-27). The Bible is clear and consistent, affirming with one voice from cover to cover that homosexual activity is sexual immorality before God.

Yet just like Adam and Eve in the Garden, we are prone not just in our culture but also in the church to subject God's Word to our judgment. Instead of obeying what God has said, we question whether God has said it. Hear the words of William Kent, a member of the United Methodist Committee to Study Homosexuality. At the end of that study, he concludes, "The scriptural texts in the Old and New Testaments condemning homosexual practice are neither inspired by God nor [are they] of enduring Christian value."[7] Kent is at least honest enough to admit what these verses assert, but then he's bold enough to say that the Bible is not God's Word.

Or hear Gary David Comstock, the Protestant chaplain at Wesleyan University:

Not to recognize, critique, and condemn Paul's equation of godlessness with homosexuality is dangerous. To remain within our respective Christian traditions and not challenge those passages that degrade and destroy us is to contribute to our own oppression. . . . Those passages will be brought up and used against us again and again until Christians demand their removal from the biblical canon or, at the very least, formally discredit their authority to prescribe behavior.[8]

Comstock's acknowledgment of what the Bible teaches leads him to label the Bible as dangerous and in need of serious editing.

Luke Timothy Johnson, Professor of New Testament at the Candler School of Theology at Emory University, takes this one step further. Johnson accepts that "the Bible nowhere speaks positively or even neutrally about same-sex love." But then he concludes:

I think it important to state clearly that we do, in fact, reject the straightforward commands of Scripture, and appeal instead to another authority when we declare that same-sex unions can be holy and good. And what exactly is that authority? We appeal explicitly to the weight of our own experience and the experience thousands of others have witnessed to, which tells us that to claim our own sexual orientation is in fact to accept the way in which God has created us. By so doing, we explicitly reject as well the premises of the scriptural statements condemning homosexuality—namely, that it is a vice freely chosen, a symptom of human corruption, and disobedience to God's created order.[9]

Johnson himself cannot escape the most obvious question behind what he is saying. If we are going to throw aside God's

Word in favor of human experience, then whose experience are we going to trust? And the obvious answer is Johnson's—and anyone else who agrees with him.

The quotes above make abundantly clear that if someone wants to advocate for homosexual activity, he or she must maintain that the Bible is irrelevant to modern humanity, inconsistent with our experience, and thus insufficient as a source of truth and guidance for our lives—that the Bible is not only deficient; it is downright dangerous.

The reality is that as soon as we advocate homosexual activity, we undercut biblical authority. And in the process of undercutting the authority of the Bible, we are undermining the integrity of the entire gospel. For if the Bible is wrong about certain issues, then who is to say what else the Bible is wrong about? This is why Daniel Heimbach, in an excellent book titled *True Sexual Morality*, writes:

> The stakes in the current conflict over sex are more
> critical, more central, and more essential than in
> any controversy the church has ever known. This
> is a momentous statement, but I make it soberly,
> without exaggeration. Conflict over sex these days is
> not just challenging tradition, orthodoxy, and respect
> for authority in areas such as ordination, marriage,
> and gender roles. And it does not just affect critically
> important doctrines like the sanctity of human life,
> the authority and trustworthiness of scripture, the
> Trinity, and the incarnation of Christ. Rather, war over
> sex among Christians is now raging over absolutely
> essential matters of faith without which no one can truly
> be a Christian in the first place—matters such as sin,
> salvation, the gospel, and the identity of God himself.[10]

Regardless of how you rank the current controversy over sexual immorality, it is clear that the most fundamental questions about what it means to be a Christian and whether we should submit to God's Word are at stake in this issue.

DARKENED HEARTS, DISORDERED MINDS

We shouldn't be surprised by this, for the gospel once again explains why so much is at stake in our view of sexual morality. The Bible connects our darkened hearts to disordered minds. As a result of rebellion in our hearts, our thoughts become "futile." If I could paraphrase Romans 1 in order to make it more personal, "Although we claim to be wise, we become fools, exchanging the truth of God for a lie, worshiping and serving created things rather than the Creator" (verses 22, 25).

In our thinking, we actually begin to believe that our ways are better than God's. We take this created gift called sex and use it to question the Creator God, who gave us the gift in the first place. We replace God's pattern with our preferences, exchanging what God's Word says about sexuality for what our observation and experience say about it. Yet we're blind to our own foolishness. It's as if we're living out Proverbs 14:12—"There is a way that seems right to a man, but its end is the way to death." The real danger here is our claim to know better than God what is best for our bodies and to justify sexual sin as a result.

Any sexual sin, including the most heinous sexual sin, can be justified and rationalized by sexual sinners. When I think of the sex trafficking of young girls that we addressed in chapter 5, or the sex scandals of church leaders that have tragically marked Christianity in our day, I cannot fathom how such action can be explained. Yet I have heard language from the lips of perpetrators that is haunting, to say the least.

I have heard adult men, for example, respond to the charge that they are manipulating young girls by arguing, "Who is to define manipulation anyway? And what sort of sexual expression doesn't involve manipulation in some way?" Ultimately, their argument continues, Why would God give them this desire if they were not designed to fulfill it? God must have made them this way. And besides, Jesus never spoke against it; instead, he welcomed children to him.

I'm sickened as I even write these words, but in a frighteningly similar way, I'm convinced that such justification and rationalization mirror our hearts and thoughts more than we want to admit. Whether we are men or women, and whether we have heterosexual, homosexual, bisexual, or transsexual tendencies, we all possess sinful sexual desires. We all have darkened hearts that tempt us toward fulfilling those desires outside of marriage between a man and a woman. We all have disordered thoughts that are prone to explain and excuse acting upon those desires, even twisting God's Word to make it say what we want it to say. We are all personally, biologically, culturally, and spiritually predisposed toward sexual sin—some of us are simply predisposed in ways that are more culturally acceptable. In the end, every single one of us is a sexual sinner.

And that means every single one of us is desperate for a Savior.

GOD SO LOVES . . .

This Savior is exactly who we find in the gospel. After we hear the Bible's exhortation to "flee from sexual immorality," God says to us, "For you were bought with a price" (1 Corinthians 6:18, 20). The good news of the gospel is that God so loves sexual sinners—all of us—that he sent his Son to pay the price for all our sexual sin. Paul writes, "God made him who had no

sin to be sin for us, so that in him we might become the righteousness of God" (2 Corinthians 5:21, NIV). As Jesus hung on
the cross, he took all of our sins upon himself. In the words of
Martin Luther,

> Our most merciful Father . . . sent his only Son into
> the world, and laid upon him all the sins of all men,
> saying, Be thou Peter that denier; Paul that persecutor,
> blasphemer and cruel oppressor; David that adulterer;
> that sinner which did eat the apple in Paradise; that thief
> which hanged upon the cross; and briefly, be thou the
> person which hath committed the sins of all men; see
> therefore that thou pay and satisfy for them [all].[11]

Oh, to think of it! That Jesus, God in the flesh, took the penalty upon himself for all our adultery and all our pornography
and every single lust we have ever had or will ever have. Indeed,
Jesus has paid a steep price for our bodies.

Sometimes we get the idea that God is only concerned about
what's in our hearts, our spirits, or our souls, and that our bodies
aren't really that important to him. But our bodies *are* important
to him, and we know this not just because of the price he paid
for them at the cross, but because of what happened in his body
before and after he went to the cross.

Jesus not only died for our bodies; he was born and lived
with a body. The greatest mystery in all of Christianity is the
Incarnation—the reality that God has come to us in a body. Jesus
was born just as we are with a life exactly like we have. We tend
to minimize the humanity of Jesus, forgetting that he ate and
drank, walked and slept, laughed and cried in a physical body
just like yours and mine. He didn't come as a spirit to die for our
sins, but as a child who would grow up and live among sinners.

Jesus lived a full life, too, which is immensely important to remember. Some people say, "If I don't think and act upon my sexual desires, then I am incomplete. I am not being true to who God has created me to be." But Jesus rebuffs this sentiment completely, for he was the most fully human, fully complete person who ever lived, and he was never married. He never indulged in any sort of sexual immorality (see Hebrews 4:15)—any sort of sexual thought, word, or deed outside of marriage between a man and a woman. Being true to who God has created you to be does not mean turning to sinful sexual desires.

In this fully human body, Jesus went to a cross and died for our sins, and then after the cross, God raised his body from the dead. This was not a resurrection merely of Jesus' spirit or soul but of his *body*, and the implications of this are huge for our bodies. The Bible says, "God raised the Lord and will also raise us up by his power" (1 Corinthians 6:14; see also 1 Corinthians 15). Just as God raised Jesus' body from the dead, he will raise our bodies from the dead. When we read this, we realize that God has made an eternal investment in our bodies. One day, God will raise our bodies up to be with him in a new heaven and a new earth. Our physical bodies on earth are therefore not irrelevant to God, for they will exist forever with him in heaven.

When you put all of this together, the truth is astounding. God cares about our bodies so much that he sent his Son in the flesh to live like us and among us. Then, though he had not sinned in any way, and though he deserved no penalty for sin, this Son went to the cross, where the price for sin was laid upon his body (see Romans 8:3). Jesus died for our sins. Then three days later, he physically rose from the dead in a body that will last forever, and he has promised to raise the bodies of all who turn from their sin and trust in him as their Savior (see 1 Corinthians 15:42-55).

Pause to let this soak in for a moment. The God of the universe cares for you deeply. He sees your body as an invaluable, priceless, eternal treasure of his handiwork. And when you trust in Christ, no matter what sexual sins you have committed with your body, you can be sure that God will one day raise your sin-sick body to be pure, holy, and imperishable with him forever.

Even as I rejoice in writing this, I am simultaneously sobered by the warnings of Scripture to all who choose not to trust in Christ—to all who spurn God's Word and persist in unrepentant sexual immorality. God has spoken, and he is clear: "Do you not know that the unrighteous will not inherit the kingdom of God? Do not be deceived: neither the sexually immoral, nor idolaters, nor adulterers, nor men who practice homosexuality, nor thieves, nor the greedy, nor drunkards, nor revilers, nor swindlers will inherit the kingdom of God" (1 Corinthians 6:9-10; see also Matthew 5:27-29; Galatians 5:19-21; Ephesians 5:5; Jude 1:7; Revelation 21:8). This is not saying that if you have ever committed sexual immorality of any sort, then you are going to hell. The Bible is referring here to those who refuse to turn from sexual immorality and trust in Christ. According to the gospel of God's grace, humbly repentant sexual sinners will enter into heaven. But unrepentant sexual sin will ultimately lead to hell.

A NEW IDENTITY

Repentance like this doesn't mean total perfection, but it does mean a new direction. As we've seen, we're all bent toward sexual sin, and that bent looks different in each of our lives. We are varied people—men and women, single and married, with different desires and different attractions—yet the gospel call is identical to every single one of us. In the words of Jesus, "If anyone would come after me, let him deny himself and take up his cross daily and follow me" (Luke 9:23). Repentance is a costly call to fundamentally say no to who you are (in your sin) in order to find an entirely new identity in who he is.

This is crucial in a culture that virtually equates identity with sexuality. If we are attracted to the opposite sex, we are told that we are, at our core, heterosexual. Likewise, if we are attracted to the same sex, we are told that we are, at our core, homosexual. The same can be said when it comes to bisexual and transsexual identity. We perceive ourselves according to our sexuality, and we view everything in our lives through this grid.

But the gospel awakens us to an entirely new grid. The gospel opens our eyes to the truth that God indeed is right and good. His character is holy and his Word is true, and at our core we have turned against him. In this sense, our identity is sinful. Yet Christ has come to endure the penalty of our sin and to take our place as sinners. In doing this for us, he has offered us a new identity—*his* identity. No longer separated from God, but now united with God. No longer stained by sin, but now clean from sin. No longer slaves, but now free. No longer guilty before God as Judge, but now loved by God as Father. No longer deserving eternal death, never to grasp all that God created us to be, but now having eternal life, experiencing more and more exactly who God has created us to be.

This is why Paul, recounting his conversion, writes in celebration, "I have been crucified with Christ. It is no longer I who live, but Christ who lives in me. And the life I now live in the flesh I live by faith in the Son of God, who loved me and gave himself for me" (Galatians 2:20). Paul is communicating here how when you turn to Christ, your entire identity is changed. You are in Christ, and Christ is in you. Your identity is no longer heterosexual or homosexual, bisexual or transsexual, addict or adulterer. Paul elsewhere writes to people who were characterized in all of these ways and more, "Such were some of you. But you were washed, you were sanctified, you were justified in the name of the Lord Jesus Christ and by the Spirit of our God" (1 Corinthians 6:11).

Rosaria Champagne Butterfield was once a feminist scholar who delighted in disparaging the Bible and all who believe it. "Stupid. Pointless. Menacing," she writes. "That's what I thought of Christians and their god Jesus, who in paintings looked as powerful as a Breck Shampoo commercial model." She described her life as a "leftist lesbian professor" in these words: "My life was happy, meaningful, and full. My partner and I shared many vital interests: AIDS activism, children's health and literacy, Golden Retriever rescue, our Unitarian Universalist church, to name a few."[12]

Through the compassionate engagement of a pastor who gently responded to a critical editorial she had written in a local newspaper, she saw and heard the gospel. This pastor and his wife showed God's love to her. She started reading the Bible and wrestling with the question, "Did I really want to understand homosexuality from God's point of view, or did I just want to argue with him?" One night she started praying and didn't stop until the morning. She writes, "When I looked in the mirror, I looked the same. But when I looked into my heart through the lens of the Bible, I wondered, *Am I a lesbian, or has this all been a case of mistaken identity? If Jesus could split the world asunder, divide marrow from soul, could he make my true identity prevail? Who am I? Who will God have me to be?*"[13]

This crisis of faith led her to what she describes as "one ordinary day" when she came to Christ. "In this war of worldviews," she writes, "Jesus triumphed. And I was a broken mess.

Conversion was a train wreck. I did not want to lose everything that I loved. But the voice of God sang a sanguine love song in the rubble of my world. I weakly believed that if Jesus could conquer death, he could make right my world."[14]

Such a testimony is not limited to leftist lesbian professors. This same testimony is a resounding reality across the pages of human history in countless men and women with varied sexual sins and proclivities who have been drawn by the gracious death of Christ to gladly deny themselves in order to experience entirely new life in him. This is the essence of what it means to be a Christian.

A COSTLY CALL

This gospel call is not only crucial in a culture that virtually equates identity with sexuality, but it is also critical in a church that continually reduces Christianity to consumerism. "Come to Christ," so many churches communicate, "and you will have all you want in this world. Health. Wealth. Happiness. Prosperity."

Imagine saying that to Rosaria Butterfield, a woman for whom the cost of following Christ was great. For her to come to Christ was to leave behind not only her lover but her entire lifestyle. So many details in her life were built around her identity as a lesbian, and to alter that identity was to unravel all those details. This is why she wrote about her resistance to the gospel, "I fought with everything I had. I did not want this. . . . I counted the costs. And I did not like the math on the other side of the equal sign."[15] The call to follow Christ in Rosaria Butterfield's life was not an invitation to receive anything she wanted in this world. It was a summons to leave behind everything she had.

Similarly, I think about men and women who struggle with gender dysphoria—a term used to describe the distress some people feel when their sense of gender doesn't match their biological or birth sex. A man may have a male body with female impulses that cause him to wish he was female and maybe even lead him to change biologically to a female. While I have not struggled with such dysphoria, I know people who have, and I can only imagine how distressing it indeed is. It's no surprise that people who struggle with gender dysphoria have historically high suicide (or attempted suicide) rates. For this reason, we must feel deep compassion for anyone who struggles with such distress.

At the same time, we know from God's Word that gender dysphoria and distress are not part of God's good design for our bodies. He has created each of us uniquely as men and women, and he has designed us to delight in this uniqueness, not to be distressed by it. Yet in a world of sin that is separated from God's good design, struggles like gender dysphoria exist. For this reason, like all men and women, those with gender dysphoria need gospel grace. We need grace and faith to believe in God's good design for our bodies, and grace and power to live as we've been fearfully and wonderfully made in his image. In the end, this means denying ourselves and trusting in Christ to be our joy and satisfaction as the men and women God has created us to be.

I am not in any way saying that this is easy, which is why we must be careful across the church not to minimize the magnitude of what it means to follow Christ. The gospel beckons each of us to a new identity with new activity, which means the homosexual person resists the temptation to turn to a gay or lesbian lifestyle, and the bisexual or transsexual person resists the temptation to act on their impulses. Likewise, the gospel beckons the heterosexual person to stop indulging in pornography, married men and women to stop abandoning their spouses, and singles to avoid sexual activity before marriage. All of these sacrifices may seem steep, but the call of the gospel is a call to gladly forsake the pleasures of this world in favor of the pursuit of Christ.

Consequently, as the church in our culture, we must make sure not to preach a gospel that merely imagines Christ as the means to a casual, conservative, comfortable Christian spin on the traditional American dream. Such a gospel won't work in the gay, lesbian, bisexual, and transsexual community—or anywhere else, for that matter. The gospel is a call for every one of us to die—to die to sin and to die to self—and to live with unshakable trust in Christ, choosing to follow his Word even when it brings us into clear confrontation with our culture (and our own desires, for that matter).

Such death to self requires an examination of sexuality in all of us. In what ways are you specifically prone to question God's good design for your body? In what ways are you tempted to sexual activity outside of marriage between a man and a woman? Do you have a tendency to think sexual thoughts about anyone besides your husband or wife? Are you enticed to act in any way upon those thoughts? Are you indeed putting those thoughts into action—as someone who is either single or married, heterosexual, homosexual, bisexual, transsexual, or otherwise?

Examine what you watch and what you wear. Are skintight clothes and low necklines your normal dress? How are you funding a sex-crazed entertainment system that poisons your soul as you find pleasure in seeing others sin sexually? How are these things that are so common in the culture keeping you from greater conformity to Christ?

God has not left you in the dark regarding what you should do. "Flee!" he says. "Stop reasoning with sexual immorality, stop rationalizing it, and run from it. Flee every form of sexual immorality as fast as you can!"

And none of us is alone as we flee. Each of us is a sexual sinner in a world full of sexual sinners. Unfortunately, in the church we have an obvious tendency to isolate certain segments of sinners who struggle with a particular sort of sexual temptation. We look at adulterers as an unfaithful lot who deserve to be left alone. We perceive gay and lesbian neighbors as enemies in a cultural conspiracy to take over the country. We view porn addicts as perverted, prostitutes as projects, and transsexuals as people who will pollute us if we get too close to them. We see other people as different from us and in some cases even dangerous to us.

But the truth is that they are all just like us, and we are all just like them. Every single one of us is seeking a way that seems right to us and that seems to bring satisfaction. The divine Word speaks into a divided world of sexual sinners and tells us that we have *all* gone astray, just like sheep who have wandered from their shepherd (see Isaiah 53:6). Whether we're male or female, married or divorced, single or cohabiting, heterosexual, homosexual, bisexual, or transsexual, each of us has turned to our own way. But the good news of the gospel is that God has laid the punishment for our sin upon his Son. And for all who daily turn from themselves and trust in him, he promises the peace and calm of Christ himself amid a cultural sea of sexual confusion.

Moreover, in that culture, God beckons us to proclaim this gospel. To care enough for one another to call each other to rest in God's design for sexual identity and to flee from every form of sexual immorality. Not to sit back and stay quiet because that's more convenient in the culture (or even in the church). Not to wait for people to come to us, but to go to them, just as Christ has come to us, in love and humility, with gentleness and patience, in the context of compassionate friendship and close relationship. To share the gospel with and to show God's love to all sorts of sexual sinners around us, knowing that eternity is at stake. For when we recognize that an everlasting heaven and an eternal hell are hanging in the balance, we realize it is not possible to believe the gospel and to stay silent on issues of sexual sin.

FIRST STEPS TO COUNTER CULTURE

Pray
Ask God to:
- Bring conviction and repentance in the lives of Christians (including you) involved in sexual immorality.
- Give Christians compassion, boldness, wisdom, and humility in addressing issues such as homosexual activity, pornography, and other forms of sexual sin.
- Open the hearts of unbelievers to see that God forgives and breaks the power of sexual sin and that true freedom is found in Jesus Christ.

Participate
Prayerfully consider taking these steps:
- Meet with a small group of others in your church to exhort one another to sexual purity and faithfulness.
- Support or become involved in a ministry that addresses issues of sexual immorality in our culture.
- Contact local government officials and exhort them to enact and implement legislation that will prevent the exploitation of women in our culture through avenues such as pornography and prostitution.

Proclaim
Consider the following truths from Scripture:
- 1 Corinthians 6:9-10: "Do you not know that the unrighteous will not inherit the kingdom of God? Do not be deceived:

neither the sexually immoral, nor idolaters, nor adulterers, nor men who practice homosexuality, nor thieves, nor the greedy, nor drunkards, nor revilers, nor swindlers will inherit the kingdom of God."

- 1 Corinthians 6:18-20: "Flee from sexual immorality. Every other sin a person commits is outside the body, but the sexually immoral person sins against his own body. Or do you not know that your body is a temple of the Holy Spirit within you, whom you have from God? You are not your own, for you were bought with a price. So glorify God in your body."

- Isaiah 1:18: "Come now, let us reason together, says the LORD: though your sins are like scarlet, they shall be as white as snow; though they are red like crimson, they shall become like wool."

For more (and more specific) suggestions, visit CounterCultureBook.com/Topics/Sexual-Immorality

UNITY IN DIVERSITY:
THE GOSPEL
AND ETHNICITY

Addie Mae Collins, Cynthia Wesley, Carole Robertson, and Denise McNair.

These four young girls suddenly lost their lives one Sunday in a church bombing just down the street from where I have served as pastor. You may wonder, *Why was their church bombed?* And the answer has nothing to do with the kind of persecution that people face around the world for their faith in Christ. No, their church was bombed because they were black, and the men who bombed it were white supremacists.

Not long ago, I had the honor of preaching alongside the pastor at Sixteenth Street Baptist Church in the very building that had been bombed fifty years before. I stood onstage with him and other pastors in the city before a room full of black and white Christians as together we remembered that horrible event, sadly one of many such atrocities that occurred across Birmingham (at one point called "Bombingham") during that time period, and we renewed our commitment to one another in Christ for the sake of the gospel in our city.

That gathering took place on Good Friday, the same day when, fifty years prior, Martin Luther King Jr. had led a peaceful march through downtown Birmingham, only to be thrown into jail. Facing harsh conditions in solitary confinement, someone delivered a published letter to him, penned by eight white Birmingham pastors, criticizing King for his methods and calling for him to maintain patience in promoting civil rights. King wrote a letter in response:

> It is easy for those who have never felt the stinging
> darts of segregation to say wait. But when you have
> seen vicious mobs lynch your mothers and fathers
> at will and drown your sisters and brothers at whim;
> when you have seen hate filled policemen curse, kick,
> brutalize, and even kill your black brothers and sisters
> with impunity; when you see the vast majority of your
> twenty million Negro brothers smothering in an air-tight
> cage of poverty in the midst of an affluent society; when
> you suddenly find your tongue twisted and your speech
> stammering as you seek to explain to your six-year-old
> daughter why she can't go to the public amusement
> park that has just been advertised on television, and
> see tears welling up in her little eyes when she is told
> that Funtown is closed to colored children, and see the
> depressing clouds of inferiority begin to form in her
> little mental sky, and see her begin to distort her little
> personality by unconsciously developing a bitterness
> toward white people; when you have to concoct an
> answer for a five-year-old son asking in agonizing

pathos: "Daddy, why do white people treat colored people so mean?"; when you take a cross country drive and find it necessary to sleep night after night in the uncomfortable corners of your automobile because no motel will accept you; when you are humiliated day in and day out by nagging signs reading "white" men and "colored"; when your first name becomes "nigger" and your middle name becomes "boy" (however old you are) and your last name becomes "John," and when your wife and mother are never given the respected title "Mrs."; when you are harried by day and haunted by night by the fact that you are a Negro, living constantly at tiptoe stance never quite knowing what to expect next, and are plagued with inner fears and outer resentments; when you are forever fighting a degenerating sense of "nobodiness"—then you will understand why we find it difficult to wait. There comes a time when the cup of endurance runs over, and men are no longer willing to be plunged into an abyss of injustice.[1]

Then, following King's explanation of his obligation to disobey an unjust law of the government in order to obey the just law of God, he piercingly indicted these pastors with the following words:

In the midst of blatant injustices inflicted upon the Negro, I have watched white churches stand on the sideline and merely mouth pious irrelevancies and sanctimonious trivialities. In the midst of a mighty struggle to rid our nation of racial and economic injustice, I have heard so many ministers say, "Those are social issues with which the Gospel has no real concern."[2]

Then he pleaded for them to apply the gospel to such social issues, saying:

> There was a time when the Church was very powerful.
> It was during that period when the early Christians
> rejoiced when they were deemed worthy to suffer for
> what they believed. In those days the Church was not
> merely a thermometer that recorded the ideas and
> principles of popular opinion; it was a thermostat that
> transformed the mores of society. . . .
> But the judgment of God is upon the Church as
> never before. If the Church of today does not recapture
> the sacrificial spirit of the early Church, it will lose its
> authentic ring, forfeit the loyalty of millions, and be
> dismissed as an irrelevant social club with no meaning
> for the twentieth century.[3]

I reread these words as I prepared to make my remarks on that Good Friday, and I was freshly grieved by the gospel-less actions of my white forefathers during those days.

But I had to be honest. As much as I wanted to distance myself from those eight pastors in 1960s Birmingham, I had to admit that I have the same gospel-denying tendencies that elicited their letter. For I am prone to prefer people who are like me—in color, culture, heritage, and history. If I walk into a room by myself and see two tables, one with a group of people ethnically like me and the other with a group of people ethnically unlike me, I instinctively move toward the group that is like me. I suppose something in me assumes that those who are like me are safer, more comfortable, and therefore better for me. Similarly, I'm prone to act as if those who are unlike me are less safe, less comfortable, and less beneficial. It seems to me, then, only a short walk from such simple preference to the kind of sinful prejudice that marked my pastoral predecessors. The difference between them and me is more one of degree than of kind.[4]

So when I preached my sermon that Good Friday, I had to confess the sinful tendency of my own heart to prefer one person over another based on particular commonalities. Furthermore, even as I write these words on this day, I have to admit that I have not resisted this tendency in my own heart and in my own church with the fierceness with which I ought to fight it. I feel inadequate to write this book on so many levels, but that inadequacy may be felt most in this chapter, for even as I have sought to develop friendships, foster partnerships, and forge initiatives that promote unity across ethnic lines, I know there is so much more that needs to be done in my own life and in the church of which I am a part.

This is all the more important when we see such racial strife, division, and violence across our culture. Police shootings of African Americans and subsequent shootings of police officers have exposed racial tension and injustice across America, and responses (or lack of responses) in the church have often revealed an unfortunate and ungodly imitation of the culture instead of countering the culture on this issue.

Such imitation is all the more evident when it comes to the related issue of immigration. I have lived and worked in a state where lawmakers have sought to enact the toughest immigration legislation in the country. Fiery debate over Alabama laws reflected fervent discussion across the United States regarding how to address the twelve to fifteen million undocumented immigrants currently living in our country. These men, women, and children live in my community (and yours), representing various ethnicities, speaking different languages, and coming from different cultural backgrounds. The church has taken small steps to reach out to them in specific ministries, but we desperately need to consider how we can—we *must*—avoid the sins of those who went before us in the Civil Rights era. Majority oppression of migrant people is certainly no better than white segregation of black people.

The gospel compels such action. By the grace of God, we must work to overcome prejudicial pride in our lives, families, and churches, a process that I'm convinced begins with changing the conversation about race altogether. Moreover, with the wisdom of God, we must labor to respect immigration laws in our country as responsible citizens while loving immigrant souls in our community as compassionate Christians. In a context where minorities will become the majority over the next thirty years, we must consider how to apply the gospel across a multiplicity of colors for the glory of Christ.

THE HUMAN RACE

We live in a culture where we are constantly submerged in discussions about race and racism. Particularly in response to recent violence, we have had conversations and hosted forums, sponsored debates and fostered dialogues, read articles and heard speeches about how to solve racial tension in our culture. But could it be that we're grasping for solutions to a problem we've grossly misdefined? And could it be that the gospel not only counters culture on this issue, but reshapes the conversation about race altogether?

Consider the starting point in the gospel for so many of the social issues we have addressed: the creation of man and woman in the image of God with equal dignity before God. As we've seen, this means that no human being is more or less human than another. All are made in God's image. It is a lack of trust in this gospel truth that has led to indescribable horrors in human history. Slavery in America, the Holocaust in Germany, the Armenian massacre in Turkey, the genocide in Rwanda, and the Japanese slaughter of six million Koreans, Chinese, Indo-Chinese, Indonesians, and Filipinos all derived from the satanic deception of leaders and citizens who believed that they were intrinsically superior to other types of people. From the first chapter of the Bible, however, this much is clear: all men and women are made in the very likeness of God.

Genesis 1 lays this foundation, but Genesis 10 expands on it, telling us that after the fall of man and the flood of the world, people were divided according to "their clans, their languages, their lands, and their nations" (Genesis 10:31). All of these divisions, however, trace their human ancestry back to one family—Noah and his sons—who trace their ancestry back to one couple, Adam and Eve. This is precisely what Paul references in the New Testament when he tells a crowd of philosophers in Athens, "From one man [God] made every nation of men, that they should inhabit the whole earth; and he determined the times set for them and the exact places where they should live" (Acts 17:26, NIV).

The Bible's storyline thus depicts a basic unity behind worldly diversity. From the beginning, God designed a human family that would originate from one father and one mother. From that common ancestry would come a diverse litany of clans dwelling in distant lands and developing new nations. Before long in the Bible, you see people with various skin colors with distinct cultural patterns dotting the human landscape.

Contemplating this may cause us to wonder, "Then what race were Adam and Eve?" The answer is both obvious and simple: the human race.

"No," we might say, "I mean what color was their skin?"

And as soon as we ask the question, we realize the problem with it—on two levels. First, we don't know the answer to that question because the Bible doesn't tell us. Now in most picture Bibles in the West, we've painted a portrait of a white Adam and Eve, but we have no basis for this assumption whatsoever. For all we know, this first couple could have been any color, or different colors, for that matter. Maybe Eve's skin was the shade of dirt or bone. If anything, genetics points to the greater probability that our first parents had darker skin, which is the dominant gene in skin color. Regardless, we find ourselves thinking and talking about people in terms the Bible doesn't even use.

Second, and more important, God's Word doesn't tell us what color Adam and Eve were because God doesn't equate membership in the human race with skin tone. Whatever color Adam and Eve (and their children) were, they contained in them a DNA designed by God that would eventually develop into a multicolored family across a multicultural world.

In this way, God's Word reminds us that regardless of the color of our skin, we all have the same roots. Fundamentally, we are all part of the same race. That's why we all need the same gospel.

A GOSPEL-LESS STARTING POINT

When we come to understand this, we realize that most discussions in our culture about race and racism are beginning from a gospel-less starting point. For in the process of discussing our diversity in terms of different "races," we are undercutting our unity in the human race. And this is not merely an issue of semantics. In our conversations, we're creating categories for defining each other that are not only woefully unhelpful; they're eventually impossible.

The category of "race" as we commonly use it is unhelpful

because it locates identity in physical appearance. You are black; I am white. These statements seem simple, but they are more than mere indicators of skin color. They carry with them a whole host of stereotypes and assumptions that are based squarely upon biological attributes. Simply because skin tone or hair texture is a certain way, we instinctively assume certain characteristics about others, either positively or negatively (most often negatively).

In addition, the category of "race" as we commonly use it becomes impossible when we meet someone who doesn't neatly fit into color classifications. I think of a good friend of mine named Deric. When Deric's mom was seventeen years old, living in a rural town in northwest Alabama, she found out she was pregnant. She was white, and the child's father was black. She panicked, not knowing what to do, and after initial deliberations with some friends, she decided to have an abortion. After all, what would people in the community think? Even interracial marriage had been illegal in Alabama until 1967. (It wasn't until 2000 that lawmakers removed the following words from the state constitution: "The Legislature shall never pass any law to authorize or legalize any marriage between any white person and a Negro, or a descendant of a Negro.")

So her friends accompanied her to the clinic, where she was taken back to lie down on a table. After sedating her, the doctor began asking her questions. He checked off box after box until he came to the last question: "Do you still want to have this procedure done?" She thought for a moment. Then, although sedated and to the surprise of both the doctor and her friends, she stood up and said, "No." She walked out of the clinic, and months later Deric was born.

So what "race" is Deric? Is he black? Or is he white? Is he both somehow? In what category are we to place Deric, and with what assumptions should we approach him?

Such categorization becomes all the more impossible with the globalization of our communities. Thabiti Anyabwile, a friend of mine and a pastor who has written extensively on this subject, lived in Grand Cayman for many years. As a "black" man, he explains the hopelessness of using "race" to distinguish men and women:

> My barber in the Caribbean looks just like me. You'd think he was an African-American until he opens his mouth. When he speaks, he speaks Jamaican patois so it is clear that he's not an African-American. My administrative assistant is also proudly Jamaican—very white-skinned. The lady in my barbershop looks a lot like my wife. You might think she is African-American or even Caymanian. She is Honduran. This notion of artificially imposing categories on people according to color—biology—is sheer folly. It's an impossibility. This is why much of the field on race and ethnicity has largely abandoned the attempt to identify men based on biological categories of race.[5]

I think of the same reality when I preach in a place like Dubai. I have never been in another setting on earth that felt more like heaven than when I have stood before a gospel-driven church pastored by a friend of mine in Dubai. Imagine looking out over a crowd of people and seeing at least seventy different nationalities represented in one room. When I stayed around to talk with church members after the gathering, I don't think I met more than one person from the same ethnicity. They were different colors from different cultures with different accents and different attributes. But as I stood among them, I was strangely aware that they (or, better put, *we*) were all alike. Every single one of us had roots that went back to Adam, and every single one of us bore the image of God himself.

This starting point fundamentally counters the starting point that currently exists for understanding and approaching this social issue in our culture. And this is not merely a matter of semantics disconnected from our everyday lives. Even as I write this, I am immersed in a culture where "black" boys and men are being shot dead in the streets by "white" police officers, seemingly without warrant. Our conversations about events like these begin from a point of division. Because we unhelpfully categorize one another in terms of different races, and because we inevitably call one another different colors with all sorts of assumptions and stereotypes associated with "black" and "white" labels, from the start we undercut our ability to discuss and address serious tension over this social issue. And until that starting point changes, then labels like these will continue to prove deadly. Literally, deadly.

Now obviously, I am not attempting to deny the clear differences that exist between diverse people. That much is based not just upon biblical foundations but upon practical observation. Instead, what I'm advocating for is a gospel-rich confession that we are one race, for when that reality is clear, we are at a much better starting point in our culture for discussing our differences.

ETHNICITY

This leads us right to where the Bible grounds our understanding of human diversity: in human ethnicity. To use the language of Genesis 10, we comprise "clans" in separate "nations" that speak different "languages" in diverse "lands." And with the globalization of the world and the migration of men and women across continents and into cities, these clans from separate nations and with different languages now often live in the same land.

Here the concept of ethnicity is immensely helpful, for it includes all of these considerations and more. Instead of being strictly tied to biology, ethnicity is much more fluid, factoring in social, cultural, lingual, historical, and even religious characteristics. While we commonly recognize approximately two hundred nations in the world today, anthropological scholars have identified thousands (some say over eleven thousand; others say over sixteen thousand) of distinct ethnolinguistic groups in the world. These groups, often called people groups, possess a common self-identity with common history, customs, patterns, and practices based upon those two primary characteristics: ethnicity and language.[6]

But these categories are not narrowly limiting. Some people groups may speak multiple languages yet consider themselves one ethnic group. The Dinka I have been around in South Sudan are one example. They speak a range of dialects comprising five separate languages, but they self-identify clearly as one people. Similarly, other people groups may speak the same language yet consider themselves different ethnic groups. The Tutsi and Hutu of East Central Africa are one example. They possess both a common language and a common culture, but they have maintained distinct social identities for the last two thousand years.[7]

Applied to the United States, it makes no sense, then, to categorize our country as a nation of black, white, brown, or other "races." Instead, we are a nation of increasingly diverse people groups. We are Anglo Americans, African Americans, Latin Americans, Asian Americans, and more. These categories can be subdivided further based upon other ethnolinguistic factors, leading us to realize that we are a nation of unique people groups with diverse histories from different lands with distinct customs and even languages.

Just last weekend, a small group of members from our church

spent an afternoon intentionally meeting men and women from different people groups in our city. As they went to international restaurants and markets, community centers and college campuses, they met Thai, Filipino, Vietnamese, Punjabi, Gujarati, Colombian, Salvadoran, Palestinian Arab, Jordanian Arab, Northern Yemeni Arab, and Moroccan Arab people, just to name a few of the ethnolinguistic groups they encountered in only a few short hours. Surely this rich diversity of people cannot be defined by skin tone, hair texture, or eye color alone.

Some might say that in abandoning categories of black and white in discussions of race and racism, we're trying to sweep under the rug centuries of history and oppression as if they never happened. By no means! Instead, by basing our dialogue more meaningfully on ethnolinguistic characteristics, we're acknowledging those real centuries of history and oppression, combined with a host of other fluid factors that can't be reduced to basic biology. Moreover, in removing race and racism from the discussion altogether, we're paving the way for us as one race to call racism what it actually is: sin borne in a heart of pride and prejudice. And in doing this, we are now setting the stage for understanding how the gospel is uniquely able to foster powerful unity in the middle of pervasive diversity.

WHAT THE GOSPEL MAKES POSSIBLE

Just as soon as God's Word introduces diverse clans, languages, lands, and nations, God's Word indicts people for their propensity to selfish pride and ethnic prejudice. Such pride is evident even in the first family as Cain, a son of Adam and Eve, kills his brother, Abel. Soon after that, "the LORD saw that the wickedness of man was great in the earth, and that every intention of the thoughts of his heart was only evil continually" (Genesis 6:5).

Within chapters of the Bible, that wickedness spills over into wars among nations and conflicts among clans. The more different peoples mix together, the more they mistreat one another. The pages of the Bible and human history are thus filled with an evil affinity for ethnic animosity.

These same pages reveal a God with a passion for all people groups. After the nations rebel against him at Babel in Genesis 11, God calls one group of people to become his own in Genesis 12. God promises to bless these ethnic Israelites, but the purpose of his blessing extends far beyond them. "In you," God says, "all the families of the earth shall be blessed" (Genesis 12:3). This promise is reiterated over and over in the Old Testament as God declares his desire for all nations to behold his greatness and experience his grace (see Psalm 96).

Moreover, God gives laws to his people, the ethnic Israelites, regarding their treatment of diverse people in their midst.[8] After the Israelites spend centuries of exile in Egypt, God commands them, "You shall not wrong a sojourner or oppress him, for you were sojourners in the land of Egypt" (Exodus 22:21). In language that follows on the heels of what we already examined in chapter 4 regarding justice for the orphan and the widow, God declares that he "loves the sojourner, giving him food and clothing," and he consequently calls his people to love the sojourner (Deuteronomy 10:18). Through the prophets, God accuses his people of extortion and robbery. "They have oppressed the poor and needy," God says, "and have extorted from the sojourner without justice" (Ezekiel 22:29; see also Jeremiah 7:6; Zechariah 7:10).

The Hebrew word for "sojourner" in these passages can be translated basically and understood practically as "immigrant." Such foreigners who had been separated from their families and land found themselves in precarious positions, in need of help from the people among whom they lived. As a result, God views them with particular compassion, and the Bible often groups the sojourner, or immigrant, alongside the orphan and the widow. The pages of the Old Testament present God as "the LORD [who] watches over the sojourners" (Psalm 146:9).

When Jesus comes to the earth in the New Testament, we are quickly introduced to him as an immigrant. Fleeing a brutal political situation in Bethlehem after he is born, Jesus' family travels to Egypt, where they live for years as sojourners in a foreign land. Upon Jesus' return to Israel and from the start of his ministry, he subtly subverts the national pride of ethnic Israelites who were anticipating a Jewish Messiah who would overthrow Rome and reestablish Israel. Though Jesus' primary focus is on "the lost sheep of Israel" (Matthew 15:24, NIV), he nevertheless reaches beyond national boundaries at critical moments to love, serve, teach, heal, and save Canaanites and Samaritans, Greeks and Romans.[9] Then Jesus shocks the preconceived systems of his Jewish disciples not only by dying on a cross and rising from the grave, but also by commanding them to proclaim "repentance and forgiveness of sins . . . in his name to all nations" (Luke 24:47). Jesus came not just as Savior and Lord of Israel; he came as Savior and Lord over all.

This realization became the foundation for the call to ethnic unity in the establishment of the church. The cultural division between Jews and Gentiles (non-Jews) was deep during the first century. Yet as the story of the church unfolds, we read how, to many Jews' surprise, Gentiles began believing in Jesus. At first, Jewish Christians didn't know how to respond. Should they even accept Gentile Christians? If so, did they need to impose Jewish customs upon them? Though Gentiles were finally accepted into the church, they felt at best like second-class Christians.

Into this atmosphere, Paul speaks to Gentile believers, saying,

You were at that time separated from Christ, alienated from the commonwealth of Israel and strangers to the covenants of promise, having no hope and without God in the world. But now in Christ Jesus you who once were far off have been brought near by the blood of Christ. For he himself is our peace, who has made us both one and has broken down in his flesh the dividing wall of hostility. EPHESIANS 2:12-14

Then he exhorts them, saying, "Through [Jesus] we both have access in one Spirit to the Father. So then you are no longer strangers and aliens, but you are fellow citizens with the saints and members of the household of God" (Ephesians 2:18-19).

These words beautifully describe the unique power of the gospel to reunite people from (and, for that matter, within) different ethnic groups. And it makes sense, doesn't it? For in the beginning, sin separated man and woman from God and also from one another. This sin stood (and stands) at the root of ethnic pride and prejudice. When Christ went to the cross, he conquered sin, making the way for people to be free from its hold and restored to God. In so doing, he paved the way for all people to be reconciled to one another. Followers of Christ thus have one "Father" as one "family" in one "household," with no "dividing wall of hostility" based upon ethnic diversity.

This, then, was the glorious reality expressed in that Good Friday gathering at Sixteenth Street Baptist Church. There I stood in a room of diverse people, some of whom had even been in that building on the day it was bombed. When they looked at my white face, they could have seen the same type of person who killed those children. But by the grace of God, they didn't. Instead, they saw a brother in Christ whose character is gratefully not bound by a haunted history and whose identity is thankfully not confined to a certain color. This is the picture that the gospel makes possible.

ONE IN CHRIST

But don't be mistaken. It's not that the men and women in that Good Friday gathering who were different from me needed to ignore the history of what my people group had done to them or to overlook the ways I am different from them. In his most famous speech during the March on Washington, Martin Luther King Jr. stood on the steps of the Lincoln Memorial and shouted, "I have a dream that my four little children will one day live in a nation where they will not be judged by the color of their skin but by the content of their character."[10] Ever since that day, some in our culture have advocated for a color-blind society that pretends our differences don't exist.

This, however, is not what the gospel compels. For the gospel doesn't deny the obvious ethnic, cultural, and historical differences that distinguish us from one another. Nor does the gospel suppose that these differences are merely superficial. Instead, the gospel begins with a God who creates all men and women in his image and then diversifies humanity according to clans and lands as a creative reflection of his grace and glory in distinct groups of people. In highlighting the beauty of such diversity, the gospel thus counters the mistaken cultural illusion that the path to unity is paved by minimizing what makes us unique. Instead, the gospel compels us to celebrate our ethnic distinctions, value our cultural differences, and acknowledge our historical diversity, even forgiving the ways such history may have been dreadfully harmful.

I have experienced particular joy by joining in friendship and partnering in ministry with pastors and members of churches who are ethnically different from me—specifically those who have historical reasons to possess animosity toward me. We have worked together when tornadoes ravaged communities in our city. We have prayed together when tragedies and crises have gripped our nation. We have preached together in churches, conferences, and city events. We have served together in specific efforts to meet the needs of the poor, the widow, and the orphan around us. In all of this, I have learned so much from my brothers and sisters who are unlike me. And the more these friendships flourish and partnerships expand, the more I am thankful to God that they are not like me.

On a global scale, I can't help but picture Steve Saint standing beside Mincaye on a stage as together they testified to the grace of God in the gospel. Mincaye, a Huaorani man from the jungles of Ecuador, years before had killed Steve's father, Nate, when Nate tried to share the gospel with Mincaye and his people. Mincaye has now become a follower of Jesus and a friend to Steve. Joining arms, one wearing Western clothes and the other wearing tribal dress, one speaking English and the other speaking his native language, one whose father had been killed and the other who had speared that father dead, they portray the power of the gospel not to eliminate differences as if they don't exist but to transcend differences as one in Christ.

This is what the Bible means when it says, "There is neither Jew nor Greek, slave nor free, male nor female, for you are all one in Christ Jesus" (Galatians 3:28, NIV). Some people misconstrue this verse much as they misconstrue King's words to say that our differences don't matter. But they do. Our peculiarities are important. We have much to learn and much to celebrate in our gender, cultural, and ethnic distinctions.

When I consider people who have profoundly influenced my life, I am grateful that many of them are from different ethnicities around the world. I think of Jeffries, a South Sudanese friend who first introduced me to the plight of the persecuted church. Jeffries has given me an entirely new perspective on joy amid suffering, and through his desire to share the gospel with his persecutors, he has taught me how to love enemies across ethnic lines. I think of Fatima, a Middle Eastern woman who has exemplified biblical hospitality in the way she and her family have welcomed me and others into their home. As a follower of Christ in a country where it was illegal for Fatima to become a Christian, she has modeled what it means to exalt Christ humbly, boldly, and wisely in the culture around her. Similarly, I think of Jian and Lin, an Asian couple whom I first met over a meal of hot pot, a spicy stew consisting of an entire chicken (and I mean an *entire* chicken). As I have shared life with Jian and Lin, God has used their simple lives and sacrificial leadership in the church to uncover cultural blind spots in my life and leadership.

I could go on and on, listing names of men and women from different ethnicities who have made indelible marks on my life. When I consider their collective impact upon me, I realize that they have shaped me not *in spite of* our differences, but *because of* our differences. All of this ultimately points to the goodness of God in the gospel, for according to Galatians 3, in Christ we are able to experience the full beauty of God's design for mankind's diversity.

THE SOJOURNER IN OUR MIDST

The gospel not only affects the ways Anglo Americans and African Americans view each other in our culture, or the way we may view people in different countries, but this gospel also affects the way followers of Christ view migrant men and women who are living right around us in our country. A cursory reading of the Old Testament, combined with a clear understanding of Christ's cross in the New Testament, calls into question the contemporary approach to immigration among many Christians in our culture. In addition to practical ignorance on this issue in the political sphere, our personal lives often reflect little concern for the sojourner in our midst. Russell Moore writes that the Christian response to immigrant neighbors has been akin to saying, "You kids get off my lawn," in Spanish.[11] But if the God of the Bible possesses particular compassion for the immigrant, even equating him or her with the orphan and the widow, and if the cross of Christ is designed to compel outreach across ethnic divisions, then how much more should we as the people of God care for immigrants from other countries in our midst?

Consider the story of Sam and Lucas. Sam and Lucas live in Mexico in the midst of desperate poverty, unable to provide for their wives' and children's basic needs. One day, a friend tells them that he has found a way for Sam and Lucas to get jobs in the United States. There they can make money and send it back to sustain their families. Sam and Lucas see no other option and agree to go. They say good-bye to their wives and children, and they leave with their friend.

Weeks later, they find themselves lying down in the back of an old SUV, covered completely by a blanket as the truck bounces down the road. Finally, they arrive at a back entrance behind a popular restaurant, where the proud owner steps out. After speaking to the driver in a foreign language, the owner gives him some cash, then opens the back door of the SUV. He uncovers the men and tells Sam and Lucas to get out quickly.

They go inside the back of the restaurant, where the owner sits them down and serves them a quick meal. As they eat, the owner introduces Sam and Lucas to what will be their job: busing tables and washing dishes. After they're finished eating, the owner escorts them by van to a decaying, shuttered, split-level home that they will share with a host of other workers like them. "I'll pick you and the others up at ten o'clock in the morning," the owner says, and off he goes. Sam and Lucas have arrived at their new home.

Sam and Lucas now have a new life. Every day they are shuttled back and forth between the place where they sleep and the restaurant where they work. It is a well-known restaurant, getting all sorts of great reviews and attracting all kinds of different people—people like you and me. But amid all the crowds that surround Sam and Lucas, absolutely no one knows them. No one even notices them. They are destitute, sending as much money as they can back to their families while resorting to alcohol and prostitution to curb their loneliness.[12]

It is not my aim here to stereotype migrant workers—although this story is true, it obviously doesn't mean that all Latino dishwashers in restaurants have the same story. It is also not my aim to oversimplify either the plight of immigrants in our country or the predicament of how to provide for them. Finally, it's not my aim here to propose comprehensive political answers for the practical legislative quagmire that illegal immigration presents in our country.

It *is*, however, my aim to show that the gospel message has implications for the issue of immigration, and particularly for illegal immigrants like Sam and Lucas. Amid necessary political discussions and inevitable personal disagreements, first and foremost the gospel reminds us that when we are talking about immigrants (legal *or* illegal), we are talking about men and women made in God's image and pursued by his grace. Consequently, followers of Christ must see immigrants not as problems to be solved but as people to be loved. The gospel compels us in our culture to decry any and all forms of oppression, exploitation, bigotry, or harassment of immigrants, regardless of their legal status. These are men and women for whom Christ died, and their dignity is no greater or lesser than our own.

Likewise, their families are no less important than our own. Many illegal immigrants, like Sam and Lucas, are in the United States for understandable reasons, fleeing brutal economic and political situations in their own countries as they fight for the survival of their own families. Others came to the United States years ago and have now begun families here. I think of Ricardo, a follower of Christ and the father of five children, three of whom are US citizens. Ricardo entered the country illegally more than twenty years ago, and for the last twenty years he has worked to support his family while serving in his community. However, if Ricardo were to go back to his village in Mexico now, he would be resigning himself and his family to abject poverty. His other option would be to split up his family, leaving his three "legal" children behind with a neighbor.[13] Surely, just as the gospel compels us to respect the personal dignity of immigrants regardless of their legal status, it also compels us to protect their familial unity regardless of legal status.

All of this is obviously complicated by out-of-date legislation that is out of sync with the current labor market in our country. Add to this our selective enforcement of immigration laws, and it becomes clear to us all, regardless of personal political persuasion, that our system needs reform. And the gospel is not silent even here, for much as we saw in chapter 3, the Bible clearly teaches that government exists under God to establish and enforce laws for the good of people (see Romans 13:1-7). We have a responsibility before God as citizens under a government to work together to establish and enforce just laws that address immigration. Among other things, such laws should involve securing our borders, holding business owners accountable for hiring practices, and taking essential steps that ensure fairness to taxpaying citizens of our country. Likewise, we have a responsibility before God as citizens under a government to work together to refute and remove unjust laws that oppress immigrants.[14] Failing to act in either of these ways would be to settle for injustice, which would put us out of sync with the gospel.

I don't presume easy answers to any of the above, but I am proposing that the gospel requires Christians to wrestle with these questions. Regardless of personal or political views, none of us can escape the reality that we're talking about our neighbors, and Jesus' command regarding our neighbors is clear. As long as immigrants, legal and illegal, live around us by God's sovereign design (see Acts 17:26-27), we're compelled to consider how to love them as we love ourselves (see Luke 10:25-37).

OFF THE SIDELINES

I think of a friend of mine named Tyler, who pastors in Arizona. Amid the massive influx of immigrants into his community (many of whom are illegal) and surrounded by the milieu of legislative discussions in his state, Tyler and the church he leads have decided to engage this issue with gospel perspective and to serve these people with gospel compassion. Together they began providing food and clothing to migrant workers through a variety of different ministries. These ministries paved the way for personal relationships to develop with migrant men, women, and children, opening other doors for members of the church not just to love but to learn from these workers and their families. This has obviously involved more time and resources, but in Tyler's words, "It wasn't long before our people began donating more than food—they started to donate their lives." This eventually led to the construction of a community center in a Latino neighborhood that is now filled weekly with English classes, after-school programs, life-skills training, and Bible studies. In addition, the church Tyler pastors began partnering with a Latino church to start a center that protects people who in the past would end up either abused by employers or working without compensation.

The church's work among Latinos then carried over into an awareness of Somali Bantu and Uzbek refugees living in the surrounding community. Consequently, hundreds of church members now serve these refugees, welcoming them at the airport, tutoring them, teaching life and business skills, and organizing ways to financially support refugee-owned restaurants.

In all of this, Tyler says, "We have enjoyed hundreds of opportunities to engage in conversations about Jesus . . . , and we've seen God change lives." But it hasn't been easy. Tyler comments, "Our work has been affirmed by many but has also been met with criticism from both inside and outside the church. . . . Because of our support of these communities, we've been accused of contributing to the breakdown of and economic drain on our educational and medical systems, and even to violent crimes like rape and murder by undocumented immigrants." One of the things I appreciate most about Tyler is his willingness to both listen to and learn from such criticism. In his words, "We've found that it's important to pause and listen to the critiques of respectable people with legitimate concerns. We especially need to listen to those who challenge us on the grounds that our work counteracts the common good. If their concern is valid, we should respond and adjust accordingly. If, however, they are misguided, we should clarify our intentions and continue the work to which we have been called."[15]

No one can expect to engage in ministry like this in our culture and experience anything less than challenges like these. What I admire most about Tyler and his church is the way they are not afraid to step off the sidelines, at great cost and in the face of certain criticism, to apply the gospel to this pressing social need in our day. The members of this church are clearly not perfect in their response to immigration. At the same time, multitudes of men, women, and children made in the image of God are grateful that the members of this church aren't passive, either.

A BETTER COUNTRY

In the end, we are all immigrants ourselves. I'm not merely referring to our ancestors who may have migrated to America many years ago. I'm referencing the very essence of what it means to be a Christian. The Bible calls believers in Christ "sojourners and exiles" who "desire a better country" and are "seeking a homeland," a "city that is to come" (1 Peter 2:11; Hebrews 11:13-14, 16; 13:14). In other words, Christians are migrants on this earth, and the more we get involved in the lives of immigrants, the better we will understand the gospel.

Unfortunately, throughout history Christians have failed to understand how the gospel affects the way we view and love people of different ethnicities. My hope and prayer is that this would not be what historians write concerning the church in our day. The body of Christ is a multicultural citizenry of an otherworldly kingdom, and this alters the way we live in this ever-changing country. By the sheer grace of God in the gospel, we are compelled to counter selfish pride and ethnic prejudice both in our hearts and our culture. For after all, this is not the culture to which we ultimately belong. Instead, we are looking forward to the day when "a great multitude that no one [can] number, from every nation, from all tribes and peoples and languages" (Revelation 7:9) will stand as one redeemed race to give glory to the Father who calls us not sojourners or exiles, but sons and daughters.

FIRST STEPS TO COUNTER CULTURE

Pray

Ask God to:

- Open the eyes of all believers (including your own) to selfish pride and sinful prejudice and to grant repentance.
- Protect and provide for immigrants and their families and to put believers in their paths to minister to them.
- Give the leadership of the United States (and other governments) wisdom in addressing the issue of immigration.

Participate

Prayerfully consider taking these steps:

- Talk with the leadership of your church about partnering in ministry with a church whose members are of a different ethnicity from yours.
- Open your home to an international student or someone from a different people group, as the vast majority of these individuals never have an opportunity to go inside the home of an American family.
- Begin a ministry to immigrants in need in your local area. Provide food, shelter, and help with the language. Most important, proclaim the gospel to them.

Proclaim

Consider the following truths from Scripture:

- Acts 17:26: "He made from one man every nation of mankind to live on all the face of the earth, having determined allotted periods and the boundaries of their dwelling place."

- Deuteronomy 10:19: "Love the sojourner, therefore, for you were sojourners in the land of Egypt."
- Galatians 3:28: "There is neither Jew nor Greek, there is neither slave nor free, there is no male and female, for you are all one in Christ Jesus."

For more (and more specific) suggestions,
visit CounterCultureBook.com/Topics/Ethnicity-Immigration

UNPRECEDENTED CRISIS: THE GOSPEL AND REFUGEES

Imagine an eight-year-old boy named Samir.

His name means "pleasant companion." He has two sisters. One is five years old. Her name is Amira, which means "princess," and that's exactly what she is to him. Samir prides himself on taking care of his princess of a sister, and he is nothing short of a "pleasant companion" for her. And then there's Raja, their baby sister, born six months ago. Her name means "hope."

Together, they lived in Syria with their father, mother, and grandmother. Samir's parents were both teachers. His dad taught Arabic in the state-run school in Syria while his mom taught music. They worked hard to provide for their family in a quaint village of about four thousand people.

Well, it used to be quaint.

Their village was situated on the border of three different provinces in Syria, and over recent years, it became trapped in a triangle of terror: the Syrian army on one side, the Free Syrian Army on the other side, and the Russian army in the middle.

Samir vividly remembers the first time a bomb landed in his village. He was inside the house playing with Amira when the door suddenly flew open. Samir's dad, out of breath from running home as fast as he could, began yelling, "Get out of the house!" A minute later, they were huddled together in a makeshift shelter while the sound of bombshells shot all around them. Shrapnel littered the streets in a sure sign to these Syrian villagers that their quaint community had suddenly become a war zone.

It wasn't long until electricity was out for most of the day. Schools could no longer function, and work came to a halt. Food and water were both becoming scarce. Bombs would fall day and night, leaving no semblance of peace at any point for Samir and his family. Anxiety began to disturb this eight-year-old's mind, with diverse side effects. Samir was turning into a cowering, stuttering version of himself, too scared to sleep and just waiting to wake up his sister and sprint with his family to the shelter at any moment.

One night he overheard his parents talking. "We can't stay here anymore," his father told his mother. "We need to go somewhere else."

Samir's mom then asked the obvious question. "Where?" For generations their families had lived and worked in this village. Syria was all they'd ever known. Where would they go, and how would they support themselves?

Samir's dad shared how he had seen and heard of relocation opportunities. If they could just get across Turkey to the Aegean Sea, then they could cross over to Greece, and there they would be free. If only they could get to Greece, then they would have passage into the rest of Europe, and they could start over.

Samir's mom immediately expressed concern. "Do you really think we can travel with your mom and three kids, including a six-month-old baby, hundreds of miles across Syria and then Turkey?" She continued, "Then how do we get across the Aegean Sea to Europe? And who's to say they won't turn us right around when we get there?"

"I don't know," Samir's dad said as he sank into silence. But after a long pause, he spoke again. "I also don't know any other option. We either stay here and die, or we risk our lives and go."

Within days, the family was packed. Everyone but the baby had a bag to carry, and just like that, generations of history and an entire family's possessions were reduced to five plastic sacks, one of which contained all the money Samir's mother and father had saved. They set out on foot, leaving what used to be the comforts of home behind for a journey into the unknown. It was a three-day trip to the Turkish border, some of it by bus, but most of it by foot in light of the various dangers associated with travel on the main roads. The first night their family slept in an abandoned coal factory. The next night was spent in a stable.

The third day posed the greatest challenge—a massive mountain to cross on foot at the Turkish border. It was a nine-hour trek, with the sounds of bullets and bombs nearby. They ran out of water about halfway through. Samir's dad was now carrying Amira, his mom was carrying Raja, and Samir and his grandmother were plodding along behind together. Every one of them would have been ready to quit had the others not been pushing them along. But they finally reached Turkey in need of rest and relief. They would find neither.

Ever since refugees began trekking across Turkey, an entire industry of exploitation has begun. Refugees need simple goods: water, food, and supplies for the journey to the coast. So a swath of smugglers are there to charge exorbitant prices for everything they need. It was no different for Samir's family. Samir's dad had no choice but to pay whatever the smugglers asked to get whatever his family needed. He saw his money slowly dwindle, yet the highest sum was still to come.

As they finally approached the coast, they found themselves joined by thousands of other refugees, a sea of humanity seeking asylum. Samir's dad checked his family into a hostel, a humble semblance of a hotel where the family crammed into a small room with one bed. Samir's grandmother slept on it with the baby while the rest of the family slept side by side on the floor. As Samir nuzzled up to his dad that night, he thought about all that he missed—his home, his friends, his life—and he considered all that he had seen in the effects of war all around him. As tears came to his eyes, he took solace in the fact that he no longer heard bombs overhead. At least here they were safe.

The next morning, Samir went with his dad to find a way to cross the sea. The system of smugglers at the coast was active, and it was nearly impossible to tell whom you could trust. A ferry across the Aegean would cost you or me about $17. But smugglers were charging refugees approximately $1,000 to $2,000 for each member of a family, including infants, to cross to the other side. Moreover, the refugees wouldn't be crossing on a ferry. They would be crossing either on a small boat or a rubber dinghy, a raft made for about thirty people, with no guarantee that it would reach the other side.

Samir heard people telling stories. The day before, thirty-four people (including fifteen children and four toddlers) had drowned when an overcrowded boat capsized due to storms and high winds. Those 34 joined approximately 2,500 people who have died trying to get to Greece. This great sea has literally become a graveyard.

The journey across the Aegean is delicate, depending on everything from weather conditions to armed criminals. Masked men on jet skis are known to attack boats, smashing into them with sticks and threatening to drown them if the passengers won't surrender whatever valuables they have with them.

After a while, Samir and his dad met a man who said he could get them across for $1,800 apiece, more than $10,000 for Samir's family. Samir's dad knew that would come close to draining his savings. But what choice did he have?

The living conditions in Turkey are harsh. There's a reason people are spending their savings and risking their lives to leave that country. So Samir's dad reluctantly agreed. "I will try to get you on a more sturdy boat," the smuggler said, "but we will see. Simply keep your phone by your side, and I will call you when it is time."

Samir and his dad left the meeting with this man and immediately went to buy life jackets, not realizing that their quality was so poor that many people had drowned wearing them. Once the life jackets were purchased, Samir and his dad went back to the hostel, where the rest of the family was waiting. They gave them the news and told them they needed to be ready at any time.

That night, they received a call from the smuggler. "Too much rain and wind," he said. "We can't go tonight." The next night, the same message arrived, followed by the next, and the next, until some nights a message never even came. Samir's dad began to worry he had made a mistake working with this particular smuggler and passage was never actually going to be a reality as long as they were working with him.

They passed the days in the hostel meeting other families, sharing one another's stories, and spurring on their hope in what might lie ahead on the other side of the sea. Such hope was fading fast until one night, the phone rang suddenly and the voice of the smuggler on the other end said, "You can travel on a rubber dinghy tonight. Come to the meeting place immediately." And just like that, Samir's dad had a choice.

He had waited for weeks, hoping his family would be on a boat more sturdy, safe, and secure than a small rubber dinghy amid the crashing Aegean waves. Now he had minutes to decide if he was ready to risk his family's life on a dinghy. In utter exhaustion from the journey by this point, Samir's dad thought, *This may be our only chance*, so he said to his family, "Grab your bags and life jackets, and let's go." Soon they were crammed into a small van with other refugees making their way through alleys toward a hidden crag in the sea.

There, a raft built for thirty people was waiting for sixty refugees arriving in the vans. The smugglers began loading the raft one by one, cramming the refugees closely in next to one another. As each of them climbed in, they were immediately cold, able to feel the freezing temperature from the water around them. One of the refugees was appointed by the smugglers to drive the boat, a task this man (and no one else on the boat) had ever done. The smugglers started the engine, pushed them out from shore, and thus began the longest three hours of Samir's short life.

Imagine being crammed into that boat. See the pitch-black darkness. Feel the shiver of the sea as its waves toss you back and forth. Hear the sound of people screaming in fear as a man who has never driven a boat before nervously navigates the Aegean Sea with sixty lives in his hands.

Samir looked over at his mom and saw fear on her face for the first time in this journey as she clutched his baby sister tightly, knowing that if she or the baby were to fall off now, there's no way the baby would live. To make matters worse, freezing water was pouring into the boat with every passing wave, which became a major problem as they approached the coast, for the raft was now completely overloaded, and it was starting to sag into the sea.

"Water!" someone cried. "We need to bail out this water!" They began trying to do so but to little avail. There was too much. So another person yelled in a panic, "Weight! We need to shed more weight!" They began throwing what little valuables they had left among them overboard. This did little to help, and something more significant was needed.

That's when Samir's dad suddenly stood up. He looked into his son's eyes, and then across at his wife, and he said, "I want you and everyone else on this boat to live. I'll do my best to meet you on shore." And without any further hesitation, he jumped. Samir screamed in horror as his dad, just like that, was gone. His mom, sister, and grandmother were wailing as well, but it was too late. The loss of weight immediately made a difference, and the raft began moving quickly toward the land. Everyone was relieved except for Samir and his family as they now watched his dad disappear into the darkness of the Aegean Sea.

After a time, they arrived on shore. People jumped out of the boat, and their clothes were quickly drenched as they all trudged ashore. For most of these refugees, shouts of jubilation suddenly filled the air. "We've made it! We're in Europe!" they cried.

Samir's family, however, didn't join the celebration. While others ran away from the sea, Samir and his family couldn't take their eyes off it. Tears streamed down his mother's face as she now faced the prospect of the journey ahead, of life ahead, apart from her husband.

"What do we do, Mommy?" Samir and Amira asked. Samir's mom was silent, not knowing what to say, when an aid worker suddenly came running over to them. She had heard the story of what Samir's father had done, and she told them that there were Greek coast guard boats patrolling these waters. There was a chance, she said, they could find him and pick him up. Samir's family now found themselves clinging to this sliver of hope as they came up the shore and wrapped themselves in warm blankets. And there they waited for an hour, then two, until a Greek coast guard ship radioed in, "The man who jumped from the rubber boat has been rescued." Not long thereafter, they brought him ashore, and Samir's family's celebration could begin.

But the journey was not over. A forty-mile walk led them to a processing center, where they would wait in line—for papers, food, water, clothing, *everything*. It didn't take long to feel more like cattle than people. But the refugee camp here was a short-term stay, and their goal was to get to the border of Macedonia as soon as possible. There, they heard, was the easiest access en route to Germany, the place where most of these refugees wanted to end up.

After a night in the camp, Samir's dad wanted them to waste no time, so the journey continued. They caught a bus to a nearby city, about fifty miles south of the Macedonian border. When they arrived in that city, Samir's dad looked at his wife, kids, and mother and realized they didn't have the energy for a fifty-mile walk. So he found a taxi driver who agreed to take them to the border for the equivalent of about $300—nearly all of the family's remaining money. Hesitantly, Samir's dad gave the driver the $300, and the family climbed into the taxi.

Twenty minutes later, though, the driver abruptly stopped and told them to get out of the car. Samir's dad protested. "I paid you to take us to the border," he said. "I gave you the money you asked to take us to the border."

The taxi driver wouldn't listen. "I'm not taking you any farther," he said. "I've taken you as far as you have paid me to take you. I will only take you farther if you pay me more."

Samir's dad responded, "I can't pay you more. I don't have any more to pay you."

The driver responded, "Then you will have to get out."

So they did. And for the next two days, they trudged along, using the last pennies they had to buy small sips of water and snacks for food. They arrived at the Macedonian border, exhausted and dehydrated. This was their destination. The destination everyone had said was *the place* where passage into inner Europe became a reality. But nothing could have prepared them for what they found when they arrived.

The Macedonian border had just been closed a couple of days before. Passage into inner Europe was now blocked, and this refugee camp made for two thousand people was now filled with fifteen thousand people. All of the established tents were taken, and the only option for shelter was a thin, small tent (made for two or three people) out in the field. That tent was barely enough for the six of them to sit in, much less lie down in. By now, it was getting close to dark, so Samir went with his dad to stand in line for food, water, and blankets, and his mom, sisters, and grandmother waited in the tent. The temperature was dropping, and it would be a cold night.

As they stood in separate lines, the dad in one and the eight-year-old in the other, the rain began to fall. Freezing rain. Relentless rain. Rain that wouldn't stop all night.

Two hours later, with a couple of blankets and a portion of food, Samir and his dad returned to the tent and unzipped it, only to discover their entire family shivering wet as water crept into the tent from above and below them. Quickly Samir and his dad crammed in and zipped the tent closed. They passed out the blankets to the girls; Samir and his dad would go without. Similarly, they distributed the food and water. It didn't take long for the meager meal to be finished. They were all exhausted, so they did their best to situate themselves to sleep, the adults propped up while the kids lay down upon them. They sat and lay there in the relative silence of the tent, with cold water seeping in among them and freezing rain pelting around them, and that's when it happened.

They broke.

They all broke.

It started when Raja, the sweet, now-seven-month-old baby girl whose name means "hope," began coughing in the cold. When Samir's dad heard the sound of his baby girl getting sick, he could no longer hold it in anymore. As she coughed, he began to cry. Earlier, while he was waiting in line for food and water, he had heard other men talking about a new government plan to export Syrian refugees from Greece back to Turkey. Up until this point, every step of the way, he had held out hope for his family in the future. But now, crammed into this cold tent with no money to his name and no hope for a better tomorrow, he couldn't hold back his tears.

He wept.

His wife, cuddled up next to him, followed in turn, and then his mom, and then Amira and finally Samir. They all cried, uncontrollably, as Samir's dad said over and over again to his family, "I'm sorry. I'm sorry. I'm so sorry!" They cried that night until they were weary from their weeping, and without another word spoken, they all fell asleep, a family with no hope for anything the morning might hold.

MILLIONS OF SAMIRS

I must tell you that this is not just one true story. It is a combination of different true accounts from different people, some of whom I have met and others whom I haven't. I had read and heard such stories, but everything changed when I walked late at night along the Macedonian border through a sea of tents swimming in mud as freezing rain fell on them. I vividly remember looking at the lines of men and women standing and listening to the sounds of their children crying and their babies coughing as they struggled for survival in a semblance of hell on earth.

These are not isolated stories. These are stories that are repeated over and over and over again among millions of people. The scope of the current refugee crisis is truly unprecedented, encompassing more than sixty million people. Never before in history have so many men, women, and children around the world been displaced, put in danger, or forced from their homes. In Syria alone, eleven million people—half the population—have been either displaced or killed.

I mention numbers like this simply to show the sheer enormity of the needs in the world, for I believe that most people in the churches across our culture are paying little, if any, attention to this. Or if we are paying attention to refugees, we are doing so through the lens of political punditry and partisan debates regarding whether we should allow a relative few of them into our country. It is a sure sign of American self-centeredness that we would take the suffering of millions of people and turn it into an issue that is all about us.

My aim in this chapter is not to propose a particular political position for my country, but instead to help us see as the church that the way so many of us think and talk about refugees today often springs from a foundation of fear, not of faith. Our opinions, conversations, and discussions so often seem to flow from a view of the world that is far more American than it is biblical, and far more concerned with the preservation of our country than it is the accomplishment of the great commission. Needless to say, this needs to change.

SOVEREIGNTY OVER SUFFERING

So how are we to think about this refugee crisis in light of the gospel?

Our starting point is with the sovereignty of God. The Bible is clear that God is sovereign (in control) over everything in the world. He is sovereign over all nature. The wind blows at his bidding, and the light of the sun shines according to his command. The stars in the sky appear because God brings them out "one by one, and calls them each by name. Because of his great power and mighty strength, not one of them is missing" (Isaiah 40:26, NIV). There is not a speck of dust on the planet that exists apart from the sovereignty of God.

God is also sovereign over all nations. The Bible says that God charts the course of countries and holds the rulers of the earth in the palm of his hand. This is good news that we must always remember, for the president of Syria is not sovereign over all, and neither are the leaders of Russia, North Korea, or the United States. God reigns and rules over all of them.

God's absolute sovereignty extends even over suffering in the world. We remember the book of Job, where God is called "the Almighty" thirty-one times, and the entire story of Job's life is told in such a way that it is clear that God is sovereign over everything and Satan is sovereign over nothing. In Job 1, the Accuser appears before God with limited ability. He must be allowed by God to afflict. Amid all the mystery that shrouds this scene, one conclusion is clear: the power of Satan is limited by the prerogative of God. Satan cannot do anything apart from divine permission. Satan is on a leash, and God holds the reins.

Ultimately, God is sovereign over life and death. If God wills, we live, James 4:15 says. Job says rightly, "The LORD gave, and the LORD has taken away" (Job 1:21). Job later asks his wife,

"Shall we receive good from God, and shall we not receive evil?" (Job 2:10). Then, in the same verse, the Bible tells us, "In all this Job did not sin with his lips."

So then, in view of suffering in the world like we are considering with refugees and a number of other issues in this book, we must be careful in our lives not to sin with our lips, or even with our thoughts. Entire theologies of suffering have developed that claim that God is doing the best he can under the circumstances, but ultimately he doesn't have control over evil and sorrow in the world. But we need to remember that amid suffering in this world, we would be leaving the Bible behind if we concluded that God is not ultimately in control. Moreover, it will not bring much comfort practically for us to consider that Satan is in control instead of God. If the power of God is limited, then how can we be confident in any promises he has made?

Obviously, there is mystery in Scripture (and debate among Bible-believing Christians) over how God's sovereignty intertwines with man's responsibility, particularly in evil and suffering. Yet the Bible is crystal clear on this truth: God is in control, and Satan is controlled. God is sovereign, and Satan is subordinate. The Bible does not present some sort of Star Wars dualism in which good and evil are equal forces warring against each other. The Bible doesn't show this kind of dualism; instead, we see domination.

It's all over the Bible. When Job is afflicted, God is in control. When Joseph is sold into slavery, God is in control. When evil kings act in Israel's history, God is still in control. When religious leaders and Roman officials sentence Jesus to death and crucify him on a cross, God is in control of it all. When Christians are preaching the gospel to the nations and being killed in the process, God is in control. When we get to the end of the Bible and we see the cosmic battle for the souls of men and women throughout history, God will be in control.

God is in control, and Satan is subordinate to him in every page of the Bible and on every page of history, including the refugee crisis that currently surrounds us. According to Acts 17:26-27, God determines the periods and boundaries of all the peoples of the earth, and he leads and guides them so that they might seek and find him.

Again, this is all over the Bible. Across the Old Testament, God raises up groups of people and sends them here, disperses nations and scatters them there. At God's appointed time, he sends Israel to Egypt, and at God's appointed time, he brings Israel out of Egypt. God orchestrates the exile from Jerusalem as well as the return to Jerusalem. Even in the New Testament, God uses suffering like the stoning of Stephen in Acts 7 to scatter the church from Jerusalem to Judea and Samaria and eventually the ends of the earth.

Consequently, when we see the migration of people in the world due to a multitude of different reasons, we can be confident it is all ultimately occurring under the sovereign governance of God. Moreover, as Acts 17 makes clear, God is ultimately working in all of this, even the worst suffering, so that people might find him.

UNPRECEDENTED OPPORTUNITY

And people are indeed finding him.

Men, women, and children who have lived in countries where there has for decades (even centuries) been no access to the gospel now have access to the gospel as a result of the refugee crisis. Syrians, Afghans, Iranians, and Iraqis who have never heard the good news of God's love for them in Christ are hearing the gospel for the first time.

As I have gone to refugee camps and spent time with friends

who are serving in those camps, I have heard story after story of God's grace. One Syrian woman said to a friend of mine, "I'm tired of being tied to a religion that doesn't offer me hope; I want to be a new person." She, her husband, and their friend all placed their faith in Christ.

Two Kurdish brothers have had their entire family killed by militants in Iraq, including their parents, whom they witnessed being murdered right in front of their eyes. When these brothers heard the good news of God's love for them in the gospel, they immediately said, "We want to follow Jesus."

Another man was born in Palestine, but years ago he fled his home country to go to Syria in search of refuge. Now he has fled Syria, and he has been separated from his wife and children, not knowing how or if he can reunite with them. When he saw my friend distributing water at a refugee camp, he pulled my friend aside and asked, "Do you speak Arabic?" When my friend responded, "Yes," the man asked, "Can you please tell me how to become a Christian?"

Even as I have written these reports from my friends, I have received a text from another friend saying that eight new believers have just been baptized in one of the refugee camps. Indeed, unprecedented opportunities abound for the spread of the gospel among men, women, and children who now have access to the gospel for the first time.

In light of these opportunities, we in the church can't stand back and spend all our time debating whether a few refugees might come to our country. Instead, many of us need to step out and consider giving our time to take the gospel to them.

After all, the gospel is particularly good news for the refugee! The gospel reveals a God who actually identifies with the refugee. Jesus, God in the flesh, came as a baby boy, and the first story we have about him following his birth is his exodus to Egypt. Jesus himself was driven to a foreign country by a murderous king.

The gospel for the refugee is good news of a God who is not distant from us. He is not detached from the people we are and the pain we experience. Instead, this God is present with us. He is no stranger to suffering, and he is familiar with our pain. He has not left the outcast and the oppressed alone in a world of sin and suffering. He has come to us, and he has conquered for us. Jesus Christ, the Son of God, has severed the root of suffering—sin itself. He was falsely accused as a crucified criminal, dying an unjust death, but he rose from the dead and now is exalted as a sin-and-death-conquering King. For all who turn from their sin and put their trust in him, he will save and satisfy them forever.

This is the greatest news in all the world, and every person in the world—including every refugee—needs to hear it.

SELFLESS LOVE

Not only do refugees need to hear the gospel, but they need to see the fruit of the gospel in selfless love that marks our lives.

Remember the story Jesus tells of the Good Samaritan in Luke 10. When a Jewish man was in need, the Samaritan took him, cared for him, provided for him, and paid for everything he needed. Without question or hesitation, the Samaritan sacrificed much for this man despite their differences.

Have you ever done this for somebody? Have you ever seen someone in need and cared for that person in this way? Have you ever sacrificed for everything someone needed, without question or hesitation? I'm guessing you have. I'm guessing that pretty much every one of us has done that for someone, and that someone is ourselves. When you or I have not been well or have been in need, we have done whatever it takes—even gone over the top—to make sure that we have the care and provision we need.

That's the point of the story in Luke 10. Jesus' command in this passage is clear: "Love . . . your neighbor as yourself" (Luke 10:27). More specifically, through the story, Jesus is saying, "Love strangers—even your enemies—the way you love and care for yourself." So how should we love refugees in the world? According to Jesus, we should love them the way we love ourselves.

Obviously, most refugees live far away from most readers of this book. But that doesn't mean we can't look for ways to love them from a distance. We can start by praying for them, confident that the God who reigns sovereign over all people has ordained prayer as a means by which we can participate with him in the accomplishment of his purposes in the world. We must not underestimate prayer. We can be confident that as we pray for the refugee, we are participating in God's provision for the refugee. So whether they're riding on a raft in the middle of the Aegean Sea or sleeping on a street outside Macedonia's border, let's plead for God's provision in their lives and families, confident that the God who hears our cry will answer according to his compassion.

Then, let's look for opportunities to give and go to them. You can find information at CounterCultureBook.com concerning ministries that are working with refugees in various ways. Whether it's giving needed resources or going on a short-term trip to share the gospel, the possibility exists for you to personally be a part of loving the refugee as yourself.

Finally, let's look for opportunities to welcome them. As men, women, and children from other countries come to our culture and our cities and communities in search of rest and refuge, let's welcome them with open arms. Let's do what the Samaritan did, going out of our way to provide for their needs and, along the way, sharing with them the greatest news in the world.

After all, as we saw in the last chapter, every follower of Christ currently finds himself or herself in a foreign land. You and I are migrants here, and we're looking for a better country. So for the sake of more than sixty million Samirs in the world, let's take advantage of the opportunities we have to pray for, give and go to, and welcome even just one of them.

FIRST STEPS TO COUNTER CULTURE

Pray
Ask God to:
- Protect and provide for refugees in imminent physical danger.
- Give churches a burden to minister to the physical and spiritual needs of refugees, both in their own communities and among the nations.
- Direct the paths and prepare the hearts of refugees such that many might hear and embrace the gospel of Jesus Christ.

Participate
Prayerfully consider taking these steps:
- Meet with church leaders and other members to strategize about ministering to refugees in your community and among the nations.
- Stay informed about the world's refugee crisis and make it a priority as you pray for unreached peoples in the world.
- Give financial support to ministries and organizations that are already ministering to refugees.

Proclaim

Consider the following truths from Scripture:

- Luke 10:27: "You shall love the Lord your God with all your heart and with all your soul and with all your strength and with all your mind, and your neighbor as yourself."

- Acts 17:26-27: "[God] made from one man every nation of mankind to live on all the face of the earth, having determined allotted periods and the boundaries of their dwelling place, that they should seek God, and perhaps feel their way toward him and find him. Yet he is actually not far from each one of us."

- Proverbs 31:8-9: "Open your mouth for the mute, for the rights of all who are destitute. Open your mouth, judge righteously, defend the rights of the poor and needy."

For more (and more specific) suggestions,
visit CounterCultureBook.com/Topics/Refugees

CHRIST IN THE PUBLIC SQUARE: THE GOSPEL AND RELIGIOUS LIBERTY

Eerie.

That's the only word that comes to mind when I think about standing a hundred yards away from North Korean soldiers who were staring right at me with weapons in their hands.

I was in the demilitarized zone (known as the DMZ), a small strip of land that cuts the Korean peninsula in half, separating the North and the South. Approximately 150 miles long and 2.5 miles wide, it serves as a buffer between these two countries and the allies they represent. Ironically, it is the most heavily militarized border in the world.

I stood in what is called the Joint Security Area, the only part of the DMZ that allows North and South Korean forces to stand face-to-face with one another. Years ago, this small village was designated as the location where negotiations between the two countries would take place. In the center of that area is a small blue building where international meetings occur. I walked into the building, where I saw a conference table with a white line running down the middle of it. During official discussions, South Korean officials sit on one side of that line while North Korean officials sit opposite them.

What was most eerie for me, though, was not coming out of that building and looking across the border at these North Korean soldiers whose eyes were fixed on my every movement (along with the few others who were with me). Instead, what was most eerie was contemplating the condition of people, and particularly Christians, living behind those soldiers.

North Korea has a heinous human rights record. Food deprivation, forced labor, sexual violence, systematic torture, and public executions all characterize this communist country. Specifically, North Korea is known for putting people of any faith in prison camps called kwan-li-so, where some are eventually killed for their beliefs. For years, North Korea has been at the top of the World Watch List, a ranking of fifty countries that exposes the places where Christians are most persecuted in the world. If a North Korean is caught with a Bible or is suspected of having any contact with South Korean or Chinese Christians, he or she may be shot. North Korean police are trained to travel to China, posing as refugees and infiltrating churches there to discover contacts in the North Korean church. They create mock prayer meetings to catch and eventually murder North Korean Christians.

Needless to say, freedom of religion for North Koreans is nonexistent. And though the conditions may not be as severe, the same can be said for men and women in many other nations. The denial of this freedom affects people of different faiths, yet followers of Christ are the most widely persecuted religious group in the world. According to the US Department of State, Christians face persecution of some kind in more than sixty different countries today.[1]

So how does the gospel compel us to live in a world where many of our brothers and sisters are suffering for their faith in Christ? And does this same gospel compel us to act on behalf of people who suffer for other faiths, whether they are Jews, Muslims, Hindus, Buddhists, animists, or atheists? The more we consider these questions, the more we realize that religious liberty is a rare commodity in the world, and one which is increasingly uncommon in our own culture.

THE FIRST FREEDOM

Yet again, questions like these lead us back to the beginning of the Bible, where God creates man in his image with a unique capacity to know him and an innate desire to seek him. Consequently, one of the fundamental human freedoms—if not the most fundamental human freedom—is the privilege of each person to explore truth about the divine and to live in light of his or her determinations. It is an essential part of the human experience to ask and answer questions like *Where did I come from?*, *Why am I here?*, and *How should I live my life?* and then to act in accordance with the conclusions.

Now obviously, different people will make different determinations regarding what to believe, whom to worship, and how to live. This is a choice God has offered to all people, for from the beginning God has given men and women the freedom to decide whether to worship him. Adam and Eve were not forced into faith or coerced into obedience when they dwelled with God in the Garden. Instead, part of their humanness was the ability (and opportunity) to act of their own will, a God-given privilege that eventually resulted in their decision to disobey him. But it was *their* decision, for even in his divine sovereignty, God did not (and does not) remove human responsibility.

This reality becomes all the more clear in the rest of Scripture, specifically in the life and ministry of Jesus. Never do we see Jesus forcing faith on people. Instead, he teaches doctrine, tells stories, and invites people to receive or reject him. In response, people listen to him, reason with him, argue with him, disagree with him, and often abandon him (ultimately to the cross). At one point, Jesus rebukes his disciples for their desire to call down condemnation from heaven upon Samaritans who reject him (see Luke 9:51-56). Then, when he sends them out in the following chapter, he encourages them to respect people's freedom to reject them (see Luke 10:5-11). We see, then, that regardless of one's perspective on the doctrines of election and free will, there is no question that the language of the Bible indicates the importance of willful choice and personal invitation. In the end, the gospel message is fundamentally invitation, not coercion. "Behold, I stand at the door and knock," Jesus says at the close of Scripture. "If anyone hears my voice and opens the door, I will come in to him and eat with him, and he with me" (Revelation 3:20).

For this reason, those who understand and believe the gospel advocate the free exercise of faith. Journeying back to the fourth century, we hear Augustine, a church father, saying that when "force is applied, the will is not aroused. One can enter the Church unwillingly, one can approach the altar unwillingly, one can receive the sacrament unwillingly; no one can believe except willingly."[2] Similarly, fast-forwarding to the twenty-first century, we hear 4,000 church leaders from 198 countries gathered together in Cape Town, South Africa, saying, "Let us strive for the goal of religious freedom for all people. This requires advocacy before governments on behalf of Christians *and* people of other faiths who are persecuted."[3]

Such respect for religious freedom is not limited to Christians. One need not believe the gospel in order to recognize that faith must be free in order to be genuine. Authentic belief requires authentic choice. Human dignity necessitates personal discovery—the opportunity to search for truth apart from threats, to settle on faith apart from force, and to come to conclusions apart from coercion.

This is why the founders of our country called faith a fundamental human right—indeed, the very first human right in what we know as the Bill of Rights. Our nation's Declaration of Independence starts by saying, "We hold these truths to be self-evident, that all men are created equal, that they are endowed by their Creator with certain unalienable Rights, that among these are Life, Liberty and the pursuit of Happiness." It goes on to say, "To secure these rights, Governments are instituted among Men." In other words, the purpose of government is to protect the rights of its people—rights that are innate, obvious, and undeniable according to reason.

In order to ensure the protection of these rights, our nation's founders drafted the Bill of Rights, the first of which reads, "Congress shall make no law respecting an establishment of religion, or prohibiting the free exercise thereof." In putting this right first, our founders acknowledged that freedom of religion is the foundation for all other freedoms. After all, if government can mandate what you believe or deny you the opportunity to live according to your beliefs, then where will its reach end? What would keep it from dictating what you can read or write, what you can hear or say, or how you must live? Indeed, the founders concluded, if God himself does not violate the religious freedom of man, then surely government shouldn't either.

What our government calls this "right" is commonly known as the "freedom of worship," but this label can be somewhat misleading because the way it is often applied in our culture unnecessarily and unhelpfully limits the "free exercise" of religion to the private sphere. When people hear the term "freedom of worship," they often envision the freedom for men, women, and children to gather together in a church building, synagogue, mosque, or other place for corporate worship. This picture may also extend to the home, where families have the freedom to pray (or not pray) at mealtimes, before bed, or at other times during the day. But even so, all of this is private, a religious freedom limited to what happens when someone is alone or in a specific gathering of a physical or a faith family.

What this label fails to acknowledge is that those who gather for worship in private settings then scatter to live out their beliefs in the public square. As men, women, and children live, study, work, and play in every sector of society, they perform duties and make decisions in alignment with their consciences and in accordance with their convictions. This is part of the "free exercise" of religion: the freedom of worship not just in episodic gatherings but in everyday life. And it is such "free exercise" that is subtly yet significantly being attacked in American culture today.

AN ALARM

Imagine you are a follower of Christ who believes the Bible. Your driving desire is to love God, and flowing from this, you long to love others. You also happen to be a professional photographer. One day a woman in your community contacts you about her upcoming event. She says to you, "My female partner and I are celebrating our commitment to each other in a formal ceremony, and we would like you to photograph it." Immediately your mind starts racing. *What should I say?* you think to yourself. And you begin to process your personal convictions.

On one hand, you want to serve the community in which you live, including the people who make up that community. You've built a business bent on using your talents to bless people just like the woman who is making this request. Yet at the same time, your love for others is a subset of your love for God, and you believe he has designed marriage as the union of a man and a woman for the demonstration of his character and the display of his gospel in the world. Consequently, you have a hard time conceiving how you can participate in a celebration of something that you are convinced God condemns. You can't escape the thought that your participation would violate your conscience. And even more important, in your heart you can't avoid the conviction that such participation would dishonor God.

In speaking to this woman, then, you decide to politely decline. In so doing, you find yourself gratefully resting in the "free exercise" of religion that has been granted to you in our country—the "freedom of worship" not just in private, but also in public.

Imagine your surprise, then, when you discover that you are being sued for your decision. And imagine your further surprise when you learn that the government on which you were leaning for this "free exercise" of religion tells you that the law requires you to compromise your conviction in such a circumstance.

This is no imaginary scenario for Elaine Huguenin, co-owner of Elane Photography in Albuquerque, New Mexico. When Vanessa Willock asked Huguenin to photograph her commitment ceremony with another woman, Huguenin politely said that she does not photograph such ceremonies. Willock, despite finding another, cheaper photographer for her ceremony, filed a complaint with the New Mexico Civil Rights Commission, claiming that Elane Photography was guilty of discrimination. The court ruled in Willock's favor, and Elane Photography was ordered to pay a large penalty.

This case became all the more concerning when it eventually went before the New Mexico Supreme Court, which upheld the ruling against Elane Photography. In a unanimous verdict, the justices ruled that "when Elane Photography refused to photograph a same-sex commitment ceremony, it violated the NMHRA [New Mexico Human Rights Act] in the same way as if it had refused to photograph a wedding between people of different races."[4] Beyond the fundamental flaw that we have already noted in equating ethnic identity with sexual activity, the stated reasoning behind this ruling was frightening, to say the least.

In a concurring opinion to the court's ruling, Justice Richard Bosson wrote that Elaine Huguenin and her husband are "compelled by law to compromise the very religious beliefs that inspire their lives." He went on to say that "the Huguenins are free to think, to say, to believe, as they wish; they may pray to the God of their choice and follow those commandments in their personal lives wherever they lead. The Constitution protects the Huguenins in that respect and much more." However, the court went on to say, "in the smaller, more focused world of the marketplace, of commerce, of public accommodation, the Huguenins have to channel their conduct, not their beliefs, so as to leave space for other Americans who believe something different." This, the court said, is "the price of citizenship" in our country.[5]

When one reads this, one realizes how dangerous the distinction is between supposed "freedom of worship" in one's private life and the "free exercise" of religion in the public square. The highest court in the state of New Mexico has said that while Elaine Huguenin is free to exalt her God in the church she attends, she is not free to express her beliefs in the business she owns. In other words, she is free to practice her faith in private for a couple of hours at the start of the week, but she is forced to deny her faith in public for multiple hours every other day of the week. In the end, Elaine Huguenin is coerced to violate her conscience and dishonor her Creator as a citizen in her culture.

Elane Photography appealed to the Supreme Court of the United States, which declined to hear the case. Thankfully, however, the Supreme Court did hear a similar, significant case regarding Hobby Lobby and Conestoga Wood in which, by a 5–4 decision, they ruled that leaders of closely held corporations do indeed have freedom to apply their religious convictions in the way they lead their corporations (in this case, the court ruled that government cannot force such corporations to violate their religious beliefs by purchasing abortion-causing drugs).[6] Doubtless similar cases will be considered in the years to come, and the narrow vote in the Hobby Lobby case, combined with current trajectories in Supreme Court nominees, make it very likely that religious liberties for Christians are increasingly endangered in America.

So what are the principles undergirding the way we process circumstances like those that Elane Photography faced? This is a question not just for the Huguenins to ask, but for all people of any faith to ask in a culture that is rapidly redefining the "free exercise" of religion. A quick perusal of cultural trends indicates a plethora of potential situations we are likely to encounter. Increasing numbers of professions require state licenses (a nearly fivefold increase over the last sixty years), and oftentimes these licenses include conditions that clash with traditional religious beliefs. More and more, employers and employees, doctors and pharmacists, teachers and administrators, insurers and investors, and ministers and ministries face governmental mandates to provide goods and services that contradict their personal convictions. More and more, companies and corporations are establishing policies for employees that require them to violate their consciences when it comes to matters of faith. Continued efforts to quell the public profession and application of faith affect how followers of Christ (and those of other religions, for that matter) are allowed to speak, what they are allowed to wear, how they are allowed to organize, and what they are allowed to do in the communities where they live.

As soon as I write this, I want to say that my aim is not to be an alarmist. But on further reflection, maybe it is. Maybe an alarm does need to be sounded, and maybe all of us need to seriously consider how to counter a rapidly shifting religious culture with clear gospel conviction.

DIGNITY IN DISAGREEMENT

Once more, we must remember that we are not exclusively talking about freedom for Christians in our culture. The same right to religious liberty that should protect followers of Christ should also protect followers of Moses, Muhammad, Krishna, and the Buddha, as well as those who believe there is no god to follow in the first place. This is one of the reasons why years ago I joined prominent religious leaders, including some I strongly disagree with, in signing a document expressing convictions concerning religious liberty. The end of that document states:

> We will not . . . bend to any rule purporting to force us to
> bless immoral sexual partnerships, treat them as marriages
> or the equivalent, or refrain from proclaiming the truth, as
> we know it, about morality and immorality and marriage
> and the family. We will fully and ungrudgingly render to
> Caesar what is Caesar's. But under no circumstances will
> we render to Caesar what is God's.[7]

That last phrase alludes to Jesus' teaching that while we have certain obligations to our government (i.e., Caesar), our ultimate obligation is to our God (see Mark 12:13-17). He is the one who has put the freedom of conscience on the human heart, and that freedom applies universally. For this reason I gladly stand for religious liberty alongside people who do not believe the same gospel that I do. I don't believe I'll spend eternity with such people in heaven, but I am more than willing to go to jail for them on earth.[8]

The gospel compels me to say this, because the gospel begins with a God who gives men and women the freedom to pursue or deny him as they please. Unfortunately, Christian history is haunted by people who missed this mammoth foundation. Constantine's legalization of Christianity in the fourth century soon turned into governmental coercion to become a Christian. Tragically, church history in subsequent centuries contains other examples of shameful attempts to spread Christianity by force or military might. Even today, wars begin and battles are fought under the facade of Christian religion. Yet history, reason, and Scripture together shout the reality that none of this was, or is, right.

This is why a level of separation between church and state is so essential. This phrase—"separation of church and state"—though widely debated regarding its specific application, signifies the unique role of these two institutions in society and their interdependent relationship with one another. The church (read: religion) exists as an arena where individuals search the deepest questions of life and apply their answers consistently in the way they live. The state (read: government), in turn, exists to enable that quest, protecting men and women as they exercise this human privilege. The state exists neither for the establishment of religion nor for the elimination of religion but for the *freedom* of religion. In this relationship between church and state, the government fosters a marketplace of ideas where religious exploration and expression are open—where men and women of all faiths are able to reason together regarding how to flourish alongside one another.

But if we're not careful, this marketplace of ideas can subtly be minimized, and religious liberty can inevitably become limited. This is increasingly evident in contemporary culture, where the search for religious truth is often supplanted by the idolization of supposed tolerance. The cardinal sin of our culture is to be found intolerant, yet what we mean by intolerant is ironically, well, intolerant. Let me explain.

As soon as someone today says that homosexual activity is wrong or sinful, he or she is immediately called "intolerant." "Offensive," "bigoted," or "hateful," as we've seen, but we'll stick with "intolerant" for now. This supposed intolerance is often based upon that person's belief in the Bible. Simply because that belief is different from others' beliefs, it receives the "intolerance" label.

But the label is strangely self-defeating. Isn't the person who assigns the "intolerance" label actually displaying a similar intolerance of that other person's belief? In the process of calling another person "intolerant," it sure seems that the name-caller is fairly intolerant him- or herself. This is common across our culture. It's as if Americans are tired of intolerant people, and we're not going to tolerate them anymore. We find ourselves in the awkward position of being intolerant of intolerant people, which means we cannot tolerate ourselves.

Apparently, our view of tolerance is a bit skewed. After all, the very notion of tolerance necessitates disagreement. Think about it. I don't tolerate you if you believe exactly what I believe. If you believe that baseball is the greatest sport ever invented, I don't tolerate you. I wholeheartedly agree with you, and I will gladly sit behind home plate with you, eating a hot dog and enjoying a game with you any day! It's only if you believe that baseball is boring and soccer is much more exciting that I will find myself having to tolerate you. In that case, I will ardently disagree with you, and I will invariably enlighten you as to all the reasons why you're wrong. But in the end, I will gladly sit in the stands with you as we watch guys run around kicking a ball on a field together.

Tolerance implies disagreement. I have to disagree with you in order to tolerate you. Sports superiority is obviously a light example, but on the deepest religious questions about life, we are bound to experience similar disagreements, aren't we? And when we come to those disagreements, it would not only be wise but helpful for us to not immediately resort to calling one another intolerant (or bigoted or hateful, for that matter). Instead, it would be wise and helpful for us to patiently consider where each of us is coming from and why we have arrived at our respective conclusions. Based upon these considerations, we can then be free to contemplate how to treat one another with the greatest dignity in view of our differences.

Further confusion about intolerance can also be clarified when we realize that tolerance applies to people and beliefs in distinct ways. On one hand, toleration of people requires that we treat one another with equal value, honoring each person's fundamental human freedom to express private faith in public forums. On the other hand, toleration of beliefs does not require that we accept every idea as equally valid, as if a belief is true, right, or good simply because someone expresses it. In this way, tolerance of a person's value does not mean I must accept that person's views.

For example, I have Muslim friends whom I respect deeply, yet I disagree with them passionately. I believe Jesus is the Son of God; they don't. They believe Muhammad was a prophet sent from God; I disagree. I believe Jesus died on a cross and rose from the grave; they don't. They believe they will go to heaven when they die; I disagree.

These are major points of disagreement, and they shouldn't be minimized. The tendency in our relativistic approach to religious truth is to say, "Hey, as long as someone believes something, that makes it right." But such thinking simply can't apply to any of the issues I mentioned above. Either Jesus is or isn't the Son of God. He can't be the Son of God and not be the Son of God at the same time. Similarly, either Muhammad was a prophet sent from God or he wasn't. Either Jesus died on the cross and rose from the grave or he didn't. Muslims will either go to heaven when they die or they won't.

These are serious questions (I would say *eternally* serious questions), and the purpose of religious freedom is to provide an atmosphere in which these questions can be explored. Such an atmosphere must be marked by the ability to articulate vigorous disagreement about beliefs while continuing to assign value and dignity to the people with whom we disagree. It is this atmosphere that is increasingly compromised in our culture today. I lament the many ways that Christians express differences in belief devoid of respect for the people with whom we speak. Likewise, I lament the many ways that Christians are labeled intolerant, narrow-minded, and outdated whenever they express biblical beliefs that have persisted throughout centuries.

Nowhere are these twin realities more clear than in the current debate over marriage. When we think back to chapter 6, we realize that many people disagree about the truths we discussed there. This does not mean, however, that Christians should view those who advocate the redefinition of marriage as arch-enemies who are conspiring to take over the culture. Instead, they are men and women seeking a way that seems right to them. Consequently, there are wonderful ways to express disagreement with them while also conveying clear love and admiration for them.

At the same time, we saw how the Supreme Court's decision on the definition of marriage not only undercut "an aspect of marriage that [has] been unquestioned in our society for most of its existence," but seemed to assert rather strongly that opposition to same-sex marriage is rooted in the hatred of homosexuals. Supporters of traditional marriage, according to Justice Scalia's dissenting opinion, were painted as "bigots" and "enemies of the human race." Such supporters were described as men and women who seek "to 'demean,' to 'impose inequality,' to 'impose . . . a stigma,' to deny people 'equal dignity,' to brand gay people as 'unworthy,' and to 'humiliat[e]' their children."[9] Such characterizations are not just dangerously unhelpful. They are simply untrue.

The ramifications for religious liberty in all of this are great. These are weighty matters to discuss, ranging from the foundations of the family to life after death. Such matters demand the ability to ask questions and explore answers in an atmosphere of dignity and respect, passionate discussion and inevitable disagreement. Furthermore, such matters demand the opportunity for all of us as citizens to arrange our lives according to what we believe as we consider how to listen to, learn from, and live alongside one another not in spite of, but in light of our differences. None of this is simple in a culture like ours. But all of this is critical for a culture like ours.

A GLOBAL PERSPECTIVE

And for cultures around the world. Scores of men and women from many faiths, including many of our brothers and sisters in Christ, live today without the kind of liberty we are considering. Millions upon millions of people are presently denied the opportunity to even explore truth that will affect their lives on earth and for eternity.

Government coercion is one of the greatest restrictors of religious liberty around the globe. This is most clear in communist and Islamist states, where countries adopt an official religion (or nonreligion) and require their citizens to conform to corresponding beliefs. In such situations, the state and the church (or antichurch) are virtually synonymous. Religious (or nonreligious) teachings become the law of the land, and men and women are penalized (if not expelled or executed) for disobedience to them.

Societal pressure follows closely on the heels of governmental regulation as family, friends, religious fanatics, community leaders, and criminal mobs intimidate, threaten, harm, or kill men, women, and children who profess certain faith. Such pressure accounts for much Christian persecution today. Syrian rebels disproportionately target Syrian Christians, abusing, raping, murdering, and beheading them. During one month alone in Egypt in 2013, thirty-eight churches were destroyed, twenty-three others were vandalized, fifty-eight homes were burned, eighty-five shops were looted, seven Christians were kidnapped, and six Christians were killed. The following month witnessed the worst attack on Christians in Pakistan's history as suicide bombers exploded shrapnel-laden vests outside All Saints' Church in Peshawar, murdering eighty-one church members and wounding more than one hundred.[10] All of these stories represent persecution of Christians by people outside the official governments of these countries.

On the whole, an average of one hundred Christians around the world are killed every month for their faith in Christ (and some estimates have this number much higher[11]). Literally countless others are persecuted through abuse, beatings, imprisonment, torture, and deprivation of food, water, and shelter.

Each occurrence of religious oppression represents an individual story of faith tested amid fire and trial. But these are not merely stories on a page for me. These are my friends. And I praise God for how they have endured the fire faithfully.

I think of Bullen and Andrew, friends of mine in central Africa whose entire lives have been lived in the midst of war. As a child, Bullen hid in a corner of his house while the rest of his family was kidnapped by militant Muslims from the north. Now twenty years old, he has no idea where his dad, mom, or sisters live, or if they are even alive. Andrew, who is the same age as Bullen, described how helicopter gunships would swoop down over his village, sending everyone scattering. Each of the kids, Andrew told me, had designated holes in the ground that they would run to and hide in whenever attacks came. In their short lives, they have seen churches bombed and Christian wives raped while their husbands were murdered. But you wouldn't know any of this by looking at Bullen and Andrew. Their dark, slender faces contain bright, contagious smiles as they talk about God's faithfulness to preserve their faith in spite of what they've witnessed. Their favorite saying is "God is greater."

I think about Ayan, a precious woman I know in the horn of Africa from a people who pride themselves on being 100 percent Muslim. To belong to Ayan's tribe is to be a Muslim. Members of her tribe find their personal identity, familial honor, relational standing, and social status exclusively in Islam. Consequently, when Ayan met a Christian and began to contemplate Christianity, she knew the cost of even considering conversion was high. "If my family or the people in my village found out that I was becoming a Christian, they would slit my throat without question or hesitation," Ayan told me. In the end, Ayan decided that Christ was worth it. Her faith in Christ forced her to flee her family and to isolate herself from her friends. Now

Ayan is spending her life for the spread of the gospel among her people in a different region. "I love my people," she said, "and I want to do whatever I can to give them a chance to know who Jesus is and how much he loves them."

I think about Fatima and Yaseen in the Middle East. Fatima is a woman I mentioned in chapter 8 who came to faith in Christ upon hearing the gospel from a friend of hers in another country. But everyone else in Fatima's family is Muslim, and Fatima struggles daily with how to live out her faith in a family that will disown her (or worse) as soon as they find out. Yaseen is a pastor in a community close to Fatima. As I sat in his house, he told me the story of how just one year prior, that very house had been bombed by a rebel group intent on removing any semblance of Christianity from his country. Of course, Yaseen could have immediately moved his family (and many would maintain he should have done so), yet Yaseen stayed, and he has seen more people in the community come to know Christ as a result (at great cost to them as well).

I think about a group of seminary students in Southeast Asia I had the opportunity to address at their graduation. Living in the country with the largest Muslim population in the world, they face both governmental pressure and societal persecution in varying degrees. Before they graduate from this seminary, though, these students are required to plant a church in a Muslim community of at least thirty new baptized believers. As these graduates walked across the stage to receive their degrees, I was captivated by the humble yet confident look on each of their faces. Every one of them had fulfilled the church planting requirement. The most solemn part of the day was a moment of silence for two of their classmates who were killed at the hands of Muslim persecutors.

I think of Jian and Lin, a couple in East Asia also previously mentioned. Jian and Lin lead a house church network in East Asia, training pastors and Christians in underground locations where, if they are caught, the state government could take their land, their jobs, their families, or their lives. Lin is a teacher on a university campus where it is illegal to spread the gospel. She meets in secret with college students to talk about the claims of Christ, though she could lose her livelihood for doing so. Jian is a doctor who left his successful health clinic to provide impoverished villages with medical care, using that as a platform for conducting house church meetings in secret. I have traveled with Jian to different parts of his country, spending time with other house church leaders. Every time we have gone, I have been reminded that if we were caught, I would be deported back to my comfortable home in the United States. Jian, however, would be detained in the confines of a prison in his country and could lose his life. Yet he presses on, loving and leading these churches in spite of constant risk.

I think of Sahil in South Asia. He and his wife both grew up in Muslim homes. She came to Christ first, and then she introduced Sahil to Christ. As soon as their families discovered they had become Christians, Sahil and his wife were forced to flee their community. In the years that followed, they grew in Christ and in their desire to see their family know Christ. Slowly they renewed contact with their family members. Slowly their family members began to respond. They eventually welcomed Sahil and his wife back to their community, and from all appearances things were going well, until one day Sahil dropped off his wife for a meal with her family while he went to be with his family. His wife sat down at the table with her family and began to drink and eat. Within moments she was dead. Her own parents had poisoned her. When I met Sahil, I met a man who had lost his wife, but he had not lost his faith. He now works as a church planter in his country.

I think of Norbu and Sunita, a couple who lived in a Tibetan Buddhist village. When they first heard the gospel, it was quickly followed up with a threat from their village leaders. "If you become Christians," they told Norbu and Sunita, "you will no longer be able to get water from the tap in our village." This was obviously a severe threat, for the tap is literally a source of life for those who live in this community. Yet Norbu and Sunita continued to contemplate conversion, which led those same village leaders to increase their intimidation. "If you become Christians," they said, "this community will not protect you." Despite such threats, Norbu and Sunita came to the conclusion that Christ is Lord, and they became his followers. Two weeks later, Norbu and Sunita were dead. The official word was that rocks from an avalanche had killed them. The unofficial truth, though, was that Norbu and Sunita had been stoned.

When I think about my friends, the faith described in Hebrews 11 immediately comes to my mind. These friends remind me of those who "were tortured and refused to be released, so that they might gain a better resurrection. Some faced jeers and flogging, while still others were chained and put in prison. They were stoned; they were sawed in two; they were put to death by the sword. They went about in sheepskins and goatskins, destitute, persecuted and mistreated—the world was not worthy of them" (Hebrews 11:35-38, NIV).

PROCLAIMING CHRIST

These stories are not surprising when you consider the words of Christ in the Gospels. "Blessed are those who are persecuted for righteousness' sake, for theirs is the kingdom of heaven," Jesus told his disciples. "Blessed are you when others revile you and persecute you and utter all kinds of evil against you falsely on my account. Rejoice and be glad, for your reward is great in heaven" (Matthew 5:10-12). On a later occasion, when he sent these disciples out like "sheep in the midst of wolves," he promised them that persecution would come. "Beware of men, for they will deliver you over to courts and flog you in their synagogues, and you will be dragged before governors and kings for my sake, to bear witness before them." He concludes, "You will be hated . . . for my name's sake. But the one who endures to the end will be saved" (Matthew 10:16-18, 22). Even a cursory reading of Gospel passages like these reveals that the more we become like Jesus in this world, the more we will experience what he experienced. Just as it was costly for him to counter culture, it will be costly for us to do the same.

And think about why persecution like this happens. It is not because Christians in other countries have secret faith that they keep to themselves. As long as a Christian is quiet about his or her faith in Christ, not saying anything to anyone about Christ, but praying and practicing faith in privacy, then that Christian faces far less risk of persecution. It is only when a Christian is public about his or her faith, applying faith in the public square and even proclaiming Christ, that persecution will inevitably occur. In other words, as long as our brothers and sisters around the world sit back and accommodate the culture around them, they can avoid suffering. It's only when they stand up and counter the culture around them with the gospel of Jesus Christ that they will experience suffering.

So this is the quandary that Christians around the world face when surrounded by governmental and societal pressure against their faith. On one hand, if they stay quiet, they can remain safe. But they know that in so doing, they will violate their consciences and disobey the commands Christ has given them to share grace and gospel truth with the people around them. However, if they do speak up, and if they do put their faith into practice in the public square, persecution is certain to come. I praise God for the Christian men and women around the world who have decided to proclaim Christ with their lips and in their lives, and as a result, while you read this book, they are experiencing pressure, suffering in prison, and enduring persecution.

Surrounded by this global reality, and driven by our love for God, we must act. We must pray and work for our persecuted brothers and sisters around the world. When one part of the body suffers, the whole body suffers (see 1 Corinthians 12). In a land of religious liberty, we have a biblical responsibility to stand up and speak out on their behalf.

Moreover, in a country where even our own religious liberty is increasingly limited, our suffering brothers and sisters beckon us not to let the cost of following Christ in our culture silence our faith. May we not sit back and accommodate our culture in relative comfort while they stand up and counter their culture at great cost. May we realize with them that privatized Christianity is no Christianity at all, for it is practically impossible to know Christ and not proclaim Christ—to believe his Word when we read it in our homes or churches and not obey it in our communities and cities. And may we remember with the great cloud of witnesses that has gone before us that while our citizenship belongs to a government, our souls belong to God.

FIRST STEPS TO COUNTER CULTURE

Pray

Ask God to:

- Prepare Christians in our own culture to respond boldly and humbly to increased governmental and cultural opposition.

- Work in the lives of rulers in our country and around the world so that there is more freedom given to live and speak according to the truth of the gospel.
- Strengthen persecuted believers around the world to persevere in faith and to continue to bear witness to Christ, regardless of the consequences.

Participate

Prayerfully consider taking these steps:

- Use your religious freedom to openly share the gospel with one person this week. Then set a goal to do the same in the weeks that follow.
- Support and/or get involved with a ministry that speaks on behalf of believers who live in persecuted contexts.
- Consider how you or someone you know might get involved on the issue of religious liberty, either legally or politically.

Proclaim

Consider the following truths from Scripture:

- Matthew 5:11-12: "Blessed are you when others revile you and persecute you and utter all kinds of evil against you falsely on my account. Rejoice and be glad, for your reward is great in heaven."
- Proverbs 21:1: "The king's heart is a stream of water in the hand of the LORD; he turns it wherever he will."
- 1 Peter 2:23: "When [Christ] was reviled, he did not revile in return; when he suffered, he did not threaten, but continued entrusting himself to him who judges justly."

For more (and more specific) suggestions,
visit CounterCultureBook.com/Topics/Religious-Liberty

LET'S RISK IT ALL

As I close this book, my heart is a wreck.

In the pages that have preceded this one, I have sought to share deep burdens that weigh heavy on my heart as I look at the culture around me. I don't think I'm alone in these burdens, for I know many followers of Christ who possess similar passions regarding the same realities. The oppression of the poor, the abortion of children, the neglect of orphans and widows, the trafficking of slaves, the decline of marriage, confusion about sexuality, the need for ethnic equality, the crisis of refugees, and the importance of religious liberty are all mammoth issues in our lives, families, churches, and culture. My hope is that if you didn't feel a burden for these things before you started reading this book, then you do now.

Yet I don't want these burdens on my heart to terminate with words on a page. I want these realities to transform the way I live.

I don't want to join the chorus of men, women, preachers, and prognosticators who are content to wring their hands in pious concern over the plight of our culture while they sit back in practical silence and do little to nothing about it. Nor do I want to apply the gospel inconsistently, keeping silent on those issues that are most costly to speak out on. Ultimately, I don't want to retreat into isolation from Christ or the culture and in doing so to waste the opportunities God has given me to follow Christ faithfully in the culture where God has placed me.

I'm guessing you don't want to waste your life in your culture either.

So I'm compelled to ask us three questions as this book closes. These questions are based upon a short biblical account of three men who one day found themselves face-to-face with Jesus on a road in their community, and they all point to the inevitable risk of following Christ in an anti-Christian age. Here's how the story goes:

> As they were going along the road, someone said to him, "I will follow you wherever you go." And Jesus said to him, "Foxes have holes, and birds of the air have nests, but the Son of Man has nowhere to lay his head." To another he said, "Follow me." But he said, "Lord, let me first go and bury my father." And Jesus said to him, "Leave the dead to bury their own dead. But as for you, go and proclaim the kingdom of God." Yet another said, "I will follow you, Lord, but let me first say farewell to those at my home." Jesus said to him, "No one who puts his hand to the plow and looks back is fit for the kingdom of God." LUKE 9:57-62

These three men were potential followers of Jesus, but from all we can tell in this text, Jesus talked them out of following him. The reason this passage comes to mind at the close of this book is because this is essentially the decision you and I are considering at this moment in our culture. Are we going to follow Jesus? Not, are we going to bow our heads, say a prayer, read the Bible, go to church, and give a tithe while we get on with the rest of our lives? But, are we going to follow Jesus with all our lives, no matter where he leads us to go or what the cost may be for us, our families, and our churches? In other words, are we going to take the risk of countercultural living?

In order to answer that central question, I'm compelled to ask these three corresponding questions: Are we going to choose comfort or the cross? Are we going to settle for maintenance or sacrifice for mission? And finally, will our lives be marked by indecisive minds or undivided hearts?

ARE WE GOING TO CHOOSE COMFORT OR THE CROSS?

The first man in the story eagerly says to Jesus, "I will follow you wherever you go." We know from other biblical accounts that this man was a teacher of the law, and it was customary for men like him to attach themselves to another teacher in order to promote their own status in society. By this time, Jesus was pretty popular with the people around him, so he seemed like a good candidate for this man's cultural promotion.

Jesus replies, "The Son of Man has nowhere to lay his head." In other words, if this man follows Jesus, he can expect homelessness to come. Christ makes clear that Christianity is not a path to more comforts, higher status, or greater ease in this world. The road Jesus walks is not paved with the prospect of self-advancement. Instead, it starts with a demand for self-denial. Jesus outright tells other disciples earlier in this same chapter, "If anyone would come after me, let him deny himself and take up his cross daily and follow me" (Luke 9:23). Clearly, choosing the cross over comfort is a requirement for following Christ.

This, I am convinced, is a needed word for every Christian (and prospective Christian) in our culture today. Gone are the days when it was socially beneficial to be in church at the beginning of the week. Gone are the days when it was publicly acceptable to follow Christ every other day of the week. Here are the days when holding fast to the gospel, actually believing the Bible, and putting it into practice will mean risking your reputation, sacrificing your social status, disagreeing with your closest family and friends, jeopardizing your economic security and earthly stability, giving away your possessions, leaving behind the accolades of the world, and (depending on where and how God leads you) potentially losing your life.

Think about it. It is not possible to love the poor and live in unabated luxury. It is not possible to care for the orphan and the widow without major implications for the makeup of your family. It is not possible to confess gospel convictions about marriage and sexuality without being criticized, passed over for a promotion at your workplace, or maybe even fired altogether. It is not possible to profess gospel truth to all and remain popular among all.

Jesus promised this. "'A servant is not greater than his master,'" he said. "If they persecuted me, they will also persecute you" (John 15:20). When you ask how the world responded to Jesus, the answer you come to is a cruel, bloody cross. It would be utter foolishness, then, for followers of this same Christ in this same world to believe that their fate will be any different. To be certain, most Christians won't literally be crucified, and to be clear, no Christian should intentionally pursue persecution. We don't ask for a cultural fight, but we do anticipate that the more we ground our lives, families, and churches in God's Word, the more we will find ourselves countering the culture in which we live and the harder it will become for us as a result.

What this practically means for our churches is yet to be perceived, but of this much I am convinced: the more serious our churches become about engaging our culture with the gospel, the more steadfastly we will need to hold on to biblical truths and the more sacrificially we will need to let go of personal preferences. Regarding biblical truths, church members and their pastors are daily surrounded by dazzling temptations to cave in to the changing tides of cultural opinion. We constantly see and hear prominent "Christian" leaders leaving behind timeless biblical truth in the name of love for their neighbor and tolerance in the culture. Yet how is it loving to lie to our neighbors, twisting truth to fit their (and our) liking, and ultimately leading them (and us) further from God? And don't we see that authentic tolerance doesn't mask truth but magnifies it, showing us how to love and serve one another in view of our differences? May God give us grace not to stand proudly in judgment of his Word while we gradually capitulate to the ways of this world.

Moreover, may these biblical truths take their rightful place over and above our personal preferences. When we observe our churches today, do they look like groups of people who gather with one another as they give their lives to spreading the gospel among unreached people, impoverished communities, abandoned orphans, lonely widows, dying babies, sex slaves, and suffering brothers and sisters around the world? Sadly, I don't believe that's the picture we portray. Instead, we spend the majority of our time sitting as spectators in services that cater to our comforts. Even in our giving to the church, we spend the majority of our money on places for us to meet, professionals to do the ministry, and programs designed around us and our kids. What in the world are we doing? Or better put, what in the *Word* are we doing? We have filled even the most Bible-believing churches with so much that is not in the Bible. I can't help but wonder what might happen if we put aside our personal preferences, let go of our extrabiblical (and in some cases unbiblical) traditions, laid down our cultural comforts, and organized ourselves solely and sacrificially around God's Word and gospel mission.

Are we going to choose comfort, or are we going to choose the cross?

That leads to the second question.

ARE WE GOING TO SETTLE FOR MAINTENANCE OR SACRIFICE FOR MISSION?

Jesus initiates the conversation with the second man in Luke 9. "Follow me," he says.

The man responds, "Lord, let me first go and bury my father." All he wants to do is bury his dad, something he not only wants to do but is also expected to do. To not give his father a proper funeral is to shame him.

Yet Jesus' reply is terse and to the point: "Leave the dead to bury their own dead. But as for you, go and proclaim the kingdom of God."

I can't imagine what it was like to hear those words. I vividly remember the day when I received that unexpected call from my brother telling me that my dad, my best friend in the world, had suddenly and unexpectedly died of a heart attack. Amid the intense pain of that moment and the indescribable sadness that marked the days ahead, I cannot imagine hearing these words from Jesus: "Don't even go to your dad's funeral. There are more important things to do."

What does this mean?

Jesus' main point is not that going to a funeral is wrong, but that his Kingdom will not take second place to anyone or anything else. For this man in Luke 9, it meant immediate abandonment to an urgent mission. Even more important than honoring the dead was proclaiming the Kingdom to those who were dying. And two thousand years later, I am convinced that a similar if not greater urgency surrounds us.

Over the course of this book, we have considered massive physical needs in the world. Yet as we contemplate these needs, if we are not careful, we run the risk of ignoring people's most pressing need. That need is not for water, food, family, freedom, safety, or equality. As urgent as all of these things are for men, women, and children around the world, they are surpassed in urgency by a much greater need.

That need—the most urgent need—is for the gospel.

This is why Jesus, when he spoke to this second man, told him exactly what he would tell his disciples before he left the earth. Jesus told this man, "Go and *proclaim* the kingdom of God," and then he told his disciples that "repentance and forgiveness of sins should be *proclaimed* . . . to all nations" (Luke 9:60; 24:47, emphasis mine).

This call to proclamation is curious. Jesus, of all people, knew the depth of people's physical needs. He had spent time with the sick, sat with the dying, and served the impoverished. When he saw the crowds, the Bible tells us "he had compassion for them," using words in the original language of the New Testament that portray a profound physical longing to provide for people with "every disease and every affliction" (Matthew 9:35-36). Yet his last words to his disciples were just like his first words to this man: in light of worldly suffering, over and above everything else, Jesus was calling them to speak.

You see, Jesus knew that as great as people's earthly needs were, their eternal need was far greater. When a paralytic was brought to him on a mat, Jesus said to him, "Son, your sins are forgiven" (Mark 2:5). He used this opportunity to teach a paralyzed man and the people around him that the ultimate priority of his coming was not to relieve suffering, as important and needed as that is. Instead, his ultimate priority in coming to the world was to sever the root of suffering: sin itself.

This is our—and everyone's—greatest need. Fundamentally, all people have sinned against God and are separated from him. Consequently, all of our lives not only on earth but also in eternity are at stake. Heaven and hell hang in the balance. God has made a way for all people to be reconciled to him through the life, death, and resurrection of Christ. All who receive him will experience eternal life, yet all who reject him suffer everlasting torment. This is the message of the gospel, and it is what people most need to hear.

Christ is not callous toward earthly needs. But he is even more passionate about eternal needs. The reason he came was to reconcile people to God. He came not just to give the poor drinking water for their bodies but to give people living water for their souls. He came not just to give orphans and widows a family now but to give them a family forever. He came not just to free girls from slavery to sex but to free them (and those who abuse them) from slavery to sin. He came not just to make equality possible on earth but to make eternity possible in heaven.

Because the gospel is the most pressing need in people's lives, the gospel informs the fundamental purpose of our lives. We who know the gospel have been given the greatest gift in all the world. We have good news of a glorious God who has come to deliver men, women, and children from all sin and all suffering for all time. Therefore, we cannot—we *must* not—stay silent with this gospel. Gospel possession requires gospel proclamation.

This is the major fallacy of social ministry in the church divorced from proclaiming the message of Christ. If all we do is meet people's physical needs while ignoring their spiritual need, we miss the entire point. Yet so often this is exactly what we settle for, and we do so because it's easier and less costly for us. It's far easier to give a cup of water to the thirsty and walk away than it is to give that same cup of water and stay to share about the living water that comes through Christ alone. But yet again, as Christians we don't have the choice of disconnecting these two. We must proclaim the gospel as we provide for others' good. We are compelled to speak as we serve. We testify with our lips what we attest with our lives.

To be clear, giving a cup of water to the poor is not contingent upon that person's confession of faith in Christ. Loving our neighbor as ourselves does not limit giving in this way. Instead, giving a cup of water to the poor is accompanied by sharing the good news of the gospel. True love for our neighbor requires nothing less. We care much about earthly suffering, but we care most about eternal suffering.[1]

Moreover, in God's good providence, it is in addressing eternal suffering that we are most effective in alleviating earthly suffering. After more than a decade of research on the effect of missionaries on the health of nations, sociologist Robert Woodberry came to the conclusion that "the work of missionaries . . . turns out to be the single largest factor in ensuring the health of nations."[2] Specifically, Woodberry contrasted the work of "conversionary Protestant" missionaries with "Protestant clergy financed by the state" and "Catholic missionaries prior to the 1960s." Woodberry observed, "Areas where Protestant missionaries had a significant presence in the past are on average more economically developed today, with comparatively better health, lower infant mortality, lower corruption, greater literacy, higher educational attainment (especially for women), and more robust membership in nongovernmental associations." In Woodberry's words, these conclusions landed on him like an "atomic bomb."[3]

But we are not surprised by Woodberry's findings when we consider what we see in Scripture. For the greatest way to achieve social and cultural transformation is not by focusing on social and cultural transformation, but by giving our lives to gospel proclamation—to telling others the good news of all God has done in Christ and calling them to follow him. The fruit of such salvation will be inevitable transformation—of lives, of families, of communities, and even of nations.

The central mission of the church in the world, then, is proclaiming the gospel to the world, and there is much work to be done, not only in our culture but among people around the world. In chapter 8, we noted that anthropological scholars have identified over eleven thousand different people groups in the world. Meanwhile, Jesus has called us to proclaim the gospel to all of them. "Make disciples of all nations," he says in the great commission, and the word for "nations" there is *ethne*, or ethnolinguistic groups. This commission is not just a general command to make disciples among as many people as possible. Instead, it is a specific command to make disciples among every people group in the world.

You may wonder how we're doing in obeying Christ's command. Missiological scholars have attempted to identify how many of these eleven thousand people groups have been reached with the gospel. A people group is classified as "unreached" if less than two percent of the population is made up of Christians who confess the gospel and believe the Bible. In practical terms, for a people group to be "unreached" means that not only do individuals in that people group not believe the gospel, but because there is no church around them, no Christians among them, and in many cases no one attempting to get the gospel to them, most of them will die without even hearing it. So how many people groups are still unreached? More than six thousand—a population of at least two billion people.[4]

I have met many unreached people around the world. I have hiked for days through Asian villages where I have stopped to ask families what they know about Jesus, only to hear them respond, "I have never heard of him." I have conversed with men in Middle Eastern cities who had heard of Jesus, but no one had ever told them the truth about who he is or what he did. Until that conversation, they had never met a Christian or seen a Bible. I have sat in African deserts with individuals who hadn't heard the gospel and didn't want to hear it. They live in people groups that are completely closed to other faiths and anyone who tries to share such faith with them.

This is why I'm compelled to ask, are we going to settle for maintenance, or are we going to sacrifice for mission? Jesus Christ has given us marching orders, and they are clear. Proclaim the gospel—the good news of God's great love for us in Christ—to every people group on the planet. So how is it possible that two thousand years later six thousand people groups are still classified as unreached?

One of the primary reasons this is possible is that we have settled for maintenance in the church. We have settled into a status quo where we're content to sit idly by while literally billions of people die without ever hearing the gospel. Surely *this* is the greatest social injustice in the entire world, over and above all the other issues we have considered. I know that is a bold statement, but I make it without reservation. Over two billion people today live on the earth as sinners against God, destined for hell and in desperate need of a Savior, and no one has told them how God loves them and has made a way for their salvation.

I stood at the Bagmati River in South Asia where every day funerals are held and bodies are burned. It is the custom among these Hindu people when family or friends die to take their bodies within twenty-four hours to the river, where they lay them on funeral pyres and set the pyres ablaze. In so doing, they believe they are helping their friend or family member in the cycle of reincarnation. As I saw this scene before me, I stood in overwhelmed silence. For as I watched these flames overtake the bodies, I knew based on Scripture that I was witnessing at that moment a physical reflection of an eternal reality. Tears streamed down my face as I realized that most if not all of the people I was watching burn had died without ever hearing the good news of how they could have lived forever with God.

When will the concept of unreached peoples become intolerable to the church? What will it take to wake us up to the dearth of the gospel among the peoples of the world? What will it take to stir our hearts and lives for men and women whose souls are plunging into damnation without ever even hearing of salvation? This cannot be conceivable for people who confess the gospel. For if this gospel is true, and if our God is worthy of the praise of all people, then we must spend our lives and mobilize our churches for the spread of Christ's love to unreached people groups all around the world. Jesus has not given us a commission to consider; he has given us a command to obey.

That command involves sacrifice on all our parts. If we have this much access to the gospel in our culture and there is this much absence of the gospel in other cultures, then surely God is leading many more of us (maybe the majority of us) to go to those cultures. If God calls us to stay in this culture, then surely

LET'S RISK IT ALL

he is leading us to live simply and give sacrificially so that as many people as possible can go.

And whether we stay or go, we have no choice but to counter culture. If we stay, then we must recognize that sacrificing pleasures, selling possessions, and shaping our lives around getting the gospel to unreached peoples in the world will inevitably and unavoidably go against the grain of a culture that constantly beckons us to seek more pleasures, attain more possessions, and spend our lives around what will bring us the most comfort in this world. Moreover, if we go, then we must realize that these people groups are unreached for a reason: they are difficult and dangerous to reach, and the cost of reaching them will be steep. But the gospel compels us to counter culture regardless of cost— to risk our lives, our families, our future, our plans, and our possessions—for the sake of one reward: the proclamation of the greatest news in order to meet people's greatest need.

This leads to the last question I'm compelled to ask us.

WILL OUR LIVES BE MARKED BY INDECISIVE MINDS OR UNDIVIDED HEARTS?

The last man in Luke 9 approaches Jesus and says, "I will follow you, Lord, but let me first say farewell to those at my home." A simple request, so it seems. He wants to say good-bye to his family and friends. Yet it also seems that Jesus knows as soon as this man returns to his family, the lure to stay will be strong. So he tells the man, "No one who puts his hand to the plow and looks back is fit for the kingdom of God." In other words, "Keep your attention and affection wholly fixed on me and the path I have called you to."

I have seen similar scenarios play out among people today. I have seen college students, young singles, and young couples sense God's call in their lives to go to unreached people, and then I have watched them go back to their parents (Christian and non-Christian alike), where they have been persuaded not to obey. "Isn't that risky?" their parents will ask. "How will you find a husband? Isn't this dangerous for your wife? What about your children? Do you really want to raise them there? Do you really want to keep our grandkids from ever knowing us?" Ironically, the scenario is sometimes reversed as couples in their retirement consider going, only to have their children question, "Are you sure this is wise at your age and stage of life?"

It is not uncommon for the lure of family love to lead to faithless living. Maybe it is brothers counseling sisters to have abortions in order to escape strenuous situations. *Surely God will forgive in this circumstance*, they think. Or maybe it's moms and dads encouraging their sons and daughters in their sexual decisions regardless of what Scripture says. *Surely it's okay if my child is doing it*, they think. Into such situations, Jesus' words are both succinct and sobering. "I have come to set a man against his father, and a daughter against her mother, and a daughter-in-law against her mother-in-law. And a person's enemies will be those of his own household. Whoever loves father or mother more than me is not worthy of me, and whoever loves son or daughter more than me is not worthy of me" (Matthew 10:35-37). Following Jesus doesn't just entail sacrificial abandonment of our lives; it requires supreme affection from our hearts.

Yet I see in the situations above as well as in my own spiritual life a subtle yet dangerous tendency toward indecision. When it comes to the call of God, I am prone to hesitate. Before I do anything, I want complete confirmation that I'm doing the right thing. I want to research every option and hear everyone's opinions. This is not bad in and of itself, for I want to be wise, but if I'm not careful, I can slowly let indecision become inaction.

I can easily become paralyzed by pressures from people around me and doubts that dominate within me. And before I know it, delayed obedience becomes disobedience.

But this is not the way it's supposed to be. If I'm walking by a lake and see a child drowning, I don't stop and ponder what I should do. Nor do I just stand there praying about what action to take. I do something. Immediately, without hesitation, I jump into the lake and save the drowning child.

The parallel is not perfect, but consider the realities we have addressed in these pages. At this moment, millions upon millions of men, women, and children are starving and dying without food and water. Scores of babies have been aborted today, and scores more will be aborted tomorrow. Orphanages, foster homes, and city streets and slums are overflowing with boys and girls who need a mom and dad. At this moment, unnumbered and unknown widows sit in their homes with no family or friends to provide for them in place of a husband whom they loved but have now lost. While you read these words, thousands upon thousands of young girls are sitting on corners and in brothels, waiting for a customer to rape them. At the same time, many men and women are being oppressed for their ethnicity, millions of refugees are being forced from their homes, and our brothers and sisters around the world are being persecuted for their faith. Ultimately, while we contemplate this gospel, over two billion people in the world have never even heard it. They are waiting to hear the good news of how God's love for them in Christ can satisfy them on earth and save them for eternity.

My purpose in putting these realities before us is not to cause us to collapse under their weight. To be certain, God alone is able to bear these global burdens. He alone has the emotional framework to perceive the world as he perceives it. But God loves us too much to allow us to live with indifference or inaction. Surely he means us to act in at least the ways we have explored at the end of each chapter in this book: *praying* to him, *participating* with him, and *proclaiming* his Word in the world around us.

Let's be sure to start with prayer. This is practically the most simple and potentially the most significant thing we can do in light of social injustice. These battles ultimately belong to God (see 1 Samuel 17:47), and he wills for us to participate with him in the accomplishment of his purposes through prayer. So in light of Christ's instruction to us, let's plead for God's Kingdom to come and his will to be done (see Matthew 6:9-10). In line with those who have gone before us, let's pray for God's judgment and mercy to be made manifest amid these massive needs (see Psalms 7, 10, 17, 18), knowing that none of our prayers are in vain (see Luke 11:1-13). In order to help you know how best to pray, in addition to the prayer suggestions at the end of each chapter, I again want to recommend the website that includes specific prayer points for each of the issues addressed in this book—CounterCultureBook.com—as well as the *Counter Culture Scripture and Prayer Guide* we have specifically created to accompany this book. My hope is that this website and resource will first and foremost fuel men and women who are falling on their knees before God in the face of global need.

May our prayers then lead to participation with God in the world around us. One of the primary ways this may play out is in our giving. In view of the historic affluence God has given us, we must consider ways to use our wealth for the sake of his worship. The New Testament pattern prioritizes giving to and with one's local church (see 1 Corinthians 16:1-4), so this is the primary place to begin. May God help us in our churches to organize our spending around the spread of the gospel in a world of urgent spiritual and physical need. We obviously want to give wisely when it comes to specific needs addressed in this book, so CounterCultureBook.com also contains links to ministries with which you or your local church might partner in giving. I assure you I'm not profiting in any way by pointing you to these organizations—even my proceeds in this book are all going toward spreading the gospel through ministries like these. My aim is simply to provide a first step as you consider how to give generously, sacrificially, sensibly, and cheerfully in our culture.

As we pray and give, I trust that God will lead us to go. I use "go" generally here to refer to the many other actions God may lead us to take. In light of six thousand unreached people groups, I trust that God will lead many of us to go to them, moving our lives and our families to live among them and share the gospel with them. I trust that he will lead others of us to work among the poor in our cities and around the world; to adopt or foster children; to start or participate in ministry to widows, unwed mothers, or immigrants; to work against abortion; to fight against slavery; to portray the gospel in biblical marriage; to strive for ethnic unity; to serve the persecuted church; to advocate for religious liberty; and on and on. The creativity of God may be most clear in the ways he calls different followers of Christ to use their time, talents, and treasures in diverse ways for his kingdom purposes. As I mentioned in the first chapter, not every one of us can or should give equal attention to every one of these issues, for God sovereignly puts us in unique positions and places with unique privileges and opportunities to influence the culture around us. For this reason, CounterCultureBook.com also includes initial ideas for you to consider as you contemplate specific ways God may call you to act upon his Word.

What must be consistent for all of us, however, is that we pray, give, and go as he leads, and as we do, that we proclaim the gospel with conviction, compassion, and courage. As I hope we've seen, once we recognize that the gospel is the central issue in any culture, we realize that this gospel compels us to confront pressing social issues in our culture. At the center of such confrontation, we prioritize gospel proclamation, for it alone has the power not only to change cultures on this earth but to transform lives for eternity.

So let us not stay silent with this gospel. Let's not allow fear in our culture to muzzle our faith in Christ. And let's not enable indecision to rule our lives. Let's not permit delay to characterize our days. We don't have to ask what the will of God is; he has made it clear. He wants his people to provide for the poor, to value the unborn, to care for orphans and widows, to rescue people from slavery, to defend marriage, to war against sexual immorality in all its forms in every area of our lives, to love our neighbors as ourselves regardless of their ethnicity, to provide for refugees, to practice faith regardless of the risk, and to proclaim the gospel to all nations. Of these things we are sure.

So pray to God, participate with God, and proclaim the gospel. And do these things not because you have a low-grade sense of guilt that you ought to act, but do them because you have a high-grade sense of grace that makes you want to act. Do them because you know that you were once impoverished in your sin, a slave to Satan, orphaned from God, and alone in this world. Yet God reached down his mercy-filled hand into your sin-soaked heart, and through the sacrifice of his only begotten Son on a blood-stained cross, he lifted you up to new life by his alluring love. You now have nothing to fear and nothing to lose because you are robed in the riches of Christ and safe in the security of Christ.

And pray to God, participate with God, and proclaim the gospel not under a utopian illusion that you or I or anyone or everyone together can rid this world of pain and suffering. That responsibility belongs to the resurrected Christ, and he will do it when he returns. But until that day, do with an undivided heart whatever he calls you to do. Some will say that these problems are complex, and one person, family, or church can't really make much of a difference. In many respects, this is true, for each of these issues is extremely complicated. But don't underestimate what God will do in and through one person, one family, or one church for the spread of his gospel and the sake of his glory in our culture.

So do these things with the unshakable conviction that God has put you in an anti-Christian age for a reason. He has called you to himself, he has saved you by his Son, he has filled you with his Spirit, he has captured you with his love, and he is compelling you by his Word to counter culture by proclaiming his Kingdom, knowing that the reward of following Christ is worth any risk to your life, your family, your future, your relationships, your reputation, your career, and your comfort in this world.

FIRST STEPS TO COUNTER CULTURE

Pray

Ask God to:

- Send out workers to other cultures and to open the door for many more unreached people groups to be reached with the gospel (whether through fully funded missionaries, business visas, etc.).
- Give many churches and Christians a burden to become involved in praying, giving, and going for the purpose of taking the gospel to the unreached.
- Provide missionaries with boldness and wisdom in making the gospel known among unreached peoples.

Participate

Prayerfully consider taking these steps:

- Give sacrificially through your local church so that missionaries and gospel efforts to the unreached might be supported.
- Plan to go on a short-term mission trip and ask God to clarify what your role should be in obeying the great commission.
- Support a missions agency, a translation team, or some other effort to get the gospel to unreached peoples.

Proclaim

Consider the following truths from Scripture:

- Matthew 6:9-10: "Our Father in heaven, hallowed be your name. Your kingdom come, your will be done, on earth as it is in heaven."
- Matthew 9:37-38: "[Jesus] said to his disciples, 'The harvest is plentiful, but the laborers are few; therefore pray earnestly to the Lord of the harvest to send out laborers into his harvest.'"
- Luke 9:57-62: "As they were going along the road, someone said to him, 'I will follow you wherever you go.' And Jesus said to him, 'Foxes have holes, and birds of the air have nests, but the Son of Man has nowhere to lay his head.' To another he said, 'Follow me.' But he said, 'Lord, let me first go and bury my father.' And Jesus said to him, 'Leave the dead to bury their own dead. But as for you, go and proclaim the kingdom of God.' Yet another said, 'I will follow you, Lord, but let me first say farewell to those at my home.' Jesus said to him, 'No one who puts his hand to the plow and looks back is fit for the kingdom of God.'"

For more (and more specific) suggestions,
visit CounterCultureBook.com/Topics/Unreached

ACKNOWLEDGMENTS

As I consider the measure of grace necessary to make this book a reality, I am grateful to God for many people on many levels.

I am grateful to God for the entire team at Tyndale, and particularly for Ron Beers, Lisa Jackson, and Jonathan Schindler, whose encouragement to me, patience with me, counsel for me, and belief in me have far exceeded what I deserve.

I am grateful to God for Sealy Yates, without whose tireless work and trusted friendship I would be lost in this process.

I am grateful to God for Mark Liederbach, who graciously read through this manuscript and offered invaluable counsel that not only shaped and sharpened the book but also served my soul.

I am grateful to God for the Radical crew—for David Burnette's trusted wisdom in the editing process, for Angelia Stewart's passionate attention to detail, for Cory Varden and Paul Akin's faithful service, for Jim Warren and Chris Hunsberger's selfless leadership, and for the humble dedication of every person on this team.

I am grateful to God for the elders, staff, and members of The Church at Brook Hills. God used their prayers for me and support of me to bring this book to fruition. Their trust in God's Word and zeal for God's glory among the nations is a testimony to God's grace in these brothers and sisters whom I deeply love in Birmingham.

I am grateful to God for the thousands of missionaries with the International Mission Board who live on the front lines of unreached peoples around the world (and the thousands, I pray, who will join them in the days ahead). I am humbled and honored to serve alongside them as we spend our lives together for the spread of the gospel among the nations.

I am grateful to God for my family. Simply put, this book would not be possible without the sacrifices they have made out of love for God, love for me, and love for men and women who read what is written here. I sit down at my table each night in stunned wonder as I look at my beautiful wife and best friend, Heather, and then I see the faces of my four children, Caleb, Joshua, Mara Ruth, and Isaiah. I am of all men most blessed.

Above all, I am grateful to God for his gospel. I shudder to think of where I would be apart from his grace and truth revealed in Jesus Christ. My singular prayer is that his grace toward me might be to great effect for him (John 3:30).

NOTES

INTRODUCTION—RETREAT OR RISK?

1. United States v. Windsor, 570 U.S. (2013).
2. Elane Photography, LLC, v. Vanessa Willock, 309 P. 3d 53 (NM: Supreme Court 2013).

CHAPTER 1—THE GREATEST OFFENSE: THE GOSPEL AND CULTURE

1. For an excellent article on this, see Dan Phillips, "The Most Offensive Verse in the Bible," *PyroManiacs* (blog), February 26, 2013, http://teampyro.blogspot.com/2013/02/the-most-offensive-verse-in-bible.html.
2. Michael Ruse, "Evolutionary Theory and Christian Ethics," in *The Darwinian Paradigm* (London: Routledge, 1989), 261–268.
3. Richard Dawkins, *River Out of Eden* (New York: Basic Books, 1995), 133.
4. In this and the following section, I am indebted to John Stott's presentation of the gospel in *Why I Am a Christian* (Downers Grove, IL: InterVarsity Press, 2003).
5. Stott, *Why I Am a Christian*, 76.
6. See Stott, *Why I Am a Christian*, 74–76.
7. Ibid., 35.
8. Ibid., 42–43.
9. Ibid., 55. For a more complete discussion of this, see John Stott, *The Cross of Christ* (Downers Grove, IL: InterVarsity Press, 2006), 89–93.
10. See Stott, *Why I Am a Christian*, 49–51.
11. Tim Keller, "The Importance of Hell," *The Redeemer Reports*, Redeemer Presbyterian Church, August 2009, www.redeemer.com/redeemer-report/article/the_importance_of_hell.
12. Elizabeth Rundle Charles, *Chronicles of the Schönberg-Cotta Family* (New York: M. W. Dodd, 1864), 321.
13. Francis A. Schaeffer, *A Christian View of the Church*, vol. 4 in *The Complete Works of Francis A. Schaeffer: A Christian Worldview* (Wheaton, IL: Crossway, 1982), 316–317, 401.
14. Schaeffer, *A Christian View of the Church*, 410.

CHAPTER 2—WHERE RICH AND POOR COLLIDE: THE GOSPEL AND POVERTY

1. Steve Corbett and Brian Fikkert, *When Helping Hurts: How to Alleviate Poverty without Hurting the Poor . . . and Yourself* (Chicago: Moody, 2009), 41.

2. "Health Facts," *Compassion.com*, accessed May 5, 2014, www.compassion .com/poverty/health.htm.

3. These points are drawn from an extensive study of seventy-five Bible passages that I led our church through concerning the gospel and possessions. For resources from this study, as well as on other topics, see www.radical.net /resources.

4. Timothy Keller, *Every Good Endeavor: Connecting Your Work to God's Work* (New York: Dutton, 2012), 59.

5. Lester DeKoster, *Work: The Meaning of Your Life: A Christian Perspective* (Grand Rapids, MI: Christian's Library Press, 1982), 3–4, 6.

6. Ibid., 2–3.

7. C.S. Lewis, *Mere Christianity* (New York: Simon and Schuster, 1980), 82.

8. "Water Sanitation and Health," World Health Organization, accessed May 4, 2014, www.who.int/mediacentre/factsheets/fs391/en.

CHAPTER 3—MODERN HOLOCAUST: THE GOSPEL AND ABORTION

1. "Worldwide Abortion Statistics," *Abort73.com*, last modified May 26, 2011, www.abort73.com/abortion_facts/worldwide_abortion_statistics/.

2. See Denny Burk's exploration of this point in his blog post "Why Aren't We Calling It the 'Royal Fetus'?," *Denny Burk* (blog), December 5, 2012, www.dennyburk.com/why-arent-we-calling-it-the-royal-fetus/.

3. I am indebted in this section to a booklet written by Gregory Koukl called *Precious Unborn Human Persons* (Signal Hill, CA: Stand to Reason Press, 1999), especially chapter 1, which provides the basis for much of my thinking here.

4. Koukl, *Precious Unborn Human Persons*, 7.

5. Ibid. The obvious and only exception to this is when a mother's life is in imminent danger, in which case one of two human lives will be lost and a determination may be made to save the mother's physical life. The arguments in this section follow Koukl's *Precious Unborn Human Persons*, 8–12.

6. Ibid., 26–27.

7. Susan Donaldson James, "Down Syndrome Births Are Down in U.S.," *ABC News*, November 2, 2009, http://abcnews.go.com/Health/w_Parenting Resource/down-syndrome-births-drop-us-women-abort/story?id=8960803.

8. Koukl, *Precious Unborn Human Persons*, 9.

9. Randy Alcorn, *Pro-Life Answers to Pro-Choice Arguments* (Colorado Springs: Multnomah Books, 2000), 293.

10. "Forced Abortion Statistics," *All Girls Allowed*, accessed May 20, 2014, www.allgirlsallowed.org/forced-abortion-statistics.

CHAPTER 4—THE LONELY IN FAMILIES: THE GOSPEL AND ORPHANS AND WIDOWS

1. "On Understanding Orphan Statistics," *Christian Alliance for Orphans*, accessed May 20, 2014, www.christianalliancefororphans.org/orphanstats/.

2. For specific examples of the use of this word *visit* in Scripture, see Genesis 50:24-25; Psalm 8:4; 106:4; Luke 1:68, 78; 7:16; Acts 7:23; 15:14, 36.

3. "Report: Over 115 Million Widows Worldwide Live in Poverty," *USA Today*, June 23, 2010, http://usatoday30.usatoday.com/news/health/2010-06-23-un -widows-poverty_N.htm?csp=34news.

4. Kirsten Andersen, "The Number of U.S. Children Living in Single-Parent Homes Has Nearly Doubled in 50 Years: Census Data," *LifeSiteNews.com*, January 4, 2013, www.lifesitenews.com/news/the-number-of-children-living-in -single-parent-homes-has-nearly-doubled-in/; J. A. Martin, B. E. Hamilton, J. K. Osterman, et al., "Births: Final Data for 2012," *National Vital Statistics Reports* 62, no. 9 (2013), www.cdc.gov/nchs/fastats/births.htm.

5. John Evans, "Hearts in Hands Ministers to Hospice Patients," *The Alabama Baptist*, April 28, 2011, www.thealabamabaptist.org/print-edition-article-detail .php?id_art=18942&pricat_art=4.

CHAPTER 5—A WAR ON WOMEN: THE GOSPEL AND SEX SLAVERY

1. Joe Carter, "9 Things You Should Know About Human Trafficking", *The Gospel Coalition* (blog), August 8, 2013, http://thegospelcoalition.org/blogs /tgc/2013/08/09/9-things-you-should-know-about-human-trafficking/.

2. *End It*, http://enditmovement.com/; "The Facts," *The A21 Campaign*, www.thea21campaign.org/content/the-facts/gjekag.

3. "Trafficking and Slavery Fact Sheet," *Free the Slaves*, www.freetheslaves.net/wp -content/uploads/2015/01/FTS-factsheet-Nov17.21.pdf and "Human Trafficking," *Polaris*, www.polarisproject.org/human-trafficking/overview.

4. "The I-20 Story," video file, *The Well House*, http://the-wellhouse.org/the -i-20-story/.

5. The transcript of the Gettysburg Address can be viewed at www.ourdocuments .gov/doc.php?flash=true&doc=36&page=transcript.

6. Walter Bauer, W. F. Arndt, F. W. Gingrich, and F. W. Danker, *A Greek-English Lexicon of the New Testament and Other Early Christian Literature*, ed. Frederick William Danker, 3rd ed. (Chicago: The University of Chicago Press, 2000), 76.

7. For an exegetical overview of the Bible and slavery, see my chapter titled "What About Slavery, Paul?" in *Exalting Jesus in 1 and 2 Timothy and Titus* (Nashville: B&H Publishing Group, 2013).

8. Frederick Douglass, *Narrative of the Life of Frederick Douglass* (Boston: Dover Publications, 1995), 3-4.

9. "Staggering Statistics," *MindArmor Training Tools*, www.mind-armor .com/staggering-statistics.

10. "Forced Sex Acts between a Trafficked Woman or Child and a 'John' Are Often Filmed and Photographed," Stop Trafficking Demand, http://stoptraffickingdemand.com/forced-acts-recorded.

11. U.S. Dept. of State, Trafficking Victims Protection Act (TVPA) 2000, Bureau

for International Narcotics and Law Enforcement Affairs (2001) (enacted). Print, Sec 102 (2).

12. "Performers Are Sometimes Forced or Coerced During the Production of Mainstream Pornography," Stop Trafficking Demand, http://stoptrafficking demand.com/trafficking-within-the-industry; "Forced Sex Acts."

13. Donna M. Hughes, "The Demand for Victims of Sex Trafficking", Women's Studies Program, University of Rhode Island, June 2005, p.26. (Cited in http://moderndayslaveryblog.wordpress.com/2011/03/29/the-link-between -pornography-and-human-trafficking/.)

14. Melissa Farley, "Renting an Organ for Ten Minutes: What Tricks Tell Us about Prostitution, Pornography, and Trafficking," in *Pornography: Driving the Demand in International Sex Trafficking*, eds. David E. Guinn and Julie DiCaro (Los Angeles: Captive Daughters Media, 2007), 145.

15. Ana Stutler, "The Connections Between Pornography and Sex Trafficking," *Help Others Restore Integrity* (blog), Covenant Eyes, September 7, 2011, www.covenanteyes.com/2011/09/07/the-connections-between-pornography -and-sex-trafficking/.

16. Miranda Devine, "Online Porn Addiction Turns Our Kids into Victims and Predators," *Sydney Sun-Herald*, August 14, 2005, http://www.smh.com.au /news/miranda-devine/online-porn-addiction-turns-our-kids-into-victims -and-predators/2005/08/13/1123353539758.html.

17. Angelu Lu, "Connecting the Dots between Sex Trafficking and Pornography," *World*, June 10, 2013, www.worldmag.com/2013/06/connecting_the_dots _between_sex_trafficking_and_pornography.

18. Paul Olaf Chelsen, "An Examination of Internet Pornography Usage Among Male Students at Evangelical Christian Colleges" (PhD diss., Loyola University, 2011), http://ecommons.luc.edu/luc_diss/150/.

19. Murray J. Harris, *Slave of Christ: A New Testament Metaphor for Total Devotion to Christ* (Downers Grove, IL: InterVarsity Press, 1999), 68.

CHAPTER 6—A PROFOUND MYSTERY: THE GOSPEL AND MARRIAGE

1. United States v. Windsor, 570 U.S. (2013).

2. Hope Yen, "Census: Divorces Decline, But 7-Year Itch Persists," *The Washington Times*, May 18, 2011, http://www.washingtontimes.com/news/2011/may/18/ census-divorces-decline-7-year-itch-persists.

3. Linda Carroll, "CDC: Only Half of First Marriages Last 20 Years," *NBC News*, March 22, 2012, http://vitals.nbcnews.com/_news/2012/03/21/10799069 -cdc-only-half-of-first-marriages-last-20-years.

4. Mark Regnerus, "The Case for Early Marriage," *Christianity Today*, July 31, 2009, www.christianitytoday.com/ct/2009/august/16.22.html?paging=off.

5. "Interview: Why Rob Bell Supports Gay Marriage," Odyssey Networks, https://www.youtube.com/watch?v=-q0iDaW6BnE.

6. For more on Don and Gwen's journey, see Don Brobst, *Thirteen Months* (Bloomington, IN: Westbow Press, 2011).

7. See Glenn T. Stanton, "FactChecker: Divorce Rate among Christians," *The Gospel Coalition* (blog), Sept. 25, 2012, http://thegospelcoalition.org/blogs /tgc/2012/09/25/factchecker-divorce-rate-among-christians/#_ftn1.

8. Francis A. Schaeffer, *A Christian View of the Church*, vol. 4 in *The Complete Works of Francis A. Schaeffer: A Christian Worldview* (Wheaton, IL: Crossway, 1982), 391–398.

9. Regnerus, "The Case for Early Marriage."

10. Russell Moore has encouraged me greatly on the realities I've expressed above. For more, see Russell D. Moore, "How Should Same-Sex Marriage Change the Church's Witness?" *Moore to the Point* (blog), June 26, 2013, www.russellmoore.com/2013/06/26/how-should-same-sex-marriage-change -the-churchs-witness/ and "Same-Sex Marriage and the Future," *Moore to the Point* (blog), April 15, 2014, www.russellmoore.com/2014/04/15/same-sex -marriage-and-the-future/.

CHAPTER 7—BOUGHT WITH A PRICE: THE GOSPEL AND SEXUAL MORALITY

1. See, for example, Ephesians 4:28 and Colossians 3:9.

2. For more on God's law, see David W. Jones, *An Introduction to Biblical Ethics* (Nashville: B&H Academic, 2013).

3. For a brief yet excellent resource on the biblical foundations expressed here and their practical implications, see Sam Allberry, *Is God Anti-Gay?* (Purcellville, VA: The Good Book Company, 2013).

4. For an excellent discussion of this, see chapter 8, "Saints and Sexual Immorality," in Kevin DeYoung, *The Hole in Our Holiness* (Wheaton, IL: Crossway, 2014), 107–122.

5. See Robert Wright, "Our Cheating Hearts," *Time*, August 15, 1994, 44.

6. For the sake of clarity, the term Paul uses in 1 Corinthians 6 and 1 Timothy 1 matches the term for "homosexuality" in Leviticus 18:22 in the Septuagint (the Greek translation of the Old Testament).

7. William M. Kent, "Report of the Committee to Study Homosexuality to the General Council on Ministries of the United Methodist Church" (Dayton, OH: General Council on Ministries, August 24, 1991).

8. Gary David Comstock, *Gay Theology without Apology* (Cleveland, OH: Pilgrim Press, 1993), 43.

9. Luke Timothy Johnson, "Homosexuality & the Church: Scripture & Experience," *Commonweal*, June 11, 2007, www.commonwealmagazine.org /homosexuality-church-1.

10. Daniel R. Heimbach, *True Sexual Morality: Recovering Biblical Standards for a Culture in Crisis* (Wheaton, IL: Crossway, 2004), 33–34.

11. Martin Luther, *Commentary on St. Paul's Epistle to the Galatians*, chapter 3, verse 13.

12. Rosaria Champagne Butterfield, "My Train Wreck Conversion," *Christianity Today*, February 7, 2013, www.christianitytoday.com/ct/2013/january-february /my-train-wreck-conversion.html.

13. Ibid.

14. Ibid.

15. Ibid.

CHAPTER 8—UNITY IN DIVERSITY: THE GOSPEL AND ETHNICITY

1. Martin Luther King Jr., "Letter from Birmingham City Jail," *The King Center* (online archive), April 16, 1963, accessed May 10, 2014, www.thekingcenter .org/archive/document/letter-birmingham-city-jail.

2. Ibid.

3. Ibid.

4. I was particularly convicted of this through a sermon by Thabiti Anyabwile entitled "Bearing the Image." That sermon was published in Mark Dever, J. Ligon Duncan III, R. Albert Mohler Jr., and C. J. Mahaney, *Proclaiming a Cross-Centered Theology* (Wheaton, IL: Crossway, 2009), 59–80. Many of the convictions I share below are based upon subsequent conversations with Anyabwile about this subject.

5. Anyabwile, "Bearing the Image," 64.

6. See *PeopleGroups*, www.peoplegroups.org/understand.aspx; www.people groups.org. See also *Joshua Project*, http://joshuaproject.net/help/definitions; and http://joshuaproject.net/global_statistics.

7. For a more extensive discussion of this, see *PeopleGroups*, www.peoplegroups.org.

8. This is not to be confused with God's holy judgment on various nations in their sin. The pages of the Old Testament reveal the sobering reality of divine punishment due to immorality and idolatry across various ethnicities. For more on the holiness, justice, and goodness of God even in this, see Paul Copan, *Is God a Moral Monster?* (Grand Rapids: Baker, 2011).

9. See, for example, Matthew 8:5-13, 28-34; 15:21-28; Luke 17:12-19; John 4:5-42; 12:20-28.

10. Martin Luther King Jr., "I Have a Dream . . . ," *National Archives*, www.archives.gov/press/exhibits/dream-speech.pdf.

11. Russell D. Moore, "Immigration and the Gospel," *Moore to the Point* (blog), June 17, 2011, www.russellmoore.com/2011/06/17/immigration-and-the -gospel/. Similar to the way Thabiti Anyabwile has impacted my understanding of racism, Russell Moore has greatly influenced my understanding of immigration.

12. Michael Linton, "Illegal Immigration and Our Corruption," *First Things*,

July 13, 2007, www.firstthings.com/web-exclusives/2007/07/illegal -immigration-and-our-co.

13. See Matthew Soerens and Daniel Darling, "The Gospel and Immigration," *The Gospel Coalition* (blog), May 1, 2012, http://thegospelcoalition .org/blogs/tgc/2012/05/01/the-gospel-and-immigration/ and Soerens and Darling, "Immigration Policy and Ministry," *The Gospel Coalition* (blog), May 8, 2012, http://thegospelcoalition.org/blogs/tgc/2012/05/08 /immigration-policy-and-ministry/.

14. Much of the above coincides with the principles outlined by the Evangelical Immigration Table as well as a resolution passed by the Southern Baptist Convention, of which I am a part. For more on this resolution, see "On Immigration and the Gospel," *Southern Baptist Convention*, www.sbc.net /resolutions/1213. For more on the Evangelical Immigration Table, a broad coalition of evangelical organizations and leaders advocating for immigration reform consistent with biblical values, see http://evangelicalimmigrationtable.com/.

15. For more on Tyler Johnson and Redemption Church, see Tyler Johnson and Jim Mullins, "One Church's Journey on Immigration," *The Gospel Coalition* (blog), October 31, 2012, http://thegospelcoalition.org/blogs/tgc/2012/10 /31/one-churchs-journey-on-immigration/.

CHAPTER 10—CHRIST IN THE PUBLIC SQUARE: THE GOSPEL AND RELIGIOUS LIBERTY

1. "About Christian Persecution," *Open Doors USA*, www.opendoorsusa.org /persecution/about-persecution.

2. Saint Augustine, *Tractates on the Gospel of John 11–27*, trans. John W. Rettig, in *The Fathers of the Church*, vol. 79 (Pittsboro, NC: The Catholic University of America Press, 1988), 261.

3. "The Cape Town Commitment," *The Lausanne Movement*, www.lausanne.org /en/documents/ctcommitment.html, IIC.6.

4. Elane Photography, LLC, v. Willock, 309 P. 3d 53 (NM: Supreme Court 2013).

5. Ibid.

6. You can read the Court's opinion at http://www.supremecourt.gov/opinions /13pdf/13-354_olp1.pdf.

7. "Manhattan Declaration," *Manhattan Declaration*, November 20, 2009, http://manhattandeclaration.org/man_dec_resources/Manhattan_Declaration _full_text.pdf.

8. In this I join with Albert Mohler, "Strengthen the Things that Remain: Human Dignity, Human Rights, and Human Flourishing in a Dangerous Age—An Address at Brigham Young University," *AlbertMohler.com* (blog), February 25, 2014, www.albertmohler.com/2014/02/25/strengthen-the-things-that-remain -human-dignity-human-rights-and-human-flourishing-in-a-dangerous-age-an -address-at-brigham-young-university/.

9. Antonin Scalia, "Let the People Decide: From the dissenting opinion by Justice

Antonin Scalia in *U.S. v. Windsor,*" *Weekly Standard* 18, no. 41 (July 8, 2013), www.weeklystandard.com/let-the-people-decide/article/738029.

10. Joe Carter, "9 Things You Should Know About Persecution of Christians in 2013," *The Gospel Coalition* (blog), October 28, 2013, http://thegospelcoalition.org/blogs/tgc/2013/10/29/9-things-you-should-know-about-persecution-of-christians-in-2013/.

11. "Christian Persecution," *Open Doors,* accessed July 7, 2015, www.opendoorsusa.org/christian-persecution.

CONCLUSION—LET'S RISK IT ALL

1. John Piper's address at the Lausanne Conference on World Evangelization in 2010 was a challenge to minister to both earthly and eternal needs. See John Piper, "Making Known the Manifold Wisdom of God Through Prison and Prayer," *Desiring God,* October 19, 2010, www.desiringgod.org/conference-messages/making-known-the-manifold-wisdom-of-god-through-prison-and-prayer.

2. Andrea Palpant Dilley, "The Surprising Discovery about Those Colonialist, Proselytizing Missionaries," *Christianity Today* 58, no. 1 (January–February 2014): 36.

3. Ibid., 38–40.

4. See www.peoplegroups.org and www.joshuaproject.net.

David Platt is deeply devoted to Christ and his Word. David's first love in ministry is making disciples—sharing, showing, and teaching God's Word in everyday life. He has traveled extensively to serve alongside church leaders throughout the United States and around the world.

Beginning in 2006 David served as the pastor of the Church at Brook Hills in Birmingham, Alabama. Currently, David is the president of the International Mission Board (imb.org). He is the founder of Radical, Inc. (radical.net), a resource ministry that exists to serve the church in accomplishing the mission of Christ.

A lifelong learner, David has earned two undergraduate and three advanced degrees. He holds a Bachelor of Arts (BA) and Bachelor of Arts in Journalism (ABJ) from the University of Georgia and a Master of Divinity (MDiv), Master of Theology (ThM), and Doctor of Philosophy (PhD) from New Orleans Baptist Theological Seminary. He previously served at New Orleans Baptist Theological Seminary as Dean of Chapel and Assistant Professor of Expository Preaching and Apologetics, and as Staff Evangelist at Edgewater Baptist Church in New Orleans.

David is the author of *Counter Culture*, *Follow Me*, *Radical*, and *Radical Together*. David is married to Heather, and they are the parents of four children: Caleb, Joshua, Mara Ruth, and Isaiah.

HOW CAN YOU COUNTER CULTURE?

It is possible to counter culture by yourself, but it's much easier with the support of other Christians. So gather a group and lead them through the *Counter Culture* Bible study. It includes six 30-minute teaching videos from David Platt, as well as material for personal study. A student version is also available. Inspire your group to take action and live out their faith every day.

ARE YOU READY TO BECOME A FOLLOWER OF CHRIST?

The call to follow Jesus is not simply an invitation to pray a prayer; it is a summons to lose your life . . . and to find new life in him. In *Follow Me*, David Platt reveals a biblical picture of what it truly means to be a Christian.

Online Discussion *guide*

Take *your* Tyndale reading
experience *to the* next level

A FREE discussion guide for this book
is available at bookclubhub.net, perfect
for sparking conversations in your book
group or for digging deeper into the text
on your own.

www.bookclubhub.net

*You'll also find free discussion guides for
other Tyndale books, e-newsletters, e-mail
devotionals, virtual book tours, and more!*